entertaining 1·2·3

also by Rozanne Gold

little meals: a great new way to eat and cook

recipes 1-2-3™: fabulous food using only three ingredients

recipes 1-2-3™ menu cookbook

entertaining
1·2·3

MORE THAN 300 RECIPES

FOR FOOD AND DRINK USING

ONLY THREE INGREDIENTS

Rozanne Gold

photographs by Tom Eckerle

LITTLE, BROWN AND COMPANY

boston new york london

First Edition

CREATIVE DESIGN/FOOD AND PROPS BY ROZANNE GOLD
FOOD STYLING BY MARIANN SAUVION/GRADY BEST

Library of Congress Cataloging-in-Publication Data
Gold, Rozanne
Entertaining 1-2-3 / Rozanne Gold : photographs
by Tom Eckerle. —
1st ed.
p.   cm.
Includes index.
1. Quick and easy cookery. 2. Entertaining.
TX833.5.G6496   1999
641.5′55 — dc21   99-12042
10 9 8 7 6 5 4 3 2 1
MV–NY
PRINTED IN THE UNITED STATES OF AMERICA

For Michael Whiteman,

who sharpens not only my mind but also my pencils

contents

acknowledgments

Ever-growing gratitude to my family: Marion Gold and Bill Gold, Dr. Leon and Gail Gold, my son, Jeremy Whiteman, and husband, Michael Whiteman.

Special affection to my creative troupe, who have brought extraordinary talent, verve, and professionalism to my "1-2-3" cookbooks: the renowned photographer Tom Eckerle; food stylists Mariann Sauvion and Grady Best; nutritionist Helen Kimmel, M. S., R. D.; wine experts Judy Rundel, who lent her brilliant palate and erudition to "grapenotes," Evan Goldstein, and Josh Wesson; to my support team, Laura Lehrman and John Ochse; and to my editor, Jennifer Josephy.

My friends provide everlasting joy. You know who you are and what you mean to me. But a special embrace to the incomparable Arthur Schwartz, who is like a brother who shares everything — including his unique collection of linens and tabletop ware (used in my photographs), his love, and his opinions, almost daily.

Special thanks to Dunnewood Vineyards and Winery; to my publishers in England (Grub Street), Israel (Modan), and the Czech Republic (Eminent); to Bernardaud Limoges; and to the Joseph Baum & Michael Whiteman Co., where I have been the culinary director for fifteen years.

Joe Baum, Michael Whiteman, and Dennis Sweeney have taught me well. Helping them create two of America's most magical restaurants (Rainbow Room and Windows on the World) as well as food and restaurant venues the world over has provided the best education any chef could ever have.

But most of all, thank you to all my readers who value simplicity and have learned the pleasures of "1-2-3."

entertaining 1·2·3

introduction

The history of entertaining

is embedded in the story of civilization. Eons ago, some unsuspecting cook dropped a handful of herbs on the family campfire and encountered a complexity of aromas and flavors never before imagined.

Reacting in a way that, ever since, has been part of our social makeup, she invited the neighbors for dinner — thereby becoming the world's first party planner! Her guests, in turn, were the world's first party animals.

Several thousand years later, as we enter the twenty-first century, *Entertaining 1-2-3* addresses contemporary issues associated with the civilizing ritual of "breaking bread together." At my side is a book called *The Host-ess of Today,* written exactly one hundred years ago, just as the last century dissolved into this one. Even then, ostentation was to be avoided and "simplicity was the ruling spirit of the day."

I think about that prehistoric woman, the hostess of 1899, and the harried hosts of today, all seeking the same social and personal gratifications that come from the pleasures of the table. *Entertaining 1-2-3* is written for an age in which leisure has evaporated, friendships are fractured by nonsynchronous lives, and time to shop, let alone cook, seems to shrink year by year. *Entertaining 1-2-3* is a book of ideas and menus designed to *simplify* (three-ingredient recipes for food and drink) and *streamline* (less time at the supermarket and less "stuff" to prepare) — all meant to increase the pleasure and frequency of entertaining at home.

My first book in this series, *Recipes 1-2-3,* introduced the concept of fabulous food using only three ingredients. I called it "the haiku of cooking." Its sequel, *Recipes 1-2-3 Menu Cookbook,* focused on melding three-ingredient recipes into artful and cohesive meals. Now *Entertaining 1-2-3,* while perhaps less doctrinaire, extends this premise: It presents more than three hundred recipes for food and drink, plus more than one hundred entertaining ideas, to be used as the three-ingredient building blocks in developing your own style.

In addition, I've included sixty complete menus perfect for today's host (who is, most often, also the cook) and for guests who value simplicity but reject culinary boredom. Who'd have thought it possible to prepare a generous holiday feast for twelve, a glamorous dinner for six, or a grand buffet for twenty-four and emerge exuberant and unexpectedly stress-free?

My pared-down ingredient lists and professional preparation tricks, do-ahead dishes and last-minute embellishments, all help convert the illusion of effortlessness into reality.

food-drink-style

Entertaining 1-2-3 means (1) easy to do, (2) beautiful to look at, (3) delicious to eat. The natural restraint required when dishes are limited to three ingredients produces food that is simple and pure and, in some cases, reaches great heights of sophistication.

This book is primarily about food and drink, recipes and menus. For instructions on setting a table, pitching a tent, catering a party for one hundred, or following party etiquette, you should consult the many excellent books on these subjects. However, if your desire is to become an accomplished host who finds that entertaining is integral to your life and no longer the exception, the 1-2-3 approach can be extraordinarily useful. It's meant to get your creative juices flowing.

My good friend Ann Feld believes that she's a culinary fumble thumbs, but she entertains often and always serves a lovely meal. Usually it's an impeccably fresh salad, a thick porterhouse steak and giant porcini mushrooms, an interesting sorbet and cookies: fairly primal, always delicious. Her husband, Dan, adds gastronomic complexity by serving a variety of single-malt Scotches alongside the steak.

Our friends Judy and John Sheldon have entertained us for twenty years — and never served the same thing twice. Judy also has such an amazing assemblage of china that each guest gets his or her own pattern for the night.

Eleanor Sigona, an accomplished cook and generous host, sets her table like a high-paid set designer, forecasting the theme of the meal to follow — be it Provençal or Tuscan.

We each have a style. Every style has its idio-syncrasies. Know them. Respect them. Flaunt them.

If you're not a great cook, choose recipes or menus that feel familiar and focus on some other aspect of the event (tabletop, flowers, conversation).

If you like to improvise, use the recipes in this book but create your own menus.

If you don't care much for serving or cleaning up, hire a waiter. (But even the king of France in the eighteenth century, after dismissing the servants at the end of a party at Versailles, himself served coffee to his guests.) *

If you don't want to make dessert, buy it. Or prepare my favorite 1-2–3 finale: quenelle-shaped scoops of refreshing sorbet served on a large chilled plate (sometimes black), topped with raspberries (sometimes gold), and garnished with fresh mint (or lemon balm or lavender).

Always buy great bread and, like the king, serve good, strong coffee. Your guests will think you are a genius.

The range of recipes in *Entertaining 1-2-3* is vast — from a simple potato "tortilla" to a sophisticated chateaubriand in a porcini crust; global — from a consommé of oysters and nori to stir-fried asparagus with Chinese (Shanxi) vinegar; simple to sublime — from a homey marmalade tart to voluptuous slow-baked pears in Sauternes aspic. The flavors and techniques in this book go deeper and are more complex than those in my previous two books and result in a "higher style" of fare. And yes, there are still only three ingredients.

* From *Home: A Short History of an Idea* by Witold Rybezynski (New York: Viking Penguin, 1986).

This book includes individual recipes and menus for those occasional morning guests; "thematic" casual lunches for friends; more than sixty hot and cold hors d'oeuvres — single bites that fill your mouth with flavor; cocktails, mocktails, and 1-2 punches. Every season has its culinary blessings, so I include twenty sit-down dinners with menus built around main courses and ingredients in their prime.

Naturally, you may find *Entertaining 1-2-3* most useful around the holidays, when entertaining competes with so many other demands on your time. I suggest ten holiday celebrations, from New Year's Day to New Year's Eve, comprising four-course dinners serving six to twelve that are doubled easily.

A familiar lament of the calorically challenged is that everything delicious is fattening. Savor the flavor with more than 150 recipes and healthy menus for calorie- and fat-slashing guests who demand good food (see Chapter 9).

Highlighted in Chapter 10 are unstructured food ideas and recipes for spontaneous entertaining.

styles of service

The way a meal is served is a fascinating variable in entertaining, for the very same menu can feel formal or casual depending on how dishes are presented.

Consider the time of day, the number of guests, and the spirit of the party when choosing a particular service style. Menus can be plated in the kitchen and placed directly on the table. Known as *service à l'assiette,* this is the style one expects in most modern restaurants.

5

Large platters can be carried by waiters, with each guest helping himself or herself with serving utensils. This is known as *service à la française,* which becomes *service à l'anglaise* when the waiter places the food on the guests' plates. More familiar perhaps is *family-style,* where platters are placed directly on the table and passed from guest to guest. In yet another style, *service à la russe,* food is presented by a waiter, who then "fixes" the plate on a gueridon, or side table. And of course there are large buffets from which guests help themselves, again and again.

I like to incorporate more than one style into a meal. It provides choreographic interest for the guests and alleviates bottlenecks in the kitchen.

When in doubt, serve from the left and clear from the right!

table decor

Creating a "look" is an expression of style. When it comes to table decor, my approach, not surprisingly, is simplicity.

Using one or two 3-hole candelabra with tall graceful tapers expresses either formality or romance. Sometimes I find a simple vessel — an old-fashioned painted can, an amphora, or a sleek glass pitcher — and fill it with three types of flowers, all the same color. Occasionally I scatter a variety of small vases or bottles, each with one flower, around the table. I may bed three pots of herbs in a basket, or create a triptych of fruits on a tall silver stand. A pyramid of scarlet strawberries, tiny purple champagne grapes, and stark white Jordan almonds placed strategically in little paper candy cups made a resplendent display for a friend's wedding shower. Not only beautiful, this simple decoration was good enough to eat. (For other edible 1-2-3 centerpieces, see page 32.)

If styles of service can change during a meal, so can the china. Serve dessert or salad on something quite different from the main course, and you'll liven up the occasion with no extra effort (or cost). Go one step further and serve two desserts on two different plates, alternating from guest to guest, and watch everyone start sharing.

My mother-in-law's hodgepodge of antique cups and saucers, used all at once, became a statement. My husband collects increasingly expensive double-helix brass candlesticks, and they all go on the table when company's coming.

A friend fills her table with old glass paperweights illuminated by a dozen votive candles. You can achieve a similar impact with those same votives in a large shallow bowl filled with glass marbles, or use your own collectibles as decoration.

Three is a powerful number, as the Japanese acknowledge with their style of flower arranging known as ikebana. This is the art form of cutting and arranging flowers into a new shape based on three main "branches" — just as 1-2-3 is the transformation of three main ingredients into a new form. It has been said of recipes that the most important ingredient is the one you leave out. This is analogous to the "free space" deliberately created in ikebana. In both cases, absence creates a kind of vitality.

There are several good books on ikebana, and once you've mastered the art of 1-2-3 cooking, you may wish to apply these principles to your tabletop.

wines 1-2-3

The world's a big place, and its people are making good wine. In the late 1970s, I was dating a wine distributor whose portfolio included Heitz, Phelps, Chalone, Mayacamas, Clos du Val, Trefethen, Spring Mountain, and Schramsberg, to name a few, and I developed a palate for California wines early on. I was then first chef to New York City mayor Ed Koch and moving in interesting food and wine circles. It was a time of experimentation, certainly, but also of discovery, for some of the wines in my own backyard — the Hudson Valley (Clinton Vineyards), the Finger Lakes (Hermann Wiemer), and Long Island (Lenz, Hargrave) — were then coming of age. Just as I was.

Today, while I'm still a passionate wine drinker and part of the team that re-created Windows on the World and the Rainbow Room, two New York restaurants known for their extraordinary cellars, it is "mission impossible" to stay current with new vintages and varietals that are produced around the globe. So I rely on my party line, three extraordinary experts on the subject of wine: Judy Rundel, Evan Goldstein, and Josh Wesson.

Judy helped with this book's grapenotes and discusses "big bottles" for parties; Evan is my California maven; Josh focuses on global wines, with some wonderful off-beat choices. I'll say more about them in Chapter 4.

the essence of entertaining

Our good friend James Beard once said that to entertain successfully, one must "create with the imagination of a playwright; plan with the skill of a director; and perform with the instincts of an actor. And, as any showman will tell you, there is no greater reward than pleasing your audience."

To fully grasp the essence of *Entertaining 1-2-3*, think about a 1-2-3 recipe that you already love. A peanut butter and jelly sandwich? A slab of peasant bread rubbed with garlic and doused with oil? An honest ham sandwich with real Dijon mustard? Toast with butter and Vegemite? A crusty roll smeared with sweet butter and filled with a wafer of bitter chocolate? An oyster crowned with caviar and a teardrop of lemon? A truffle omelette?

Whatever it is, put it on a beautiful plate and call a friend, or two. Everybody loves a party.

1-2-3 timeline

If a successful dish begins with quality ingredients, so does a successful party: good food, planned with style, cooked with care.

Entertaining can be a joy or a job — it depends on your outlook. But one thing's for sure: The more you do it, the easier it gets! Even the simplest approach, however, requires organization. A timeline is helpful; a succinct shopping list is essential; some kind of budget (for food, wine, flowers, and the like) is probably necessary.

So that your next party won't be your last, get organized. Molly O'Neill said it skillfully in her book *The Pleasure of Your Company*: "Overstated planning is the backbone of understated elegance."

7

1

one month to two weeks before

- Develop the idea/concept.
- Decide on the date and guests.
- Invite guests (send invitations for more formal events; call for informal events).

2

two to one week before

- Create a menu with wines (within your budget).
- Make a shopping list.
- Hire any help.
- Rent anything you might need.

3

final countdown

- Choose linens; arrange the tabletop and the centerpiece flowers.
- Prepare *mise-en-place* (get everything ready) and cook.
- Open the wines; serve the meal.
- Clean up.

morning guests

Morning meals lift my

spirits when they exceed expectations with their simplicity. A freshly made baguette, some fruit-juicy jam, and a great cup of joe make me cheerful. A toasted bagel with wasabi cream cheese (see page 102) makes me ecstatic.

Breakfast is a state of mind that rarely depends on what occurred the night before. I've discovered (having been one so often!) that morning guests are easy to charm because they're eager to start the day bright and refreshed. You just need to know *how* bright and lively the meal needs to be.

Breakfast can be "continental-style" or as bountiful as one of my seasonal "menus for six," when both host and guests have the luxury of time to linger over food and conversation.

Spring and summer menus can be enjoyed sit-down- or buffet-style, indoors or out. Winter and fall breakfasts beg for closeness around a warm table.

For those who prefer, or need, to sleep in and eat late, "elevenses," as they are called in Great Britain, are the perfect solution (see page 25). These late-morning snacks provide immeasurable pleasure, especially when served to your guests in bed.

Morning Quaffs
by the pitcher

- Mimosa, c. 1925 (page 79)

- Tequila Sunrise, c. 1930s (page 80)

- Amrus (page 85)

- Strawberry Frullato (page 85)

- Carrot-Apple Smoothie (page 85)

- Berry Bongo (page 86)

- Ginger-Pineapple Frappe (page 87)

- Moroccan Grape Drink (page 86)

- Rhubarb Lemonade (page 87)

  Multiply the recipes by the number of guests. Place all the ingredients in a large jar with a tight-fitting lid. Do not add any ice at this point. Refrigerate until ready to serve. Shake well and transfer contents to a decorative or clear glass pitcher. Serve each drink in its appropriate glass, with a bucket of ice and tongs on the side.

Morning Fruits
on a platter or in a bowl

cold

- Fresh Cherries on Ice, Sweet Lemon Mascarpone (page 193)

- Oranges and Grapefruit in Black Currant Syrup (page 159)

- Honeydew and Blueberries, Blueberry Drizzle (page 239)

- Ginger-Poached Pineapple (page 155)

- Blood Orange Salad (page 225)

- Mangoes in Lime Syrup (page 53)

warm

- Rhubarb Compote with Toasted Almond Streusel, Brown Sugar Syrup (page 164)

- Strawberries Catalan (page 147)

- Half-Pound Baked Apples, Ginger Cream (page 20)

- Fruit Compote in Honey-Lemon Syrup (page 250)

- Whole Spiced Pears, Mulled Syrup (page 216)

1-2-3 Breakfast Ideas

- Cook wheat berries in water for up to 2½ hours, until soft and tender. Add honey and poppy seeds, and serve for brunch on a chilly day.

- On a hot summer morning, pretend you're in Sicily: Spoon some gelato onto a split soft roll or a brioche. Drink coffee.

- Breakfast oasis: Toast pita bread over an open fire. Have small bowls of za'atar and extra-virgin olive oil for dunking. Drink Mint Tea (see page 26).

- Make a sweet breakfast omelette: unsalted butter, farm-fresh eggs, and a fancy jam — such as cloudberry or greengage plum — as a filling.

- Bake an egg in a custard cup, placed in a water bath, for 8 minutes. Turn out onto a piece of toast (cut into a large circle) and drizzle with truffle oil. Pass the pepper mill.

- Make giant apple turnovers: Cook peeled apple chunks with confectioners' sugar, then mash coarsely. Mound on squares of puff pastry, fold over, and bake. Drizzle with icing made from confectioners' sugar and water.

- Mix leftover linguine with well-beaten eggs, salt, and pepper. Fry like a thick pancake in olive oil until crisp on both sides but creamy in the center.

- Make fancy breakfast quesadillas with large flour tortillas: jalapeño jack cheese and crisp bacon; smoked salmon and goat cheese flavored with herbs; cream cheese and pepper jelly. Bake in a hot oven.

- Slice ripe cantaloupe into thin wedges, removing the rind with a sharp knife. Drape with paper-thin slices of speck (smoked prosciutto) or Black Forest ham. Serve with a glass of prosecco, an Italian white sparkling wine.

- Buy large yeast-raised glazed doughnuts. Fry in a little butter, pressing down with a spatula, and flip like pancakes. Serve with grilled ham steak.

- Gently warm smoked trout. Serve with soft-scrambled eggs cooked in a bit of bacon fat and crisscrossed with slices of crisp bacon.

- Toast or steam a few tortillas. Top with two poached eggs and prepared salsa. (Also great with fresh lime juice hollandaise.)

- Grill or broil a thick slice of gravlax. Serve with poached eggs and homemade melba toast.

- Cover small dried figs with low-fat milk and refrigerate overnight. Serve with a warm almond croissant.

- Make a real *pain au chocolat:* Split a wedge of yeasty peasant bread, butter lightly with softened sweet butter, and slip in a 1/8-inch-thick piece of Valrhona semisweet chocolate.

- Cut English muffins (I prefer Wolferman's) in half and toast well. Peel and slice fresh pears, pile high on muffin halves, and cover with thin slices of Brie (rind removed). Melt under the broiler.

- Toss a sprightly fruit salad. Mix segments (without membranes) of oranges and pink grapefruit with ginger marmalade. Let marinate in the refrigerator for 2 hours, until very cold. Serve in scooped-out orange shells.

- Split croissants in half lengthwise, toast lightly, and . . . shingle thinly sliced fresh apricots on top, sprinkle with confectioners' sugar, and broil until the sugar begins to caramelize; fill with mascarpone and homemade strawberry jam; fill with sliced apples sautéed in butter; top with ripe raspberries and drizzle with aromatic honey; serve with a small pot of melted chocolate (with a cinnamon stick) for dunking; spread with cold crème fraîche and hot apple butter; slather with lemon curd and top with ripe blackberries.

Recipes à la Carte

normandy oats with cider syrup and soft whipped cream

2½ cups apple cider
3 cups old-fashioned rolled oats
⅔ cup heavy cream

- Put apple cider in small saucepan. Bring to a boil, lower heat to medium, and cook for 30 minutes, whisking often, until cider is reduced to a syrup (about ½ cup). Set aside.
- *To make oatmeal:* Bring 5¼ cups water and ¼ teaspoon salt to a boil in medium pot. Add oats and cook over medium heat for 5 minutes, stirring frequently. Add 2 tablespoons heavy cream. Cook for a minute or so more, until oatmeal is the desired thickness.
- Meanwhile, in medium bowl whip remaining cream until soft peaks form.
- To serve, divide hot oatmeal equally among 6 flat soup plates. Top with whipped cream and drizzle with cider syrup. Serve hot.

serves 6

sturgeon with chive flowers and lemon oil

1¼ pounds smoked sturgeon
1 bunch fresh chives, preferably with flowers
3 tablespoons lemon oil *

- Slice sturgeon very thinly on a slight bias, using a long, thin-bladed, sharp knife.
- Arrange overlapping slices on large platter or divide evenly among 6 large plates.
- Arrange several long chives and chive flowers around fish. Chop remaining chives into ¼-inch lengths and scatter on and around fish.
- Drizzle ½ tablespoon lemon oil on and around each portion of fish.

serves 6

   * Use a top-quality brand such as Colavita.

toasted bagels with salt-cured tomatoes and ricotta cheese

12 ripe medium tomatoes (about 4½ pounds), preferably 6 red and 6 yellow
6 bagels *
15-ounce container ricotta cheese

- Slice tomatoes ⅓ inch thick. Discard ends. Place in large bowl and sprinkle with 2½ teaspoons kosher salt. Mix gently. Let sit for 30 minutes.
- Cut bagels in half and toast well in oven or toaster oven. You want them to get golden brown and crisp.
- Drain tomatoes but reserve juice. Reserve 6 slices for garnish. Layer tomatoes on toasted bagel halves. Spoon on a little tomato juice. Top each with 2 heaping tablespoons ricotta cheese. Garnish each with half a slice of tomato.
- Crush 2 tablespoons whole black peppercorns using the bottom of a bottle or a heavy glass. Scatter over bagel halves.

serves 6 or more

> * Buy large fresh bagels with a crusty exterior from a good bagel shop. Frozen bagels will not be satisfactory.

sable with dill cream

1 cup sour cream *
1 large bunch fresh dill
1½ pounds smoked sable

- Put sour cream in food processor. Wash dill and dry. Coarsely chop enough dill so that you have ⅓ cup packed. Save remaining dill for garnish.
- Add ⅓ cup dill to food processor. Add ⅛ teaspoon salt (or more to taste) and freshly ground black pepper. Process until smooth. Chill until ready to use.
- Slice sable thinly on the bias. Arrange in overlapping slices on platter or 6 large plates.
- Drizzle dill cream around fish. You will need about 2½ tablespoons cream for each portion. Garnish with small sprigs of remaining dill.

serves 6

> * You may substitute light sour cream.

scrambled eggs, hollandaise-style

16 extra-large eggs
10 tablespoons unsalted butter
2 large lemons

- Using a large wire whisk, beat eggs until light and fluffy. Add ½ teaspoon salt and freshly ground white pepper.
- Butter large metal bowl (one that will fit over pot of water to create double-boiler) with 2 tablespoons butter.
- Grate rind of lemons so that you have 1½ teaspoons grated zest. Cut lemons in half and squeeze 2½ tablespoons juice. Set aside.
- Place buttered bowl over pot of simmering water. You do not want the bottom of the bowl to touch the water. Add eggs and stir, using a flexible rubber spatula. Cut remaining butter into small pieces and periodically add to egg mixture, stirring constantly. The eggs will eventually begin to thicken.
- Add lemon zest and juice, and any remaining butter. Continue to cook until eggs meld into a smooth, thick, saucelike consistency, about 15 minutes. Add salt and white pepper to taste. Serve hot.

serves 6

sorrel frittata

16 extra-large eggs
½ pound fresh sorrel *
5 tablespoons unsalted butter

- Preheat oven to 400°.
- Put eggs in bowl of electric mixer. Add ½ teaspoon salt and freshly ground white pepper. Mix thoroughly until smooth and somewhat frothy.
- Wash sorrel and dry well. Remove bottom ¼ inch of stems and discard.
- Melt 4 tablespoons butter in 12-inch nonstick skillet. Add sorrel and cook over medium heat for 1 minute, until sorrel wilts. Sprinkle with a little salt. Do not overcook, or sorrel will turn an unpleasant khaki color.
- Add beaten eggs and cook for 5 to 6 minutes over medium heat, loosening eggs at sides of pan from time to time. Cook until set on the bottom but still runny on top. Thinly slice remaining 1 tablespoon butter and scatter on top.
- Bake until just set, about 3 to 4 minutes. (Time will vary.) Place under broiler for 1 minute. Remove from oven. Cut into wedges and serve warm or at room temperature, not piping hot.

serves 6

* You may substitute tender, young fresh spinach leaves.

eggs fontina ranchero

**1¾ cups medium-hot *salsa verde* with
    tomatillos** *
6 extra-large eggs
6 ounces Danish fontina cheese

- Preheat broiler.
- Pour *salsa verde* into heavy 10-inch nonstick skillet. Bring to a boil and lower heat. Break eggs directly into salsa: Place 1 in center and others in a circle. Add a grinding of black pepper and a pinch of salt.
- Remove rind from cheese and grate cheese on large holes of box grater. Mound cheese over each raw egg. Cover and cook over medium heat for 6 to 8 minutes, or until whites are just set.
- Put under broiler for 1 to 2 minutes, until yolks are cooked as you like. (It tastes great if the yolks are still a little runny.) Serve immediately.

serves 6

* I use Old El Paso.

goat cheese soufflé

12 extra-large eggs
12 ounces fresh goat cheese flavored with herbs
4 tablespoons unsalted butter

- Preheat oven to 400°.
- Separate eggs. Place yolks in bowl of electric mixer. Place whites in another bowl and set aside.
- Break cheese into small pieces and add to egg yolks. Melt 3 tablespoons butter in small saucepan. Add to egg yolk–cheese mixture. Whip until smooth. Add ¼ teaspoon salt and freshly ground black pepper. Mix again and transfer to large bowl.
- Using electric mixer, beat egg whites with ½ teaspoon salt until stiff. Fold whites into cheese mixture using a flexible rubber spatula.
- Butter 8- or 9-cup soufflé dish (about 8¼ inches in diameter) with remaining 1 tablespoon butter. Place foil collar around soufflé dish, tightly securing with string, so that foil extends 3 inches above dish. Pour in egg mixture and bake for 40 minutes. Remove from oven and serve hot.

serves 6

breakfast sausages
on rosemary branches

**12 to 18 small breakfast sausages (1 ounce
each) ***
12 to 18 sturdy rosemary branches
12 to 18 small cherry tomatoes

- In 12-inch nonstick skillet, brown sausages on all
sides until almost cooked through. Let cool.
- Preheat oven to 450°.
- Strip rosemary branches of all leaves except
1 inch at top. Save leaves for another use. If rosemary branches are very long, cut them in half
and then strip leaves.
- Thread each rosemary branch as follows:
Puncture a cherry tomato with hard end of rosemary branch and push tomato to just below tuft
of rosemary leaves. Next, place a sausage
lengthwise on rosemary skewer. You may need
to trim the bottom so that no more than ¼ inch
of the branch protrudes from the sausage.
- Using small pieces of aluminum foil, cover rosemary leaves and tomato on each branch. Place
branches on baking sheet and bake for 5 minutes, or until hot. Remove foil and serve.

serves 6

*
I use Jones All Natural Little Pork Sausages.

peppery pastrami hash

3 large baking potatoes
1 pound cold pastrami, in 1 piece
3 tablespoons unsalted butter

- Wash potatoes. Place in pot and add water to
cover. Bring to a boil, then lower heat. Cover and
simmer for 40 to 45 minutes, or until potatoes
are tender but not too soft. Drain and refrigerate
until cold.
- Peel potatoes and cut into small cubes. Cut cold
pastrami into small cubes.
- Place potatoes and pastrami on large cutting
board. Using a large chef's knife, chop potatoes
and meat finely until they come together to look
like uncooked hash. Season with lots of freshly
ground black pepper.
- Melt 2 tablespoons butter in 10-inch nonstick
skillet. Add hash mixture and press flat with
spatula. Cook over medium-high heat for
20 minutes, until a brown crust forms.
- Carefully slip onto plate. Cover plate with
upside-down pan, then invert both plate and
pan so hash ends crisp side up. Add remaining
tablespoon of butter to pan. Cook over medium-
high heat for 10 minutes, until crisp.
- Slide out onto plate. Cut into 6 wedges.

serves 6

19

crisp potato cake

1¾ pounds Idaho potatoes
1 medium red onion
5 tablespoons vegetable oil

- Wash potatoes and place in large pot with water to cover. Bring to a boil, lower heat, and cook for 15 to 20 minutes, until potatoes are just tender. Rinse under cold water. Peel and let cool.
- Grate potatoes on large holes of box grater. Put in bowl. Peel onion and grate on large holes of grater. You will have about 3 tablespoons onion puree. Add to potatoes along with 1 teaspoon salt and freshly ground white pepper.
- In 10-inch nonstick skillet, heat 2½ tablespoons oil. Pack in potato-onion mixture and cook over medium heat for 10 to 12 minutes, or until bottom is crisp.
- Slide potato cake onto plate. Place pan upside down over cake, then invert both plate and pan so that cake is cooked side up. Carefully pour remaining oil around edge of potato cake and cook for 10 minutes, or until both sides are browned and crisp.

serves 6

half-pound baked apples, ginger cream

6 large Rome apples (½ pound each)
8 tablespoons Ginger Sugar (see page 300)
¾ cup heavy cream, well chilled

- Preheat oven to 400°.
- Wash and dry apples, but do not peel. Core apples, then place in shallow baking pan side by side.
- Fill each apple with 1½ to 2 teaspoons Ginger Sugar. Put ⅛ inch water in bottom of pan. Bake for 30 minutes. Most of the water will evaporate. Sprinkle 2 tablespoons Ginger Sugar in bottom of pan and add ¼ cup water. Bake for 20 minutes more.
- Meanwhile, put cream in chilled bowl. Add remaining ginger sugar and beat with a wire whisk until thickened but still spoonable.
- Remove apples from pan. Add about ¼ cup hot water to pan and loosen caramelized sugar to make a thin caramel sauce. Reduce over high heat, if necessary. Spoon sauce over hot apples, then spoon on cream. Serve warm.

serves 6

marmalade tart

Pastry dough for 2 9-inch pie crusts *
¾ cup good-quality, very thick orange marmalade
½ cup confectioners' sugar

- Preheat oven to 350°.
- Roll out dough to make 2 thin 9½-inch-diameter circles. Place 1 pastry circle on baking sheet lined with parchment paper. Spoon marmalade evenly over pastry, leaving a 1-inch border.
- Use a cookie cutter to cut a 1½-inch-diameter circle from center of second pastry circle and discard center. Brush edges lightly with water and place pastry on marmalade. Press edges of pastry circles together tightly. Trim edges with a small sharp knife.
- Bake for 35 minutes, or until golden brown. Remove from oven and let cool for 15 minutes.
- In small bowl, mix together confectioners' sugar and 1 tablespoon cold water until smooth. Spread evenly over top crust of warm tart, being careful not to cover hole in center. Serve warm or at room temperature.

serves 8

  * Use frozen pie shells or packaged pie crust mix.

cream cheese riffs:

"chocolate"
strawberry cheesecake
honey-walnut
maple-raisin
orange-rum

Here's a way to turn breakfast into a coffee klatch. Dress up a basket of breakfast breads, or even a simple offering of toast, with an array of flavorful, colorful, and slightly addictive cream cheeses, lightly sweetened.

Pack the cream cheeses into ramekins or small coffee cups and chill until ready to serve. Bring to room temperature for easy spreading.

"chocolate"

8 ounces cream cheese
⅓ cup Nutella *
1 tablespoon confectioners' sugar

- Put ingredients in bowl of electric mixer. Using the paddle, mix until ingredients are thoroughly incorporated. Do not overmix. Cover and chill.

makes 1 heaping cup

> * Hazelnut spread with cocoa, available in most supermarkets.

strawberry cheesecake

8 ounces cream cheese
3 tablespoons strawberry preserves
¼ cup confectioners' sugar

- Put ingredients in bowl of electric mixer. Using the paddle, beat just until smooth. Cover and chill.

makes 1 heaping cup

honey-walnut

½ cup coarsely chopped walnuts
8 ounces cream cheese
3 tablespoons wildflower honey

- Put walnuts in a small nonstick skillet. Heat 1 to 2 minutes over medium heat, stirring often, until toasted. Let cool.
- Place cream cheese and honey in bowl of electric mixer. Using the paddle, beat just until smooth. Add nuts and mix. Cover and chill.

makes 1¼ cups

orange-rum

8 ounces cream cheese
¼ cup sweet orange marmalade
½ teaspoon rum extract

- Place all ingredients in bowl of food processor. Process briefly until just blended. Do not over-process. Cover and chill.

makes 1 heaping cup

maple-raisin

8 ounces cream cheese
3 tablespoons real maple syrup
Heaping ⅓ cup raisins

- Place all ingredients in bowl of food processor. Process briefly until all ingredients are incorporated. Do not overprocess. Cover and chill.

makes about 1¼ cups

Seasonal Menus for Six

winter

- Normandy Oats with Cider Syrup and Soft Whipped Cream (page 15)

- Scrambled Eggs, Hollandaise-Style (page 17)

- Breakfast Sausages on Rosemary Branches (page 19)

- Olive Oil Biscuits, Hot from the Oven (page 133)

- Oranges and Grapefruit in Black Currant Syrup (page 159)

spring

- Sturgeon with Chive Flowers and Lemon Oil (page 15)

- Apple Cider Cucumber Salad (page 60)

- Goat Cheese Soufflé (page 18)

- Crisp Potato Cake (page 20)

- Strawberries Catalan (page 147)

summer

- Sable with Dill Cream (page 16)

- Sorrel Frittata (page 17)

- Toasted Bagels with Salt-Cured Tomatoes and Ricotta Cheese (page 16)

- Honeydew and Blueberries, Blueberry Drizzle (page 239)

fall

- Mangoes in Lime Syrup (page 53)

- Eggs Fontina Ranchero (page 18)

- Peppery Pastrami Hash (page 19)

- Half-Pound Baked Apples, Ginger Cream (page 20)

"Elevenses": Late-Morning Snacks

Pithiviers of Apricots and Almond Paste
  (page 143)

Earl Grey Tea

❧

Red Delicious Apple Tarts (page 64)

Rosemary Lemonade (page 86)

❧

Puits d'Amour (page 229)

Viennese Coffee (page 27)

❧

Red Papaya Tart (page 234)

Thai Coffee (page 26)

❧

Marmalade Tart (page 21)

Ice-Cold Milk

❧

Amrus (page 85)

Little Nut Cakes (page 250)

Café au Lait (page 27)

❧

Whole Spiced Pears, Mulled Syrup (page 216)

Cinnamon-Raisin Toast

Chamomile Tea

Cocktail Sandwiches: Smoked Salmon–
  Horseradish and Open-Faced Cucumber-
  Feta (page 98)

English Breakfast Tea

❧

Star Anise Tea Eggs (page 121)

Oranges

Rice Cakes

Green Tea

❧

Plugged Honeydew with Prosciutto (page 137)

Grissini and Sweet Butter Curls

Prosecco

❧

Oysters, Black Radish, Chipolata Sausages
  (page 222)

Melba Toast

Sherry

Espresso

Teas and Coffees

mint tea

**3 tablespoons loose green tea leaves
(from China)**
1 cup fresh mint leaves
Sugar to taste

- Place tea in 6-cup nonreactive teapot. Pour in 1 cup boiling water, then discard water, leaving wet tea leaves in pot. Add mint leaves and sugar. Fill pot with 6 cups boiling water. Let steep for 10 minutes, stirring occasionally. Serve hot in small glasses or teacups.

serves 6

lemon "tea"

2 large lemons
4 tablespoons sugar
1 tablespoon orange-flower water

- Wash lemons well and cut into quarters. Place in a nonreactive medium saucepan with 6 cups water and bring to a boil. Cover and cook over medium heat for 20 minutes. Strain into nonreactive, flameproof teapot. Add sugar and orange-flower water. Bring just to a boil and serve.

serves 6

thai coffee

Sweetened condensed milk
Finely ground espresso beans
1 blade lemongrass or 1 long cinnamon stick

- Place ½ inch sweetened condensed milk in small drinking glass. Place ground espresso in a stainless-steel single-cup coffee filter that sits on top of glass and pour boiling water over espresso. Or make a separate pot of strong espresso and pour ½ cup espresso over condensed milk. Use lemongrass or cinnamon stick as stirrer. This is also delicious chilled and served over ice.

serves 1

café au lait

3 cups freshly brewed strong coffee
1 cup milk, scalded or steamed
Sugar as desired, or 4 wafers good-quality
    bittersweet chocolate

- Pour hot coffee into 4 large cups or ceramic French bowls made expressly for this purpose. Using a spoon, add milk and its foam to coffee. Serve with sugar or a piece of chocolate on the side.

serves 4

viennese coffee

- Top each cup of freshly brewed strong coffee with heavy cream that has been whipped with Vanilla Sugar (see page 299). Use a strong Viennese roast.

serves 1

middle eastern coffee

- Use a finjan, which is a long-handled brass or copper pot that is narrow at the top and collects the foam of the coffee. Into the pot, put 1 tablespoon very finely ground coffee beans, about 1 teaspoon sugar (or to taste), and about ½ cup water. Over very low heat, bring to a frothy boil. When the foam rises, remove from heat until it settles. Add a few cardamom pods and repeat process. Pour into small coffee cup, spooning in some of the foam.

serves 1

COFFEE-MAKING EQUIPMENT

I always grind my own beans immediately before using. I own two 12-cup coffeemakers and use one or both as needed, transferring the contents to an attractive insulated pot.

   For espresso, I use a large traditional Neapolitan-style coffeepot.

---

casual lunches

Simplicity rules, especially

around lunchtime. Once considered the big meal of the day, lunch has given way to food that is lighter and simpler, but no less stylish and satisfying.

The following menus are deliciously uncomplicated and best served in an informal setting.

Begin with a simple hors d'oeuvre, which you may select from Chapter 5. Offer sparkling water, a glass of wine, or a refined glass (copita) of sherry. Then move on to a proper three-course meal comprising a light starter; a main course with one, or sometimes two, appropriate side dishes; and an unfussy dessert.

As always, to help preserve the sanity of the host, I have included a balance of hot and cold dishes, simple techniques, and recipes that can be prepared ahead of time.

To make some of my menus more elaborate, insert a cheese course before dessert or expand the number of hors d'oeuvres and the time allotted for them.

Want to simplify? Serve a light meal consisting of an elegant soup and stylish sandwich or salad, as listed on page 31. You may replace any of the menus' desserts with a big bowl or platter of whole and cut fresh fruit.

Presenting a bowl of ice water for dunking grapes or other small fruits is a lovely idea. Provide each guest with a beautiful plate, a dessert fork, and a knife. Homemade cookies (see page 32) are a thoughtful addition.

Most of the menus, serving four or six, can be easily doubled.

And should the occasion arise to dazzle unexpected guests, try my "1-2-3 Lunch Ideas" (see pages 65–67) and my recipes for spontaneous entertaining (see Chapter 10). These include sophisticated fare made with minimum time and effort.

Little Soup Meals

Roasted Tomato and Onion Soup (page 191)

Provolone-Pesto Pizza (page 123)

❧

Sweet Garlic-Fennel Soup (page 204)

Smoked Trout and Watercress Salad, Walnut Oil–Green Sauce (page 261)

❧

Lentil Soup with Sherry Vinegar (page 63)

Edam-Up Quesadillas (page 241)

❧

Oyster Bisque (page 252)

"Hearts" of Bibb, White Balsamic Vinaigrette (page 227)

❧

Pumpkin Soup with Cider Syrup (page 267)

Pear, Endive, and Boursin Salad (page 141)

Chilled Asparagus Bisque with Crabmeat (page 31)

Cocktail Sandwiches: Smoked Salmon–Horseradish and Open-Faced Cucumber-Feta (page 98)

Mesclun Salad, Raspberry Vinaigrette (page 55)

❧

Turnip and Potato Soup, Salt Pork "Croutons" (page 145)

Herring Salad with Dill Havarti (page 257)

❧

Carrot, Leek, and Chestnut Soup (page 214)

Salad of Arugula and Currants (page 52)

Serve the soups with a crusty baguette or Olive Oil Biscuits, Hot from the Oven (page 133).

Keep the wine selection simple: a glass of "unassuming" white or red.

Follow "Little Soup Meals" with a simple dessert: Fresh Fruit in Season (page 32), Great Fruit and Cheese Combinations (page 120), or Homemade Cookies (page 32).

fresh fruit in season

Delicious three-ingredient centerpieces you can eat.

winter

Blood oranges • star fruit • New Zealand currants

Clementines • cherimoya • winter melons

Seckel pears • lady apples • string of cranberries

spring

First strawberries • pineapple • kiwifruit

Loquats • raspberries • cultivated blueberries

Papaya • finger bananas • early cherries

summer

Apricots • guava • watermelon

Cavaillon melon • champagne grapes • lychee nuts

White peaches • blackberries • figs

fall

Asian pears • pomegranates • tangerines

Italian plums • Forelle pears • roasted chestnuts

Persimmons • local apples • whole walnuts

great cheese and fruit combinations

(page 120)

homemade cookies

- Cocoa Clouds (page 225)
- Coconut Kisses (page 53)
- Chickpea Flour Cookies (page 202)
- Crispy Oatcakes (page 119)
- Marmalade Tart (page 21), cut into slivers

Brunch, Italian-Style

Roasted Pepper Salad with Anchovies and Crushed Almonds

Penne Pasta à la Vodka

Chicken-Stuffed Ravioli with Fresh Sage Butter

Granita di Caffè

Every so often my husband and I are struck by a food memory: Like those fat anchovies and roasted peppers, lubricated by a bitter-edged Negroni, eaten in front of the ancient Marconi e Milano Hotel in Venice.

Or the first time we strolled around the Piazza Navona in Rome, eating coffee granita for breakfast, piled high on a brioche and topped with whipped cream.

Then there's that sexy *ristorante* Enoteca Pinchiorri (via Ghibellina 87) in Florence, where we first experienced pasta with vodka. We were in love.

And what about those wood-grilled sardines at Il Romazzino in, appropriately enough, Sardinia. But that's another story . . . and another menu.

For this menu, make the first course early in the day and the dessert the day before. Serve the peppers on a large platter or divvy them up among four large plates. The main course can be plated in the kitchen, with some of each pasta placed on each large plate, or passed on separate platters at the table. Let guests break off pieces of Italian bread to accompany the first and main courses.

grapenote
What could be more stylish than an Italian dry Rosé? Sip a Chiaretto Bardolino or a Sicilian Rosato from Regaleali.

roasted pepper salad with anchovies and crushed almonds

4 large red bell peppers (1½ pounds)
2-ounce can rolled anchovies with capers in oil
½ cup (about 3 ounces) shelled almonds,
    with skins

- *To roast peppers:* Place whole peppers on baking sheet 6 inches from preheated broiler. Broil on all sides until they begin to blacken, about 10 minutes. Place hot peppers in paper bag, then seal bag and allow peppers to steam and soften.
- When peppers are cool, peel off skin using your fingers or a sharp knife. Cut peppers in half lengthwise and remove seeds. *Note:* Do not wash peppers, because you want to collect their juices. Place peppers and juices on a platter.
- Remove rolled anchovies with capers from oil and set aside. Drizzle oil over peppers and add a grinding of black pepper.
- Using a large sharp knife on a cutting board, chop almonds coarsely. Place in nonstick skillet and toast over medium heat until golden brown. Return nuts to board and use a rolling pin to crush them to a coarse powder. Sprinkle over peppers.
- Unroll anchovies. Place flat anchovies on top of almonds and scatter with capers. Let marinate for 30 minutes before serving.

serves 4

penne pasta à la vodka

1 pound penne pasta, preferably tricolor
12 ounces Italian Gorgonzola cheese
6 tablespoons lemon vodka

- Bring large pot of salted water to a boil. Add pasta and cook for 10 to 12 minutes, until al dente.
- Remove rind from cheese, then cut cheese into small pieces. Place in large nonstick saucepan with 4 tablespoons vodka. Warm over medium heat until cheese melts. Add remaining 2 tablespoons vodka and lots of freshly ground black pepper. Keep warm.
- Drain pasta in colander, shaking off excess water. Add pasta to melted cheese sauce and heat for 1 to 2 minutes, tossing until pasta is thoroughly coated with sauce. Serve immediately on 4 warm, large plates.

serves 4

chicken-stuffed ravioli with fresh sage butter

1½ pounds small chicken-stuffed ravioli
8 tablespoons unsalted butter
3 bunches fresh sage (½ cup coarsely chopped leaves, plus 12 whole leaves)

- Bring large pot of salted water to a boil. Add ravioli and cook until al dente, about 8 minutes or according to package directions.
- Melt 7 tablespoons butter in large nonstick skillet. Add chopped sage, pinch of salt, and freshly ground black pepper. Cook over medium heat until butter just begins to brown and bubble. Add whole sage leaves. Toss for 1 minute and keep warm.
- Drain ravioli in colander, saving ¼ cup cooking water.
- Put hot pasta, melted sage butter, and remaining 1 tablespoon unmelted butter in large bowl. Toss well, adding enough cooking water to make a smooth sauce.
- Divide evenly among 4 warm, large plates, placing the whole cooked leaves on top. Serve immediately.

serves 4

granita di caffé

3 cups freshly brewed double-strength coffee or espresso [*]
½ cup plus 1 tablespoon sugar
½ cup heavy cream

- In medium saucepan, heat coffee and ½ cup sugar, stirring until sugar is dissolved; do not boil. Remove from heat and let cool.
- Pour sweetened coffee into shallow metal pan and freeze for 2 to 3 hours, until mushy, stirring with a fork every 30 minutes. Do not let mixture freeze solid.
- Whip cream with remaining 1 tablespoon sugar.
- Before serving, put frozen slush in bowl of electric mixer and beat for a few seconds. Spoon into chilled wineglasses and top with whipped cream.[**] Serve immediately.

serves 4

[*] This is also delicious made with a flavored coffee such as hazelnut, cinnamon, or vanilla.

[**] If you do not wish to serve this granita with cream, add 2 tablespoons Benedictine, sambuca, or Strega to the coffee mixture before freezing.

35

Fondue: It's Back!

Wine and Cheese Fondue

Course #1: Vegetables for Dunking

Course #2: Pear and Toasted Almond Bruschetta

It's the year 2000. Do you know where your fondue pot is? Better dust it off, or if you've recklessly donated it to charity, buy a new *caquelon* — an authentic earthenware pot made just for fondue. These pots are available at good cookware shops.

La fondue, as the Swiss call their beloved dish, is a party in itself. This fondue does the two-step (which hasn't come back — yet). For the first course, you dunk lovely steamed vegetables *into* the pot. Next comes a course of sweet pear *bruschetta, over* which you pour the fondue.

Quality is critical here. Use real aged Swiss Gruyère for a nutty flavor and properly creamy texture. The wrong cheese may remind you why fondue disappeared in the first place.

grapenote

If it's authenticity you're after, the classic wine accompaniment is Swiss Chasselas or Fendant. Or try a minimally wooded Chardonnay from Australia, such as Oxford Landing, Jacob's Creek, or Queen Adelaide.

wine and cheese fondue

2 pounds Swiss Gruyère cheese
3 tablespoons all-purpose flour
2 cups Chardonnay or other dry white wine

- Using a sharp knife, remove rind from cheese. Grate cheese on large holes of box grater. Mix with 1½ tablespoons flour.
- Place floured cheese in medium heavy saucepan or fondue pot. Add wine and ½ teaspoon salt, and bring to a boil. Lower heat to medium and stir vigorously with wooden spoon until cheese is completely melted, about 5 minutes. Add remaining 1½ tablespoons flour, stirring constantly. Cook for about 2 minutes, until floury taste is gone.
- The result should be a smooth, thick, creamy sauce. If too thick, add more wine that has been warmed. You also may make half the amount for the first course and then repeat the process for the second course.

serves 6

course #1: vegetables for dunking

1 pound fresh baby carrots, preferably organic
¾ pound thin fresh asparagus
2 fennel bulbs

- Peel carrots. Snap off woody ends from asparagus. Peel bottom 3 inches of asparagus with vegetable peeler. Steam carrots for 5 minutes over boiling water. Add asparagus and steam for 2 minutes. Let cool.
- Remove outer pieces of fennel, cutting away any brown spots. Cut fennel into wedges.
- Serve vegetables on large platter. Dunk them in hot fondue (see the preceding recipe) to coat, then eat.

serves 6

37

course #2:
pear and toasted almond
bruschetta

6 large slices semolina bread with sesame
    seeds, sliced on the bias, or 6 slices brioche
    loaf
3 large ripe pears
¾ cup (2 ounces) sliced almonds, lightly toasted

- Toast bread lightly on both sides. Peel pears
  and remove any seeds. Slice pears and place
  on toasted bread in an overlapping pattern.
  Sprinkle toasted almonds over pears. Pour remaining warm fondue (see recipe on page 37)
  over *bruschetta*. Serve on individual plates with
  forks and knives.

serves 6

38

Easy as a Summer Breeze

Asparagus Tonnato

Sage Shrimp and Crispy Pancetta

Borlotti Beans with Tomato and Roasted Garlic

Granita di Limetta

There is a certain irony about cooking in summer, for generally we grill food that has considerable heft — big burgers, juicy sirloins, meaty ribs. In contrast, this menu satisfies with cool flavors and rewards with a bearable lightness of being.

Tonnato refers to the creamy, lemony tuna sauce that normally graces thin slices of *vitello,* or roasted veal, and has become a quintessential summer dish. A similar preparation applied to chilled jade green asparagus promises to be equally estival.

Soak the beans overnight and prepare them, along with the roasted garlic, early in the morning before the summer sun heats up your kitchen. Ultra-ripe summer tomatoes need only to be julienned and added minutes before your guests arrive.

Make the bracing granita in the afternoon, a good a time to fix yourself a refreshing Lime Rickey: Simple Syrup (see page 299), lime juice, and seltzer.

grapenote
Keep this meal easy and serve one wine all the way through. The grassiness of asparagus and the sage in the shrimp dish call for Sauvignon Blanc. Try Hogue Cellars from Washington State or Alderbrook from Sonoma; both have a little weight and a breezy touch of oak.

asparagus tonnato

1 6-ounce can light tuna packed in olive oil *
2 large lemons
1½ pounds thick fresh asparagus

- Put tuna and oil in blender. Grate lemon rinds so that you have 2 teaspoons grated zest. Put 1 teaspoon zest in blender and reserve remaining zest in dampened paper towel. Squeeze ¼ cup lemon juice and add to blender. Puree until very smooth. Transfer tuna sauce to small bowl. Cover and refrigerate.
- Cut 1 inch from bottom of asparagus stalks and discard. Peel lower half of stalks with vegetable peeler.
- Bring large pot of salted water to a boil. Add asparagus and cook over medium heat until bright green and tender, about 5 minutes. Be careful not to overcook.
- Drain immediately and plunge into bowl of ice water to prevent further cooking. Remove from water and pat dry.
- Divide asparagus into stacks in center of 4 large chilled plates. Spoon tuna sauce evenly over midsection of asparagus. Garnish with reserved lemon zest.

serves 4

   *
Use a brand imported from Italy if possible.

sage shrimp and crispy pancetta

1½ pounds (20) uncooked large shrimp, in their shells
6 ounces pancetta, cut into ¼-inch dice
28 fresh sage leaves (about 2 bunches)

- Remove shells from shrimp, leaving tails on. Set aside.
- Put diced pancetta in large nonstick skillet. Cook over low heat until fat is rendered and pancetta begins to turn golden and crispy.
- Add shrimp, raise heat slightly, and cook over medium heat for 2 minutes, until shrimp begin to turn opaque.
- Coarsely tear 24 sage leaves, add to pan, toss gently, and cover. Reduce heat and cook over low heat for 1 to 2 minutes. Uncover pan. Add ¼ teaspoon butcher-grind black pepper and 2 tablespoons water. Cook for 1 minute more, stirring with wooden spoon.
- Serve immediately. Garnish with remaining sage leaves.

serves 4

borlotti beans with
tomato and roasted garlic

½ pound dried borlotti (cranberry) beans *
1 clove plus 1 large head garlic
¾ pound ripe plum tomatoes

- Soak beans overnight in cold water.
- Preheat oven to 400°.
- Drain beans in colander. Place in medium pot with cover. Add enough fresh water to cover beans by 1 inch and bring to a boil. Finely mince 1 clove garlic and add to beans along with 1 teaspoon salt and ¼ teaspoon whole black peppercorns. Cover pot and lower heat. Simmer for 1½ hours, or until beans are tender.
- Meanwhile, wrap garlic head in aluminum foil, folded to make a packet. Place in shallow baking pan and roast for 1 hour.
- Cut tomatoes in half lengthwise. Scoop out seeds and flesh and set aside. Cut tomato shells into long julienne strips. Add to beans for the last 5 minutes of cooking.

- Drain beans and tomato julienne, saving ¼ cup cooking liquid. Place beans and tomato in bowl. Cut cooked head of garlic in half through the center to expose all the cloves. Squeeze pulp onto beans and mix well, adding reserved cooking liquid.
- Puree reserved tomato seeds and flesh in blender until very smooth. Add to beans with salt and freshly ground black pepper to taste. Mix gently. Serve immediately or reheat gently before serving.

serves 4 (makes 4 cups)

* You may substitute dried small white beans.

41

granita di limetta

10 large limes
¾ cup sugar
1 extra-large egg white

- Grate rinds of 3 limes so that you have 2 teaspoons grated zest. Cut enough limes in half to produce 1 cup lime juice.
- In medium pot, bring 2½ cups water and sugar to a boil. Lower heat and simmer for 1 minute.
- Transfer sugar syrup to bowl. Add lime juice and zest. Let cool. Beat egg white with fork until frothy. Add beaten white to lime syrup and place in large, shallow metal pan.
- Place in freezer. After 20 minutes, remove from freezer and stir with fork, crushing any lumps and breaking up ice crystals. Return to freezer. Continue this process every 20 to 30 minutes for up to 3 hours. Spoon into chilled glasses and serve immediately.

serves 4 or more

Tropical Flavors

Shiitake-Scallion Satés

Seared Tuna with Coconut Milk and Wasabi

Orange-Cucumber Salsa

Macadamia Rice with Basil

Star Fruit, Star Anise Syrup

With its overlay of tropical flavors and merger of trendy foodstuffs, this menu tastes like an island vacation.

Choose an hors d'oeuvre with the taste of the tropics, such as Pickled Pink Shrimp (page 102), Singing Clams (page 101), or Plum-Glazed Stuffed Mushrooms (page 106).

Prepare the menu as follows: The day before your luncheon, or the morning of, make the dessert. About one hour before lunch is to be served, make the salsa and assemble the satés. Refrigerate them on a baking sheet until you are ready to serve the first course. Glaze them just before baking.

Mix the coconut milk and wasabi, and let the flavors marry before you begin to cook. The rice and tuna should be prepared as close to serving time as possible.

For an interesting and exotic bread accompaniment, serve Curry Crisps (page 110), kept whole.

In winter, this menu will bring a bit of sunshine. In summer, it will provide a cooling zephyr.

grapenote
Begin with a Sake-tini (see page 81). Switch to a Sem-Chard from Australia — it has body and a touch of sweetness. Or take your palate in a different direction with a Grenache-Shiraz blend from Rosemount, also from "down under."

shiitake-scallion satés

1 pound medium-large shiitake mushrooms
12 thin scallions
6 tablespoons hoisin sauce, plus more for
**   serving (optional)**

- Soak 12 6-inch bamboo skewers in cold water for 15 minutes.
- Preheat oven to 425°.
- Wipe mushrooms with damp towel. Remove stems and discard. Cut larger mushroom caps in half on the bias. Leave smaller caps whole. You will need 24 pieces.
- Remove any roots from scallions. Cut white and pale green parts into 1½-inch pieces. You will need 36 pieces.
- Drain skewers. Spear 1 piece of scallion so that it is perpendicular to the skewer. Place mushroom on top of scallion so that the cap faces you. Repeat with a scallion, then a mushroom, and end with a scallion. Repeat process until you have 12 skewers.
- In small bowl, mix hoisin sauce with 4 tablespoons water until thoroughly incorporated. Using a pastry brush, glaze scallions and mushrooms with hoisin mixture.
- Place skewers on baking sheet and bake for 5 minutes. Serve 2 skewers per person, with an extra teaspoon of hoisin, if desired.

serves 6

seared tuna
with coconut milk
and wasabi

13½-ounce can unsweetened coconut milk
1 tablespoon wasabi powder *
6 9-ounce 1-inch-thick tuna steaks

- Mix coconut milk and wasabi powder in small bowl using a wire whisk. Make sure wasabi is thoroughly dissolved in milk. Let sit for 30 minutes.
- Transfer mixture to small saucepan. Bring to a boil, whisking constantly. Lower heat to medium and reduce mixture to 1½ cups. This will take about 5 minutes. Add ½ teaspoon salt and stir. Remove from heat.
- Sprinkle a thin layer of salt in 2 large nonstick skillets. Season tuna steaks with freshly ground black pepper.
- Place skillets over high heat. When hot, add tuna steaks. Cook for 2 minutes and turn. Cook for 1 to 2 minutes more, until tuna is seared on the outside but still rare on the inside.
- Remove tuna from skillets and let sit for 1 minute. Reheat coconut-wasabi sauce gently over low heat.
- Cut tuna on the bias into ½-inch-thick slices. Pour sauce over fish. Serve immediately.

serves 6

* Available in Asian markets and some specialty-food stores.

orange-cucumber salsa

4 large oranges
4 kirby cucumbers
½ cup rice-wine vinegar

- Grate the rind of 1 or 2 oranges so that you have 1 teaspoon grated zest.
- Using a small sharp knife, cut rind from all oranges and discard. Cut oranges into ¼-inch-thick slices. Cut slices into ¼-inch cubes. Remove any seeds. Place diced oranges in medium bowl along with any accumulated juices. You should have 2 cups.
- Peel 2 cucumbers. Wash remaining 2 cucumbers. Cut all 4 cucumbers into ¼-inch cubes. You should have 2 cups. Add to bowl with oranges.
- Pour vinegar over oranges and cucumbers. Add salt and freshly ground black pepper to taste. Cover and marinate in refrigerator for 1 to 2 hours. Serve chilled.

serves 6

macadamia rice with basil

1½ cups jasmine rice
2 ounces (scant ½ cup) salted, roasted macadamia nuts
1 bunch fresh basil

- Put 8 cups water and ½ teaspoon salt in medium pot. Bring to a boil. Add rice and cook over high heat for 18 to 20 minutes, or until cooked through and tender to the bite but not too soft.
- While rice is cooking, chop nuts coarsely, one at a time, with a sharp knife so that they do not crumble. You will have about ½ cup chopped nuts.
- Wash basil leaves and dry. Stack large leaves and roll tightly. Using a large sharp knife, cut into very fine julienne. You should have about ⅓ cup packed leaves. Save tiny whole leaves for garnish.
- When rice is done, drain immediately in fine-mesh sieve or colander. Return drained rice to pot and stir in nuts quickly until incorporated. Transfer rice to platter or large shallow bowl.
- Scatter julienned basil on rice and scatter small basil leaves around edge. Serve immediately.

serves 6

star fruit, star anise syrup

6 large star fruit (carambola) (6 ounces each)
1½ cups sugar
12 star anise *

- Wash star fruit. Trim ends and peel only pointed edges of fruit. Cut widthwise into ¼-inch-thick slices. You will see "stars." Remove any seeds.
- Put 6 cups water, sugar, and star anise in medium pot. Bring to a boil and continue boiling for 5 minutes.
- Add star fruit slices. (If sugar syrup does not cover fruit, add a little water.) Continue to cook over high heat for 2 minutes. Remove from heat.
- Let fruit cool in liquid. Transfer fruit and syrup to bowl, reserving 1 cup syrup. Cover fruit and refrigerate until very cold.
- In small saucepan, reduce reserved syrup over high heat to ½ cup. Syrup will be very thick.
- To serve, arrange fruit in large flat soup plates. Add 2 star anise to each. Add some of the poaching liquid. Drizzle with thickened syrup.

serves 6

*
Available in Asian markets, specialty-food stores, and spice stores.

A Perfect Pranzo

Orange and Black Olive Salad

Swordfish Peperonata

Orzo Baked with Spinach and Taleggio

'Sgroppino: Venetian Lemon Slush

It's flavor-packed. It's quick. It can be prepared in thirty minutes. It's Italian.

This menu reads like a colorful map of Italy. You'll find oranges and olives in Calabria; *peperonata,* a lovely pepper compote, in Basilicata; Taleggio, a rich cow's milk cheese, in Lombardy. Serve with a basket of thickly sliced semolina bread — from an Italian bakery, of course.

'Sgroppino, a neologism translated loosely as "get the monkey off your back," is a newfangled dessert drink from Venice. It always contains lemon sorbet and prosecco, a sparkling wine from the Veneto, plus a third rather variable ingredient: vodka or grappa or fresh strawberry puree. It is served in a wide-rimmed coupe, and given sufficient quantities of vodka or grappa, you might well translate *'sgroppino* as "hair of the dog."

Pranzo means lunch, the principal meal of the day, served around noon.

grapenote
The menu is a road trip to Italy, so select a heavy-duty Italian white: a Greco di Tufo from the Molise or a Garbi, a blend from the Marches.

47

orange and
black olive salad

4 large oranges
4 ounces (about 24) large oil-cured black olives
4 tablespoons extra-virgin olive oil

- Begin preparation 30 minutes before serving this salad.
- Grate the rind of 2 oranges and set aside. Peel all the oranges with a small sharp knife, removing the rind and all the white pith. Slice oranges into ¼-inch-thick slices, capturing the juice.
- Place orange slices in an overlapping pattern on 4 large plates.
- Pit olives. Place 1 olive in center of each orange slice and scatter a few around each plate.
- Drizzle 1 tablespoon olive oil over oranges. Also drizzle reserved orange juice over top.
- Sprinkle lightly with salt and grated orange zest. Let sit for 20 minutes at room temperature before serving so that the flavors mingle.

serves 4

swordfish *peperonata*

4 6½-ounce swordfish steaks
¼ cup extra-virgin olive oil
**2 medium red and 2 medium yellow
   bell peppers**

- Season swordfish with freshly ground black pepper and coat each steak lightly with ½ tablespoon olive oil. Let sit while you prepare the *peperonata*.
- Cut peppers into long, thin strips, no more than ¼ inch wide, making sure to remove all the seeds.
- Heat remaining oil in large nonstick skillet. Add peppers, ½ teaspoon whole black peppercorns, and ½ teaspoon sea salt. Cook, stirring occasionally, until peppers are soft and lightly browned, about 20 minutes. Set aside.
- Heat an iron-ribbed grill pan or nonstick skillet until hot. Cook both sides of swordfish over medium-high heat so that fish is browned on the outside and moist inside. This will take about 8 minutes total.
- Meanwhile, warm peppers briefly. Serve fish with warm peppers on top.

serves 4

orzo baked with spinach and taleggio

½ pound orzo pasta
10-ounce package frozen chopped spinach,
   thawed
5 ounces Taleggio cheese *

- Preheat oven to 400°.
- Bring large pot of salted water to a boil. Add orzo and cook for 10 minutes. Add spinach and cook for 2 to 3 minutes more, or until orzo is tender. Remove to colander and drain well.
- Cut rind from cheese, then cut cheese into small pieces.
- Put orzo mixture in 9-by-11-inch shallow oval casserole. Add cheese and mix well. Add salt and freshly ground black pepper to taste. Mix well and bake for 8 minutes.
- Serve immediately, or cover and reheat later for 5 minutes or more at 400°.

serves 4 (makes 3½ to 4 cups)

  * You can find this Italian cheese in any specialty-cheese store, or substitute Pont l'Evêque.

'sgroppino: venetian lemon slush

1 pint ripe strawberries
1 pint lemon sorbet
1½ cups prosecco or other brut sparkling wine,
   well chilled

- Remove stems from strawberries. Wash well.
- Cut berries in half and puree in food processor until smooth. You will have about 1⅓ cups puree. Refrigerate for at least 1 hour, or place in freezer until very cold, about 20 minutes.
- When ready to serve, place lemon sorbet in bowl of electric mixer. Break up into small pieces.
- Slowly and alternately add strawberry puree and sparkling wine. Beat gently to form soft mixture. Be careful not to overbeat.
- Serve immediately in frozen wide-rimmed goblets.

serves 4

Pacific Trim

Crispy Rice with Bay Scallops and Rosemary Oil

Drunken Chicken, Served Chilled

Salad of Arugula and Currants

Mangoes in Lime Syrup

Coconut Kisses

Pacific trim: a combination of Asian and Italian flavors with a California sensibility. It feels light and healthy, fresh and colorful.

Unexpectedly, the first course is hot and needs to be prepared at the last minute. The rest of the meal is cold — very cold — and should be made in advance.

The hot rice, fried at the last possible minute, becomes crisp and stays crunchy, whereas the chicken must be made two days in advance to soften in a luxurious bath of sweetened wine.

Serve this meal with long, thin grissini. (They've always reminded me of chopsticks, despite their Italian origin.) This is a lunch of contrasts — temperatures, textures, flavors, and cultures.

grapenote

Try a bracing and appropriately named cocktail, Pacific Rim (see page 82), before lunch. With lunch, sip a soft, delicate varietal such as Viognier (California or French) or a trendy Spanish white — either an Albariño or a slightly weightier Godello (both Galician grapes).

crispy rice
with bay scallops
and rosemary oil

**6 tablespoons rosemary oil,* plus more for
    drizzling (optional)**
2 cups Arborio rice
1 pound bay scallops

- In medium pot, warm 2 tablespoons rosemary oil over medium heat. Add rice and cook, stirring frequently, for 2 minutes, until rice is coated with oil.
- Meanwhile, bring 6 cups water to a boil. Slowly add boiling water to rice, ladle by ladle, allowing each ladleful to be absorbed before adding the next. Continue to cook for 20 to 25 minutes, until rice is tender. Add kosher or fine sea salt and a grinding of white and black peppers to taste. Keep hot.
- In 12-inch nonstick skillet, heat 3 tablespoons rosemary oil over high heat, then add scallops. Cook quickly until they lose their opaque quality and begin to turn golden. Add rice and stir. Flatten into a thick pancake. Lower heat to medium-

high and continue to cook until rice is browned and crispy on one side.
- Using a large spatula, turn pancake over, adding remaining 1 tablespoon rosemary oil. Continue to cook over medium-high heat for several minutes, until crisp on other side. Sprinkle with kosher or fine sea salt.
- Cut pancake into 6 or 8 portions. Serve on large plates. Drizzle with additional rosemary oil, if desired.

serves 6 to 8

* I use Consorzio brand. It is available in many supermarkets and specialty-food stores.

drunken chicken,
served chilled

**3 whole chicken breasts, bone in and skin on
(about 4 pounds)**
2 teaspoons sugar
**2 cups white wine (Sauvignon Blanc,
dry Riesling, or dry Seyval Blanc)**

- Clean chicken breasts. Wash and pat dry. Cut breasts in half through the breastbone to make 6 pieces. Rub chicken with a total of 2 teaspoons salt. Cover and refrigerate for 12 hours or overnight.
- Bring water to a boil in bottom of large steamer. Lower heat to medium. Place breasts in steamer basket. Cover and steam over medium heat for 20 minutes. Remove and place in shallow casserole.
- Combine sugar and wine, and pour over hot chicken. Cover and marinate in refrigerator for at least 2 days. Turn breasts several times during marinating.
- Drain chicken. Place on cutting board and, using a cleaver or heavy chef's knife, cut crosswise into ½-inch-thick slices. Arrange on serving platter. Dust with coarsely ground white pepper.

serves 6 to 8

Note: This recipe is adapted from Mai Thayer, *New Chinese Classic Cookbook* (Tulsa, Okla.: Council Oak Publishing, 1998).

salad of arugula
and currants

½ cup currants
3 or 4 large bunches arugula, well chilled
¼ to ⅓ cup extra-virgin olive oil

- Place currants in small bowl. Cover with 1½ cups boiling water. Let sit for 15 to 20 minutes.
- Meanwhile, wash arugula well and spin dry. Place in large bowl. Drain currants, saving 2 tablespoons soaking liquid. Add currants to arugula and toss.
- Add enough olive oil to coat and 1 to 2 tablespoons soaking liquid. Season with salt to taste.
- Transfer to platter and serve.

serves 6 to 8

mangoes in lime syrup

3 or 4 large ripe mangoes (about 1 pound each)
⅞ cup sugar
8 large limes

- Peel mangoes. Slice into long, thick wedges, cutting carefully around the pit. Place in bowl.
- In large nonreactive saucepan, combine 2 cups water and sugar. Grate rind of enough limes to get 1 tablespoon grated zest. Add zest to saucepan. Squeeze 6 limes to get ½ cup juice. Add juice to saucepan. Bring to a boil and continue boiling for 3 minutes.
- Pour syrup over mango slices. Let cool. Cover and refrigerate until very cold.
- Very thinly slice remaining 2 limes. Serve mangoes in flat soup bowls and garnish with lime slices.

serves 6 to 8

coconut kisses

1 cup sweetened condensed milk
2⅔ cups (7 ounces) shredded coconut
¾ teaspoon rum extract

- Preheat oven to 350°.
- Combine milk, coconut, and rum extract in medium bowl. Add ⅛ teaspoon salt and stir with wooden spoon. Mixture will be sticky.
- Drop mixture by level tablespoons on cookie sheet lined with parchment paper. Bake for 10 to 12 minutes, until lightly browned. Remove from pan while hot. Put on wire rack and let cool completely. Store in airtight container.

makes 3 dozen cookies

Bistro Fare

Chicken Liver and Shiitake Pâté

Mesclun Salad, Raspberry Vinaigrette

Bistro Chicken with Goat Cheese and Basil

Homemade Potato Chips with Sea Salt

Lemon-Kissed Prune Sablés

At its core, bistro cooking is home cooking: uncomplicated good food, familiar and satisfying, yet strangely sophisticated. Not just a *spirit* of cooking, bistro food is also a style of preparation. Patricia Wells, in her lovely book *Bistro Cooking,* says, "Order a roast chicken and a whole golden bird arrives tableside to be carved in front of you. . . . Salads are not arranged like fussy still lifes. Rather the entire salad bowl arrives at the table, ready to be tossed and served."

The following menu, meant for family and friends, offers an opportunity to re-create the bistro experience at home: simple ingredients, perfectly cooked, meant to be carved and tossed at the table.

Prepare the pâté a day ahead and the dessert (a crumbly cookie of French origin) the morning of your party.

Serve this meal with a crusty baguette, the trademark of a real bistro experience, and a carafe of fruity Beaujolais.

Although the origin of the word *bistro* is speculative, one explanation is that it's an abbreviation for *bistouille,* which refers to a mixture of coffee and brandy in northern France. Why not serve one after dessert?

grapenote
Beaujolais, darling, the darling of bistro wine.

chicken liver
and shiitake pâté

6 ounces shiitake mushrooms
1½ pounds fresh chicken livers
4 to 6 tablespoons garlic oil, store-bought or
homemade (see page 299)

- Remove tough ends of mushrooms with a small sharp knife. Cut mushrooms into ½-inch pieces. Drain chicken livers; pat dry.
- In large nonstick skillet, heat 2 tablespoons garlic oil. Add mushrooms and livers. Cook over low heat until livers begin to lose their pink color and mushrooms soften, about 10 minutes. Stir often. Do not overcook livers. Remove livers and mushrooms with slotted spoon. Place in bowl of food processor.
- Cook juices left in pan until reduced to 3 tablespoons. Add to processor. Process mixture until smooth. Add 2 tablespoons garlic oil and kosher salt and freshly ground black pepper to taste. Process briefly.
- Transfer mixture to shallow bowl. Drizzle with remaining 2 tablespoons garlic oil, if desired. Cover and refrigerate until ready to use.

serves 6 (makes 2½ cups)

mesclun salad,
raspberry vinaigrette

5 ounces mesclun salad mix *
¼ cup extra-virgin olive oil
1½ tablespoons raspberry vinegar

- Wash salad mix and dry well. Place in large bowl. Chill until ready to use.
- In small bowl, whisk together olive oil and vinegar, using a small wire whisk. Add salt and freshly ground black pepper to taste, and whisk again until lightly emulsified.
- Pour dressing over greens just before serving. Toss lightly. Taste for salt and pepper. Toss and serve.

serves 6

> * Ingredients may include lolla rosa, arugula, baby green and red romaine, baby leaf lettuce, and mizuna, available in most supermarkets.

bistro chicken with
goat cheese and basil

**2 large bunches fresh basil (3 cups packed
leaves)**
**8 ounces fresh goat cheese, preferably flavored
with garlic and herbs, well chilled**
5-pound roasting chicken

- Preheat oven to 350°.
- Wash basil well and pat dry. Put basil and cheese
in food processor. Add freshly ground black pepper and process until basil is incorporated and
cheese is smooth. Set aside.
- Starting at neck of chicken, slip your fingers
under breast skin, carefully separating skin from
flesh. Continue downward and, with your index
finger, separate skin around thighs.
- With your fingers or a spoon, push cheese mixture
under skin to cover entire breast and thighs. Use
all the mixture. You will have an approximately
¼-inch-thick layer of cheese under the skin. (You
may press on skin to evenly distribute cheese.)
- Truss chicken. Sprinkle lightly with salt and
freshly ground black pepper. Roast in heavy shallow baking pan for 1½ hours, or until meat thermometer registers 160° in the thigh.
- Remove from oven. Let rest for 10 minutes before
serving. Carve as desired.

serves 6

homemade potato chips
with sea salt

3 large Idaho potatoes, about 1½ pounds
1 quart, approximately, vegetable oil
⅓ cup finely chopped curly parsley

- Peel potatoes with vegetable peeler. Slice potatoes paper thin, using mandolin or thin-bladed
sharp knife. Place potatoes in large bowl. Cover
with cold water. Let sit for two hours.
- In medium-large pot, heat several inches of oil
until very hot. Small bubbles will appear on surface. The temperature should be about 350°.
- Remove potato slices from water and pat very
dry. Add to oil, a few handfuls at a time. Stir frequently with slotted spoon until potatoes are
golden and crisp. This will take 5 to 7 minutes.
As potatoes are cooked, transfer them to sheet
pan lined with paper towels. Sprinkle with fine
sea salt. Continue to cook until all potatoes are
cooked, salting them as soon as they are removed
from hot oil.
- Serve chips immediately, sprinkled with chopped
parsley. Or, if serving later, reheat them in 400°
oven for several minutes to warm, then sprinkle
parsley.

serves 6

56

lemon-kissed
prune sablés

12 ounces lemon-essence pitted prunes *
18 ounces refrigerated sugar cookie dough **
8 ounces mascarpone, at room temperature

- Place prunes in saucepan with cold water just to cover. Bring to a boil. Cover saucepan and lower heat to medium. Cook for 10 minutes. Remove from heat and let sit for 8 hours or overnight. Prunes will plump, and juices will thicken.
- Preheat oven to 350°.
- To make sablés, use refrigerated dough, not frozen. Cut major portion of dough into 6 2-ounce portions. Slice remaining dough into ¼-inch-thick slices.
- Using a rolling pin and a 4-inch round cookie cutter or metal ring, roll the 2-ounce portions of dough into flat round circles that are ¼ inch thick. You will have 6 sablés.
- Place sablés and other dough slices on baking sheet. Bake for 12 minutes, or until small cookies are golden brown around edges and larger cookies barely take on color. Remove from oven and using a spatula, transfer to a wire rack to cool completely.

- Remove prunes from liquid and pat dry. Reduce prune liquid over high heat to a thick, syrupy glaze.
- *To assemble sablés:* Spread each large cookie with 2 tablespoons mascarpone, leaving ⅛-inch border around edge. Place 7 prunes on each cookie to cover mascarpone, pressing down with a spatula to flatten slightly. Using a pastry brush, spread a little prune syrup on top of prunes. (Do not use too much, as you don't want the sablés to be moist.) Crumble smaller cookies with rolling pin. Sprinkle crumbs around edges of sablés or over one half of each sablé.

serves 6

*
  Sunsweet is one brand.

**
  Nestlé and Pillsbury are two brands.

The Southern Table

Crackling Pork Shoulder with Fresh Thyme and Garlic

Smoky Grits and Sweet Pea Casserole

Apple Cider Cucumber Salad

Peaches and Bourbon Sorbet, Bourbon Syrup

Pecan Pralines

Inexpensive pork shoulder generally succumbs to sweet, sticky slathers or is shredded, Carolina style, in a sauce of vinegar. Instead, my recipe intensifies the porkiness of this robust cut of meat. The shoulder gets a royal rub of garlic; a paste of fresh thyme, coarse salt, and pork fat; and finally more garlic packed profusely into the flesh. An unusual baking method, with the temperature rising incrementally, ensures a crackling crust and a meltingly moist interior.

The grits get groovy in a casserole with lightly smoked cheddar cheese and fresh green peas. The best-tasting grits are made from stone-ground hominy, because the germ is still intact.

Cool cukes, splashed with cider vinegar and maple syrup, temper the rich flavors and textures.

Dessert is a delight in both preparation and taste: An unopened can of peaches, placed in the freezer, becomes sorbet, and bourbon becomes a sugar coating.

grapenote
Consider some of the lovely white wines coming from the American South: Chardonnay from Château Elan in Georgia or Williamsburg Winery in Virginia. Also from Virginia is Oakencroft Monticello Chardonnay Reserve, with notes of soft oak, fruit, and smoke.

crackling pork shoulder with fresh thyme and garlic

5½- to 6-pound pork shoulder
2 large bunches fresh thyme
8 large cloves garlic

- Preheat oven to 350°.
- Trim most of the fat from pork shoulder. Chop fat into very small pieces to make ⅓ cup.
- Remove enough leaves from thyme to make ⅓ cup packed. Set aside any remaining thyme branches.
- Press 2 cloves garlic through garlic press and rub all over pork shoulder. Mince remaining garlic and chop with thyme leaves, pork fat, and 1 teaspoon kosher salt to make a paste.
- Make ¼-inch-wide, 1-inch-deep holes in pork and fill with garlic-thyme mixture. Also insert mixture around bone. The idea is to infuse the flesh with as much flavor as possible.

- Put remaining thyme branches in bottom of roasting pan or large shallow casserole. Place pork shoulder on top.
- Roast for 45 minutes, then turn up heat to 400° and roast for 25 minutes more. Turn up heat again to 450° and roast for an additional 25 minutes. Check the meat's temperature with a meat thermometer. It is done if the thermometer reads about 145°. Remove from oven and let rest for 10 minutes before carving.

serves 6 or more

smoky grits and
sweet pea casserole

1 cup fresh or thawed frozen green peas
8 ounces smoked cheddar cheese
1 cup old-fashioned grits *

- Preheat oven to 350°.
- Bring small pot of salted water to a boil. Add peas and cook until almost tender. Drain well.
- Grate cheese on large holes of box grater. Set aside.
- In medium heavy saucepan, bring 5 cups water and 1 teaspoon salt to a boil. Slowly add grits, lower heat to medium, stir, and cover. Cook for 10 minutes, stirring once or twice so that no lumps form. Remove cover.
- Add peas, all but 1 cup grated cheese, ½ teaspoon butcher-grind black pepper, and salt to taste. Stirring frequently, cook uncovered for 10 minutes, until grits are thick.
- Pour mixture into 9-by-11-inch or 10-by-10-inch shallow casserole or baking dish coated with nonstick vegetable spray. Top with remaining 1 cup cheese and bake for 15 minutes. Serve immediately.

serves 6 or more

*
Do not use quick-cooking grits.

apple cider
cucumber salad

1½ seedless hothouse cucumbers (about
**   1 pound)**
9 tablespoons apple cider vinegar
6 tablespoons pure maple syrup

- Peel 1 cucumber and leave the half cucumber unpeeled. Slice both into very thin rounds with a sharp knife. Place in small bowl. Add salt and freshly ground black pepper to taste.
- In another small bowl, whisk together vinegar and maple syrup. Pour over cucumbers and toss gently.
- Cover and refrigerate for at least 1 hour. Before serving, adjust seasonings, adding salt and/or vinegar to taste.

serves 6

peaches and bourbon sorbet, bourbon syrup

28-ounce can peach halves in heavy syrup
6 tablespoons bourbon
½ cup sugar

- Freeze unopened can of peaches for at least 12 hours.
- Dip unopened can in very hot water for 10 seconds to loosen filling. Open both ends of can with can opener and force filling out. Cut frozen filling into 1-inch chunks and place in bowl of food processor.
- Puree until smooth, slowly adding 3 tablespoons bourbon. Transfer peach sorbet to bowl and refreeze until ready to serve.
- *To make bourbon syrup:* Put ½ cup water and sugar in small saucepan. Bring to a boil and cook over high heat for 5 minutes. Add remaining 3 tablespoons bourbon, lower heat, and simmer for 5 minutes, or until syrup is reduced to ⅓ cup. Let cool completely before serving.
- Remove sorbet from freezer 10 minutes before serving. Place scoops of sorbet in wineglasses and drizzle with bourbon syrup.

serves 6 or more

pecan pralines

1½ cups sugar
1½ cups heavy cream
1 cup (4 ounces) pecan halves, lightly toasted and broken in half

- Combine sugar and heavy cream in large saucepan. (You need a large pan because the mixture will foam up.) Add a pinch of salt and bring to a boil. Continue to cook over low heat, keeping a low boil going, for 50 minutes. Mixture will have the color of coffee with milk.
- When mixture registers 240° on a candy thermometer (or forms a firm ball in cold water), remove from heat.
- Add pecans and stir well. Quickly drop by the tablespoon onto waxed paper. Let harden.

makes 16 to 20 pralines

Big Lunch

Lentil Soup with Sherry Vinegar

Cheshire Pork Chops with Mixed Peppers, Hot Pepper Oil

Alabaster: Potato and White Turnip Puree

Sautéed Cherry Tomatoes (page 188)

Red Delicious Apple Tarts

This big, inclusive, family-style meal, polished enough for guests, says "Come on to my house."

Lentil soup, chockablock with shallots, is deliciously simple and tastes as if it were cooked all day. A basket of Garlic Croûtes (see page 109) provides aroma and crunch.

Half-pound pork chops are comfort food when stuffed with Cheshire cheese, cheddar's rich and crumbly relative. Unembellished side-kicks include a sauté of cherry tomatoes and a mash of turnips and potatoes. The latter, a Shaker dish known as alabaster, is named for its silvery white hue.

The soup can be prepared the day before and the fresh apple tarts in the morning. The rest of the menu takes forty-five minutes to prepare.

Big on flavor and short on stress, this is a meal to remind us of life's inherent goodness.

grapenote

To dress up this menu, begin with a glass of Amontillado sherry during or before the soup. Next try a lovely Syrah (Correas) or Malbec (Elsan) from Argentina, or a lush Merlot (Dunnewood) from California.

lentil soup
with sherry vinegar

½ pound shallots
1 pound dried brown lentils
3 to 4 tablespoons sherry vinegar

- Peel shallots and finely chop.
- Put lentils, shallots, and 5 cups cold water in medium heavy pot. Add ¼ teaspoon whole black peppercorns and 1 teaspoon salt. Bring to a boil. Lower heat and cook for 45 minutes.
- Add more water if necessary, cover, and cook for 30 minutes more.
- Remove from heat. Pour half of soup in food processor and process until very smooth. Return pureed soup to pot and stir to combine. Add vinegar and salt and freshly ground black pepper to taste.
- Reheat gently and serve. If serving later, add more water to reheat, as soup will thicken. Adjust seasonings.

serves 8 (makes about 8 cups)

cheshire pork chops
with mixed peppers,
hot pepper oil

8 8-ounce center-cut rib pork chops, 1 inch thick
12 ounces Cheshire cheese or good-quality sharp cheddar
2 9½-ounce jars pepper salad in oil

- With a very sharp knife, make a deep horizontal pocket in each pork chop. Cut cheese into four pieces and stuff each pocket so that no cheese is showing.
- Press down lightly on each chop and season lightly with salt and freshly ground black pepper.
- Drain peppers in fine-mesh strainer, reserving oil. In each of two large nonstick skillets, heat 2 tablespoons reserved oil. When oil is very hot, add pork chops. Lower heat and cook until chops are golden brown, about 3 minutes. Turn chops over. Add drained peppers and cook pork until browned and cooked, still remaining a bit pink and juicy, about 4 minutes.
- Serve immediately, topping chops with peppers and oil.

serves 8

alabaster: potato and white turnip puree

2½ pounds white turnips
2½ pounds large red potatoes
8 tablespoons unsalted butter

- Scrub turnips and potatoes, but do not peel. Place in large heavy pot and add water to cover. Bring to a boil. Cover and cook for 35 to 40 minutes, or until turnips and potatoes are very soft.
- Drain turnips and potatoes in colander. Peel under cool running water. In large bowl, mash well with potato masher. Add butter a little bit at a time. Mash again. Add salt and freshly ground white pepper to taste, then whip with a wire whisk until smooth and fluffy. Serve immediately.

serves 8 (makes about 7½ cups)

red delicious apple tarts

2 sheets frozen puff pastry (17¼ ounces)
4 large Red Delicious apples
½ cup cinnamon sugar

- Let puff pastry thaw at room temperature.
- Preheat oven to 400°.
- Cut each sheet of puff pastry into 4 equal pieces. Place on 1 or 2 large baking sheets, making sure pastry edges do not touch.
- Wash apples and dry well, but do not peel. Lay each apple on its side and cut through the core to make paper-thin round slices. Discard seeds.
- Place apples in a tightly overlapping row down the center of each piece of pastry. Sprinkle with 1 tablespoon cinnamon sugar.
- Roll up edges along two long sides to make border, using a little water to affix sides to bottom.
- Place tarts on baking sheet.
- Bake for 25 to 28 minutes. Place under broiler for 30 seconds to brown lightly. Remove from oven and let cool. Serve immediately or within several hours of baking.

makes 8 tarts

1-2-3 Lunch Ideas

- Freeze a jar of cocktail sauce. Poach jumbo shrimp or buy them cooked. Serve shrimp with a scoop of cocktail sauce "sorbet" and lemon wedges or grated fresh horseradish.

- Add diced mangoes and chopped cilantro to store-bought chicken salad.

- Top paillards of grilled swordfish with canned caponata and a splash of lemon juice. Or top grilled chicken breasts with caponata and a splash of balsamic vinegar.

- Buy fresh gnocchi or cavatelli pasta. Serve with a quick pesto cream made with prepared pesto and reduced heavy cream.

- Roll thinly sliced ham and Gruyère cheese in skinless boneless chicken breasts. Wrap tightly in plastic wrap and steam. Chill, then thinly slice.

- Make a frittata of Genoa salami (first render fat in a nonstick skillet), eggs, and small cubes of boiled potatoes.

- Sauté lots of fresh cherry tomatoes in Garlic Oil (see page 299) and pour over hot, steamy linguine. Add a little of the pasta cooking water to the tomatoes.

- Serve grilled fresh tuna with salsa and Rosemary Mayonnaise (see page 299).

- Spread a fillet of sole with scallion cream cheese and a thin slice of smoked salmon. Roll up like a jelly roll and bake at 350°.

- Wrap thick slices of smoked mozzarella cheese in blanched romaine leaves. Brush with olive oil, then grill or sauté.

- Add curry powder and golden raisins to store-bought tuna salad. Serve with poppadums (crisp Indian flatbreads).

- Great sandwich: sourdough bread, Gorgonzola, and speck (smoked prosciutto). Heat in a cast-iron grill pan or toast in the oven.

- Puree a small can of light tuna in olive oil with a small can of anchovies and capers. Blend until smooth, then chill. Use as a sauce for thin slices of cold veal roast or cold poached chicken.

- Pour hot yellow polenta over a 1/3-inch-thick slice of Italian Gorgonzola cheese. Sprinkle toasted pignoli (pine nuts) on top.

- Sauté large slices of shiitake mushrooms in unsalted butter until soft. Pour over a large oval "burger" of ground veal (mixed with small bits of butter, salt, and pepper) that has been broiled or grilled.

- Thread jumbo shrimp and spicy sausage (andouille or chorizo) on bamboo skewers. Grill or broil, then place atop couscous.

- Make a cucumber sandwich. Thinly slice cucumbers, sprinkle with sea salt, and press down. Let sit, weighted, for 1 hour. Press out water and pile thickly between slices of pumpernickel bread spread with sweet butter. Add freshly ground black pepper.

- Sauté plump sausages (just pork or pork and veal) in a nonstick skillet. When the fat is rendered, add green grapes and cook over high heat until caramelized. Splash with white balsamic vinegar.

- Stuff boneless chicken breasts with cream cheese mixed with chopped roasted red peppers (fresh or jarred). Bake until golden. Make a sauce from the pan drippings pureed with additional peppers.

- A great emergency meal: Make a spice rub of good-quality chili powder, salt, and freshly ground black pepper. Rub on a thick swordfish steak. Grill and serve on hot creamed corn.

- Grill baby lamb chops on long metal skewers, seasoning them well with salt and freshly ground black pepper. Serve with cilantro butter or a shower of fresh mint and chopped scallions.

- Make a risotto with butter and Barolo wine. Sauté rice in butter, slowly add Barolo, and whisk in small pieces of cold butter at the end.

- Buy fresh gnocchi. Prepare Piedmontese-style *(alla bava),* with butter and melted fontina cheese.

- Make a simple pasta dish — a specialty of Siena called *pici*. Toss cooked pasta with lots of extra-virgin olive oil and toasted bread crumbs.

- Sauté chicken livers in fat rendered from pancetta. Add small cubes of pancetta, then deglaze pan with dry Marsala.

- Fry jumbo shrimp in Garlic Oil (see page 299). Sprinkle with sea salt. Flambé with a few tablespoons of grappa.

- Steam large lobster tails, or bake on a bed of coarse sea salt. Serve with fresh tarragon butter. (Freeze butter and thinly slice. Place on warm lobster.)

- Spread flounder fillets with thick prepared pesto. Roll up like a jelly roll and put in a shallow casserole. Pour white wine over fish and bake until barely opaque. Reduce juices and pour over fish.

- Steam fresh mussels in salted water to cover. Add heavy cream and saffron threads. Serve as a soup.

- Marinate turkey tenderloins in honey mustard and yogurt for several hours. Remove from marinade and grill. Serve sliced on the bias.

- Buy the best-quality sushi from a reputable source. Top with salmon caviar and serve in a bento box with a glass of cold sake.

- For great, quick dessert ideas for lunch, see "Ten-Minute Desserts" on pages 304–305.

classy cocktails and party wine

Where there's food,
there's drink.

To hone the cocktail hour to an art form, apply my 1-2-3 principles to drink making:

1. The best drinks are made with the best raw materials (including freshly made ice cubes).
2. Temperature is a critical factor. Serve mixed drinks and cocktails in chilled glasses. Serve wines at the correct temperature (see "Serving Temperature of Wine" on page 76). Serve other drinks with lots of ice (American-style) or prechilled.
3. Use the appropriate glassware.

Bartending Bylaws

Dale DeGroff is, hands down, America's best-known bartender and maestro mixologist. He worked with us at our three-star (and sadly closed) restaurant Aurora in midtown Manhattan — and then at the celebrated Rainbow Room, where he manned the famous bar where *Sleepless in Seattle* was shot and where hundreds of celebrities sipped his drinks. Almost single-handedly, he brought the cocktail back to life.

His advice on cocktail making at home? "Offer one cocktail, but make it a great one."

Anthony Dias Blue, friend and wine writer extraordinaire, says to keep things simple. "What you don't need is people sidling up to your bar expecting a Singapore sling or a mai tai." He suggests making the bar self-service, and his rule of thumb is to allow twelve servings per bottle (most drink recipes call for a two-ounce serving, and a bottle of booze is generally twenty-five ounces).

Today the average number of drinks per guest (not counting wine at dinner) is two. In Jim Beard's day, the average was four. He said that some guests might have only one, others might have eight!

Times have changed, and so has the desirability of particular drinks. Some old-fashioned drinks (except maybe the old-fashioned) are making a comeback — especially the mythic martini. And then there are newfangled concoctions such as the cosmopolitan, the metropolitan, and the lemon drop, as well as martini spin-offs, from the Sake-tini (see page 81) to the chocolate martini (infused with Godiva Liqueur and garnished with a chocolate kiss or chocolate coins).

Times have changed in other respects, too. Many guests are opting for sparkling water and nonalcoholic "mocktails." You'll be a great host if you offer one of these (see page 83). Even a jug of freshly squeezed blood orange juice shows that you have considered the needs of all your guests. To that end, there are also some decent nonalcoholic wines and beers on the market, and it would be nice to include one of these.

In my mother-in-law's day, guests helped themselves from graceful glass pitchers of chilled martinis or manhattans as they wished, straight up into a specialty glass (also known as the cocktail glass) or over ice into a "rocks" glass. Appropriate garnishes such as lemon twists, cocktail onions, and olives were offered. In those days, maraschino cherries also were de rigueur.

Close to the heart of my 1-2-3 philosophy is a terrific little book called *The 3-Bottle Bar* by H. I. Williams, lent to me by none other than the cocktail kid himself, Dale DeGroff. This "Hospitality Poured from 3 Bottles," as the subtitle boasts, consisted in the year 1943 of whiskey (rye or bourbon, blended or straight), gin, and dry white wine.

Today my three-bottle bar would be a top-shelf vodka, a superlative gin, and a good Scotch. There will always be a taker.

In keeping with today's trends, you might create a signature libation, such as a special infused vodka, for which you and your parties become known. My favorite combinations are rosemary-lemon, strawberry-basil, orange-tarragon, ginger-lime, and horseradish-fennel. Steep these flavorings in the bottle for three to four days. Strain the infused vodka, return it to the bottle, and store it in the freezer. Serve in small, elegant, chilled glasses or use in mixed drinks.

71

The Party Line on Party Wine

Most preprandial experiences fall into the stand-up cocktail party category, where entertaining means offering a variety of delectable choices to lots of friends. That also means heading straight for the magnums in your local wine store and reserving premium wines for your sit-down dinners.

Following is a list of recommended party wines from my personal wine guru Judy Rundel, who in addition to running the New York Wine Tasting School with her husband, John Sheldon, works in a prominent wine shop surrounded by "big bottles" in a range of styles, tastes, and countries of origin (all priced at around $8 to $15).

big bottles

Here are some of Judy's suggestions.

whites

SAUVIGNON BLANC (California)
Corbett Canyon (very good varietal character for the money)
Delicato (less aggressively Sauvignon)
R.H. Phillips (between the two in character)

CHARDONNAY (all, unless otherwise indicated, light, fresh, and relatively unoaked)
Argyle (Oregon)
Puech Cocut (France)
Walnut Creek (Chile)
Fetzer Sundial (California), bigger, fuller, richer, and more expensive than the others
Lindemans (Australia), a Sem-Chard blend and therefore a tad fruitier

WHITE BLENDS (widely available)
Georges Duboeuf Table Wine (France)
Torres Viña Sol (Spanish)

reds

MERLOT (all fairly light and soft, except Fetzer, which is big and jammy — and pricier)
Undurraga (Chile)
Bel Arbor (California)
Fetzer Eagle Peak (California)

Nathanson Creek (California), light style but does taste like Zinfandel

CABERNET

Delicato

Lindemans, a Shiraz-Cab blend, and therefore gustier and spicier

There's a decent Chianti in mags — Rocca della Macie — and a Citra Montepulciano d'Abruzzoti, which is really rustic and chewy. Judy likes Mistura from R.H. Phillips, which is a light, fresh, fruity Rhône-type blend. She also recommends Georges Duboeuf Table Red — light and fruity, great for making sangria — and Torres red, the Sangre de Toro.

regular size

In this category, I create a little wine bar for my guests with one or two unexpected white varietals, such as an Alsatian Pinot Blanc, a California Sauvignon Blanc, or a French Viognier, as well as lighter-style reds, such as an Oregon Pinot Noir, a good-quality Beaujolais, or a crianza Rioja. During cocktail time, serve all these in the same style white-wine glass, since they are not "big" wines needing lots of oxygenation or intellectualization.

sparkling

Cocktail time in our house is a great excuse to pop a few corks. Sometimes a good sparkler eliminates the need for any other beverage.

Try nonvintage French champagne from Veuve Clicquot, Deutz, Pol Roger, or Taittinger, or a good-quality sparkling wine from California: Domaine Carneros, Iron Horse, or Schramsberg, or the less expensive Piper Sonoma or Mirassou. (More from Evan Goldstein on pages 74–75). It's also a savvy touch to support a local sparkling wine maker such as Gruet, if you happen to be in Santa Fe, or Clinton Vineyards (sparkling Seyval), if you're entertaining in the Hudson Valley.

This is a good time to go global — with prosecco, a sparkling wine from Italy's Veneto region, or with cava, a Spanish sparkling wine made in the traditional champagne method. Judy suggests a cava from Segura Viudas — "a brut reserva with real character."

The flute-style champagne glass is the right way to serve champagne. It is elegant (the coupe has become terribly outmoded), and its shape preserves the "mousse," or sparkle. As an aperitif, figure six glasses from a bottle of champagne and five glasses from a bottle of wine. Wine with dinner is another story (see page 88).

For extra-special occasions, few symbols scream "party" more than a big bottle of champagne, generally purchased for its celebratory quality rather than any particular merit given to its wine-making or aging properties. The sizes are as follows:

Magnum (2 bottles)

Jeroboam (4 bottles)

Methuselah (8 bottles)

Salmanazar (12 bottles)

Balthazar (16 bottles)

Nebuchadnezzar (20 bottles)

california wines

The party line continues as Evan Goldstein, the youngest person ever to pass the prestigious English-based Master Sommelier exam and the influential and beloved director of the Sterling Vineyards School of Service and Hospitality in the Napa Valley, speaks about wines for entertaining, California-style.

"We're blessed with a year-round entertaining climate," Evan says, "and with California's cornucopia of fresh produce, artisanal oils, vinegars, cheeses, sublime seafood (there's more than just Dungeness crab), our wine country picnics are the envy of the free world."

After years of teaching, experimenting, and listening, this chef turned oeno star has shared his many thoughts about California's grapes and resultant wines.

Evan advises, "When you have more than a couple of guests, provide at least two wines side by side, one red and one white, of diverse but congenial contrasts: Pinot Noir and Sauvignon Blanc, Merlot and Riesling, or Rhône-style red and white wines.

"California's sparkling wines are food-friendly accompaniments to a meal, and are not just meant for 'toasting', especially if there's a bit of Asian spice or heat in the menu. Try the bubblies of Mumm Napa Valley, Iron Horse Vineyards, and Roederer Estate, three of California's finest.

"A meal can have only one focus. If you want to show off the wine, pick a food as a background note and vice versa. The first crab of the season from San Francisco Bay doesn't want competition from a complex, aggressive Chardonnay. But one of Napa Valley's aged Cabernet Sauvignons likely won't demand anything more than a simply prepared cut of red meat."

Where does Evan find value: For whites, avoid the heavy hitter Chardonnays and look for Sauvignon Blanc, Pinot Blanc, Riesling, and less expensive Chardonnay. In reds, Zinfandel and Rhône-style wines are your likely values.

"Don't overlook Rosé," he says. "I honestly don't know whether it's the suggestive power of its appearance, but Rosé wine, with its clearly refreshing nature and fruit-forward flavor, is totally soothing. My favorites include Saintsbury Vin Gris, Simi Rosé of Cabernet Sauvignon, and Swanson Rosato di Sangiovese.

"Turn your friends on to dessert wines. We have spectacular examples out here. Whether it's Navarro's sumptuous late-harvest Riesling, Bonny Doon Vin de Glaciére Muscat, or Ficklin's spot-on Tawny Port, they're sure to surprise and impress."

And don't forget two Evan axioms regarding entertaining. "First, the company at the table supersedes all wine and food matching — friends and family are ultimately more significant than whether a Sauvignon Blanc picks up on the note of tarragon in the vinaigrette; and second, everyone has different tastes, so there are no magic bullets."

Here are a handful of great value wines from Evan.

whites

Sterling Vineyards Sauvignon Blanc
Steele Pinot Blanc
Napa Ridge Chardonnay
Chappellet Chenin Blanc
Navarro Gewürztraminer
Bonny Doon Pacific Rim Riesling

Tessera Chardonnay
Duckhorn Sauvignon Blanc
Beringer Alluvium
Zaca Mesa Roussanne

reds

Tessera Merlot
Flora Springs Sangiovese
Benziger Cabernet Sauvignon
Seghesio Zinfandel
Rabbit Ridge Allure
Cline Côtes d'Oakley
Monterey Vineyard Pinot Noir
Boeger Zinfandel
Qupé Syrah
Joseph Phelps Vin du Mistral
McDowell Syrah

wines of the world

Josh Wesson, coauthor of the seminal book *Red Wine with Fish,* and president of Best Cellars wine stores (upbeat, highly original, and brilliantly accessible, like the man himself), says that "party wines, like vice presidents and Rodney Dangerfield, rarely get the respect they deserve. More often than not, they end up banished to some foldout table, stuck between the honey mustard, hot sauce, and three-bean salad.

"By way of understatement, it's unfortunate that any crowd-pleasing wine should be so shamed that it's made to turn its label and hide amongst the condiments — especially when there's so much great-tasting, modestly priced wine coming from all over.

"In fact, there's probably never been a better time to seek out and serve inexpensive, good-to-go international offerings than now."

Some of Josh's favorite $10-and-under selections include the following.

sparkling

Seaview Brut (Australia)
Marques de Gelida Brut (Spain)
Brut d'Argent (France)

whites

LIGHT-BODIED
Famega Vinho Verde (Portugal)
Babich Sauvignon Blanc (New Zealand)
Poggio del Lupo Orvieto (Italy)

MEDIUM-BODIED
Alice White Chardonnay (Australia)
Hugel Pinot Blanc (France)

FULL-BODIED
Bois du Renard Chardonnay (France)
Willm Pinot Gris (France)
Rosemount Semillon (Australia)

reds

LIGHT-BODIED
Georges Duboeuf Beaujolais Regniè (France)
Farnese Montepulciano d'Abruzzo (Italy)
Borsao (Spain)

Impala Merlot (South Africa)
Guigal Côtes du Rhône (France)
McGuigan Shiraz (Australia)

FULL-BODIED
Château Grand Cassagne Syrah (France)
Cape Bay Pinotage (South Africa)
Cantele Primitivo (Italy)

sweet

Cascinetta Moscato d'Asti (Italy)
Yalumba Clocktower Tawny Port (Australia)
Osborne Pedro Ximénez Sherry (Portugal)

A few final notes from Josh: "When shopping for party bottles, buy the youngest available — party wines generally don't benefit from aging.

"If you care about wine and food pairings, remember that wines and foods fall in love for one of two reasons: Either something in the wine and food tastes similar — for example, sweet with sweet — or something in the wine and food tastes different — for example, sweet with sour.

"Finally, don't forget to have fun after you pull the cork. A party wine's primary job is to make you smile."

SERVING TEMPERATURE OF WINE

The temperature at which a wine is served has a significant effect on its bouquet and taste. Here are several rules.

- **Serve high-quality dry white wines cool, around 54° to 61°F (12° to 16°C).**
- **Serve sparkling wines, softer whites, and Rosés well chilled, 43° to 50°F (6° to 10°C).**
- **Serve red wines, wines that are complex and mature, or wines that are tannic or bitter relatively warm, 64°F (about 18°C).**
- **Chill sweet wines to 54°F (about 12°C). Our palates are more sensitive to the sweetness in wines the warmer they are.**

Sips and Bits

For unexpected guests or for a short cocktail
hour before a long dinner, try one of these classy
1-2-3 pairings.

Fino sherry • roasted almonds • green olives

Champagne • aged Parmigiano-Reggiano • champagne grapes

Sake • iced clams on the half shell • wasabi crackers

Vodka • smoked salmon • dark Russian bread

Aquavit • herring • hard sharp cheese

Ouzo • pistachios • stuffed grape leaves

Raki • watermelon • feta cheese

Off-dry Riesling • prosciutto • melon

Chardonnay • cold lobster • hot melted butter

Rosé wine • spanakopita • Kalamata olives

Beaujolais • Hungarian salami • marinated oil-cured olives

Gewürztraminer • taramasalata • pita chips

Sweet vermouth • bresaola • sesame bread sticks

Bourbon • variety of chilled oysters • unsalted pretzels

Dry Marsala • *pinzimonio* (selection of raw vegetables) • extra-virgin olive oil
  (with coarse sea salt and cracked black pepper)

Prosecco • *affettato* (selection of Italian cold cuts — rolled, folded, and flat) • grissini

Sauternes • fois gras • brioche toast

1-2-3 Snacks

Mix any of these three-ingredient combos
in one bowl for a quick taste thrill.

Kalamata olives • *herbes de Provence* • extra-virgin olive oil

Mixed nuts • candied ginger • minced rosemary

Chow mein noodles • smoked almonds • diced dried pineapple

Cashews • sun-dried cherries • coconut chips

Peanuts • *ras el hanout* • sultanas

Shelled sunflower seeds • toasted hazelnuts • chopped dried apricots

Walnut halves • garlic oil • chili powder

Shelled pistachios • fennel seeds • raisins

Three-Ingredient Cocktails

classic

Here they are, in the years they were born.

martini, c. 1890s

1 teaspoon dry vermouth
2½ ounces gin
1 unpitted green olive

- Stir vermouth and gin in mixing glass filled with ice cubes. Strain into chilled martini glass. Garnish with olive.

serves 1

daiquiri, c. 1898

¾ ounce freshly squeezed lime juice, plus 1 lime wedge
1 tablespoon Simple Syrup (see page 299)
2 ounces white rum

- Shake all ingredients very well with ice cubes. Strain into chilled cocktail glass. Garnish with lime wedge.

serves 1

piña colada, c. 1954

2 ounces unsweetened pineapple juice
2 ounces white rum
1½ ounces coconut cream

- Whirl all ingredients in blender with crushed ice. Pour into large goblet, highball glass, or wineglass.

serves 1

mimosa, c. 1925

Freshly squeezed orange juice
2 dashes Grand Marnier
Champagne or sparkling wine

- Chill champagne flute in freezer. Fill one-quarter of the way with orange juice. Add Grand Marnier, then top off with champagne. Stir gently.

serves 1

gibson, c. 1940s

2¾ ounces gin
A few drops dry vermouth
3 cocktail (pearl) onions

- Pour gin over ice in mixing glass. Add dry vermouth and stir. Strain into chilled cocktail glass and add onions.

serves 1

tequila sunrise, c. 1930s

5 to 6 ounces freshly squeezed orange juice,
**   plus 1 orange slice**
1¾ ounces tequila
2 dashes grenadine

- Pour orange juice and tequila over a few ice cubes in highball glass. Add grenadine so that it sinks slowly through mixture. Garnish with orange slice and a straw.

serves 1

sidecar, post–WWI

¾ ounce freshly squeezed lemon juice
¾ ounce Cointreau
1½ ounces brandy

- Shake all ingredients vigorously with ice. Strain into chilled cocktail glass.

serves 1

margarita, c. 1930s

1 ounce freshly squeezed lime juice, plus
**   1 lime wedge and 1 lime slice**
2 ounces tequila
⅔ ounce triple sec

- Rub rim of cocktail glass with lime wedge and dip into saucer of salt. Pour all liquid ingredients over a few ice cubes in shaker and shake vigorously. Strain into prepared glass. Garnish with lime slice.

serves 1

new wave

caipirinha

The national drink of Brazil, it's been around for eons but is new to the American bar scene. Great for a party.

2 or 3 small lime wedges
2 teaspoons superfine sugar
2 ounces cachaça (high-proof spirit distilled from sugar cane)

● Place lime wedges in large rocks glass. Sprinkle with sugar. Using a pestle or the back of a spoon, muddle until all the juice is released and the sugar is dissolved. Add crushed ice and pour in cachaça. Stir and serve.

serves 1

kamikaze

1½ ounces vodka
⅔ ounce Cointreau
⅔ ounce freshly squeezed lime juice, plus 1 lime wedge

● Place all ingredients except lime wedge in shaker with ice. Shake vigorously, then strain into chilled cocktail glass. Add thin lime wedge and stirrer, and serve.

serves 1

sake-tini

4½ ounces vodka
3 ounces super-premium sake
Thin cucumber slices

● Pour vodka and sake over ice in mixing glass. Swirl to integrate. Strain into 2 chilled cocktail glasses and garnish with cucumber slices.

serves 2

lemon-tini

6 ounces Absolut Citron vodka
2 ounces freshly squeezed lemon juice, plus
2 strips lemon rind
1 ounce Cointreau

- Fill large shaker two-thirds full of ice cubes. Add vodka, lemon juice, and Cointreau. Shake until well blended. Strain into 2 chilled cocktail glasses. Top with squeeze of lemon juice and long, thin twist of lemon rind, if desired.

serves 2

pacific rim

Created in 1993 by Ginger DiLello at Philadelphia Fish and Company.*

3 ounces vodka
½ ounce ginger liqueur
1 strip crystallized ginger

- Fill large mixing glass two-thirds full of ice cubes. Add vodka and ginger liqueur. Stir until well blended and chilled. Strain into chilled cocktail glass. Garnish with crystallized ginger.

serves 1

> * Adapted from Gary Regan and Mardee Haidin Regan, *New Classic Cocktails* (New York: Macmillan, 1997).

mexi-freeze

6-ounce can frozen lemonade concentrate
6 ounces tequila
2½ tablespoons grenadine

- Put lemonade, tequila, and grenadine in blender with lots of crushed ice. Blend on high until smooth and thick.
- *Optional:* Moisten rims of 4 chilled wineglasses or martini glasses with tequila. Dip in salt to coat. Carefully fill glasses.

serves 4

autumn leaf

An original recipe created by me for my Thanksgiving guests.

½ cup fresh (unpasteurized) apple cider *
½ ounce arrack or Pernod
1 teaspoon freshly squeezed lemon juice,
plus 1 strip lemon rind

- Put 4 ice cubes in large old-fashioned or rocks glass. Add cider and arrack, and stir. Add lemon juice and stir again. Serve with long, thin twist of lemon rind and stirrer.

serves 1

> * Available in the produce section of many supermarkets.

mocktails

You may also use any of the smoothies and fruit drinks on pages 85–87 as mocktails.

verjus spritzer

½ cup *verjus* (juice pressed from unripe grapes) *
Raspberry-flavored seltzer
1 long, thin strip lemon rind

- Place a few ice cubes in large wineglass. Pour *verjus* over ice. Fill glass with seltzer. Run lemon rind over rim, twist gently, and place in glass.

serves 1

* Available in specialty-food stores and some super-markets.

adam and eve

1½ teaspoons pomegranate molasses *
¾ cup apple juice
Ginger ale

- Put pomegranate molasses and apple juice in large highball or rocks glass. Stir. Add ice cubes and fill with ginger ale. Serve with stirrer.

serves 1

* Available in Middle Eastern markets.

cider sparkler

1 small sugar cube
Several drops angostura bitters
Dry sparkling nonalcoholic apple cider

- Put sugar cube in champagne flute and sprinkle with bitters. Top with sparkling apple cider.

serves 1

83

brighton beach

8½-pound piece ripe watermelon
3 cups unsweetened pineapple juice
1 cup currant-flavored vodka

- Remove any seeds from watermelon. Save black seeds for garnish.
- Cut watermelon into small pieces, discarding rind. Place in food processor or blender in batches and puree until completely smooth. Transfer to large bowl or gallon jar. Add pineapple juice, vodka, and large pinch of salt. Stir or shake well. Place in freezer for 1 hour or chill for several hours in refrigerator. Serve very cold over ice. Scatter with reserved seeds.
- *Optional ideas:* Serve punch in scooped-out watermelon with small pieces of watermelon floating on top. Or make ice cubes from additional pineapple juice to which you have added watermelon seeds for a great look. Or make a granita: Break up frozen punch and place in food processor immediately before serving. Serve in punch cups with spoons.

serves 12 (makes 12 cups)

tropica

This drink was inspired by dear friends, Jennifer and Donn Resnick.

12 juice oranges, plus more for floating
6 cups guava nectar
1½ cups premium gin

- Cut oranges in half and squeeze enough juice to make 4 cups. Place in large bowl or jar. Add guava nectar and gin. Add large pinch of salt. Shake or stir well. Freeze for 1 hour or refrigerate until very cold. Thinly slice remaining oranges and float on punch. Serve over ice.

serves 12

cocktails and hors d'oeuvres

COCKTAILS AND MOCKTAILS: cocteau (martini glass) (page 89),
autumn leaf (rocks glass) (page 82), cider sparkler (champagne flute) (page 83),
with shanghai glazed walnuts (page 111)

little radishes with whipped goat cheese and toasted cumin (page 96), brie croustades with black caviar (page 222),
endive with sun-dried tomato and orange pâté (page 96), smoked salmon kisses (page 100),
smoked salmon roulades (page 122), two-tone mussels (page 121)

SHRIMP-IN-A-SNAP:

wasabi-stuffed (page 102) and pickled pink (page 102),

shrimp cocktail with tomato sorbet

sake olives with grapefruit (page 111), star anise tea eggs (page 121),
FLAVORED SALTS: paprika salt — sesame salt — curry salt (pages 110–11),
shiitake-scallion satés (page 44)

rib bits (page 124) with
silver-dollar corn cakes with bacon and crème fraîche (page 125)

LEFT TO RIGHT: the world's best pimiento spread (page 116),
med-rim eggplant with sun-dried tomatoes (page 199), fresh cod brandade (page 114)

garlic croûtes (page 109),
pita chips (page 109), curry crisps (page 110)

a rainbow of cheese truffles (page 120)

Smoothies and Fruit Drinks

amrus

A love potion from the South Pacific!

1 large ripe mango
½ cup milk
3 tablespoons Simple Syrup (see page 299)

- Peel mango and cut into 1-inch pieces. Place in food processor with milk, Simple Syrup, and 6 ice cubes. Process until thick and very smooth. Pour into 2 chilled wineglasses. Dust with coarsely ground black pepper.

serves 2

strawberry frullato

Voluptuous!

1 pint ripe strawberries
4 tablespoons sugar
1¼ cups milk

- Save 2 berries with stems for garnish. Remove stems from remaining berries. Wash well and dry. Cut berries in half and place in bowl with sugar. Let sit for 15 minutes. Place berries, accumulated juices, and milk in blender with 8 to 10 ice cubes. Blend on high until smooth and frothy. Pour into 2 glasses, then garnish each glass with a whole berry placed on the rim.

serves 2

carrot-apple smoothie

Tastes just like apricots: perfect if you don't own a juicer.

½ pound (4 medium) carrots
1¼ cups apple juice, well chilled
1 small bunch fresh mint

- Peel carrots and slice thinly. Place in small saucepan with 1 cup water. Bring to a boil. Lower heat to medium and cover saucepan. Cook for 20 minutes, until carrots are very soft. Place carrots and cooking liquid in blender with apple juice. Add a few mint leaves and puree until very smooth. Chill well. Serve in wineglasses over ice. Garnish with mint sprigs.

serves 2

berry bongo

Sexy!

**16-ounce package frozen unsweetened
    mixed berries (strawberries, blackberries,
    blueberries, and raspberries)**
2 cups cranberry juice
3 tablespoons wildflower honey

- Place frozen berries in blender with cranberry
  juice. Process on high until smooth. Add honey
  and continue to blend until thick and smooth.
  Serve immediately or keep chilled in refrigerator.
  Stir briskly before serving. Serve in tall glasses or
  wineglasses.

serves 3 or 4

moroccan grape drink

Exotic!

4 cups grape juice
1 tablespoon orange-flower water
½ teaspoon ground cinnamon

- Mix all ingredients in large jar. Cover tightly.
  Shake well and place in refrigerator until very
  cold. Serve straight up in wineglasses or over
  ice in rocks glasses.

serves 4

rosemary lemonade

1 cup sugar
**⅔ cup freshly squeezed lemon juice, plus lemon
    slices for garnish**
**1 teaspoon chopped fresh rosemary, plus
    rosemary sprigs for garnish**

- Combine sugar, 1 cup water, and 1 tablespoon
  lemon juice in medium saucepan. Add chopped
  rosemary. Mix well and bring to a boil. Remove
  from heat and let steep for 5 minutes. Strain out
  rosemary.
- Cool syrup and add 3 cups water and remaining
  lemon juice. Refrigerate until cold. Serve over ice,
  garnished with lemon slices and rosemary
  sprigs.

serves 6

ginger-pineapple frappe

Exhilarating!

1 cup unsweetened pineapple juice
½ cup plain low-fat yogurt
3 tablespoons stem ginger in syrup *

- Put all ingredients in blender. Add 6 ice cubes. Process on high until mixture is smooth and creamy and ice particles have disappeared. Serve immediately in chilled wineglasses. You may add a little additional ginger syrup if you like it sweeter and spicier.

serves 2

* Available in specialty-food stores. I use Raffetto.

rhubarb lemonade

2 pounds fresh rhubarb
⅓ cup freshly squeezed lemon juice, plus lemon slices or wedges for garnish
⅓ cup sugar

- Wash rhubarb and cut into small pieces. Place in large saucepan. Add 3 cups water and cook on low for about 20 minutes. Pour through a fine-mesh sieve, pushing the fruit down with a spoon to release juices. Add lemon juice, sugar, and ½ cup water. Heat to dissolve sugar. Refrigerate until very cold. Serve over ice, garnished with lemon slices or wedges.

serves 4

pineapple lemonade

2 cups sugar
1 medium ripe pineapple
6 tablespoons freshly squeezed lemon juice, plus thinly sliced lemons for garnish

- Place sugar and 2 cups water in medium saucepan. Bring to a boil, lower heat, and simmer for 5 minutes, until sugar is dissolved and liquid is clear.
- Peel pineapple and discard core. Cut fruit into small pieces. Place in food processor and process until smoothish pulp results. Transfer to large jar.
- Add hot syrup and lemon juice. Stir well and refrigerate for several hours. When cold, add 2 or more cups water. Add ice and serve garnished with thinly sliced lemons.

serves 6

87

Wine with Dinner

The sun, with all those planets revolving around it and dependent on it, can still ripen a bunch of grapes as if it had nothing else in the universe to do. — GALILEO

I've always loved this quote. After all, the sun, grapes, and *terroir* (the soil, earth, or total natural environment) are the three ingredients that make a bottle of wine.

As in *Recipes 1-2-3* and *Recipes 1-2-3 Menu Cookbook,* I've included grapenotes with almost every recipe or meal here. These appear mostly as dinner suggestions, but adding wine to a lunch or brunch transforms a simple meal into a celebration.

And which comes first, you might ask, the food or the wine? Although creating a dish to accompany a particular wine is refreshingly quirky, most of us decide what we are going to eat first and then choose a compatible wine.

Along with my wine mentor Judy Rundel, I have devoted great care to matching wines to the components of each menu. Small "tasting" portions of wine are sufficient to enjoy a successful food-and-wine match — where certain qualities of the wine can bring out desirable qualities in the food and vice versa. Sometimes the experience is transcendental.

You should keep a notebook of such "marriages" to guide your future wine choices. It is variety and quality, not price or quantity, that make this approach to entertaining so terrific. So plan on getting six glasses of wine per bottle, and use the proper glass for each wine.

The larger the glass, the better, since swirling or oxygenating any wine will make it taste better, even to the inexperienced palate. Just opening the cork is not sufficient. Decanting is better; swirling is best.

Conventional wisdom dictates the order of wine service: dry before sweet, young before old, ordinary before fine, light before heavy. Or, as the great gastronome Brillat-Savarin put it in *The Physiology of Taste* (1825), "The progression of wines and spirits is from the mildest to the headiest and most aromatic."

However, with some experimentation, this order can be redirected. For example, when my husband and I were chosen Hospitality Professionals of the Year by the Food and Beverage Association of America, we created an Upside-Down Wine Dinner, where a sweet wine was paired with the first course; red wine was served before white; and dessert was accompanied by a cocktail (see page 90). Breaking the rules was lots of fun.

Another great idea is to have a BYOB party, especially for wine-savvy friends with great cellars who know that the best way to enjoy a great bottle of wine is to share it.

After-Dinner Drinks

molly's milk (aka the dubliner)

Created by Dale DeGroff at our famous Rainbow Room Bar.

1 ounce Irish whiskey
1 ounce Irish Mist
Heavy cream, lightly whipped

- Pour spirits over lots of ice in mixing glass. Stir briskly. Strain into chilled cocktail glass and spoon ½ inch cream on top.

serves 1

grasshopper

¾ ounce green crème de menthe
1 ounce white crème de cacao
1½ ounces heavy cream

- Pour all ingredients into shaker with ice cubes. Shake vigorously. Strain into chilled cocktail glass.

serves 1

cocteau

Instead of a cocktail, have a Cocteau — created by me to honor the artist.

2 to 2½ ounces Armagnac
½ ounce yellow Chartreuse
½ ounce crème de cassis, plus more for floating

- Pour all ingredients into shaker with ice cubes. Stir vigorously. Strain into chilled cocktail glass. Float more cassis on top, letting it filter down into the drink.

serves 1

brandy elixir

3 cups brandy
1 vanilla bean, split
8 large sprigs fresh tarragon

- Steep all ingredients in clean glass jar with cover for 2 weeks. Strain and store in lead-free decorative bottle. Serve in brandy snifter.

serves 12

Drinks with Dessert

Asti Spumante • sorbet • fresh berries

Grasshoppers (see page 89) • frozen Yodels • Jordan almonds

Vin Santo • biscotti • sweet ripe cherries

Château d'Yquem • Roquefort cheese • dried pears

Malmsey Madeira • gooey brownies • vanilla ice cream

Asti Spumante • giant strawberries with stems • big meringue shells

Gamay Beaujolais • cheesecake • raspberry sauce

Armagnac • prunes • nougat

Muscat de Beaumes de Venise • halvah • candied orange rind

Ruby Port • chocolate truffles • candied ginger

Hungarian Tokay (5 puttonyos) • Australian glacéed apricots • whole walnuts

Kirsch • French Gruyère • Crispy Oatcakes (see page 119)

Ice wine • grilled marshmallows • graham crackers

Sauternes • Fig Newtons • macadamia nuts

Sweet Wines

My first taste of dessert wine was a doozy. I was twenty-three years old, chef for Mayor Ed Koch of New York, and invited to the apartment of Sol Zausner, the distinguished gourmet known for bringing crème fraîche to this country. He handed me a small stemmed glass, into which he slowly poured a lustrous, leggy liquid of unknown origin to me. Surely this was liquid gold: cold, sweet, and smooth, with a richness and bright intensity I had never experienced.

Forever lingering on my palate is that sip of Château d'Yquem 1937.

It is a wonderful act of generosity and savoir faire to offer a dessert wine to your guests: sometimes in lieu of dessert, often paired with dessert. But I like to serve it as a second dessert, a sweet parting shot, if you will, at the end of a languorous dinner, just after coffee.

Favorites from the party line include Muscat de Beaumes de Venise, Bonny Doon Vin de Glaciére Muscat, Château Climens, Tokaji Aszù, Hermann Wiemer Late Harvest Riesling, Quady Electra, Denoix Cinq from France (a fruit-kissed dessert wine made from five berries and cherries), Bergerac Monbazillac (a great value for Sauternes/Barsac style), Grahams Vintage Port, Navarro Late Harvest Riesling, Château Fesles Bonnezeaux Late Harvest Chenin Blanc (Loire), Quintra DO Vesuvio Vintage Port (1992), and Inniskillen, Sweet Vidal (Canada).

Oh yes, and Château d'Yquem, any year.

5 hors d'oeuvres

If there is one phrase that conveys the essence of entertaining, it certainly is *hors d'oeuvres*.

These morsels that precede most dinners, generally consumed standing upright, often are the best part of the party. Sometimes they *are* the party — a delightful sweep of flavor-resonant miniatures that are served, with plenty of drink, until no one remains standing.

However seductive they may be, hors d'oeuvres are meant to whet, not sate, the appetite.

According to the late, great James Beard, "the hors d'oeuvre is a rite rather than a course and its duty is to enchant the eye, please the palate, and excite the flow of gastric juices . . . so that the meal to follow will seem doubly tempting and flavorful."

Today the term applies to innumerable expressions: from canapés to crudités, from satés to sushi, and they fit into many styles of service. They can be presented on a sideboard, all at once; passed by a waiter, one by one;

93

served at the dining table; or a desirable combination of them all.

At New York's magical Rainbow Room and Windows on the World (which our consulting firm, Joseph Baum & Michael Whiteman Co., re-created in 1987 and 1997, respectively), hors d'oeuvres are a way of life. Thousands of hand-crafted tidbits are produced daily for myriad parties and formal dinners. There is usually a choice of at least four cold and four hot hors d'oeuvres from an extensive list, allowing eight pieces per person for the first hour of a party and six for the next hour.

For an elaborate cocktail reception at home, use the same formula. If the cocktail party is to become the meal, add a sideboard or small buffet of two or three items. A side of cured salmon (see page 223), a pasta such as Penne Pasta à la Vodka (see page 34), and perhaps a salad (see pages 55 and 227) are all you need.

For a more structured dinner party, where the bulk of the conversation is meant for the table, begin with a variety of three to five hors d'oeuvres — or just one that is carefully chosen to make a big and confident statement, especially if served with champagne.

Sometimes hors d'oeuvres can take the form of "Sips and Bits" (see page 77) or, less frequently, cheese, crackers, and fruit in thoughtful combination (see page 120).

The distinguishing feature of all hors d'oeuvres, however, is their small size. Some are finger food, where a lack of utensils establishes a direct rapport with the food; some are presented dramatically on large platters, antipasto-style, where guests help themselves to small portions on small plates.

In that spirit, almost anything can become an hors d'oeuvre — even soup, served in decorative demitasse cups on a beautiful silver tray.

Quick and Easy

cold

- Little Radishes with Whipped Goat Cheese and Toasted Cumin

- Endive with Sun-Dried Tomato and Orange Pâté

- Prosciutto and Melon Batons

- *cocktail sandwiches:* Smoked Salmon–Horseradish; Open-Faced Cucumber-Feta

- Cherry Bombs

- Celery Bites

- Smoked Salmon Kisses

- Zucchini Thimbles with Goat Cheese and Chili Oil

- An Unusual Hummus

- Singing Clams

- *shrimp-in-a-snap:* Wasabi-Stuffed; Pickled Pink

- *1-2-3 dips for crudités or chips:* Green Peppercorn Dip; Za'atar Pesto; Dilled Champagne Cream

- Crème Fraîche Garlic Dip, Teardrop Tomatoes (page 231)

- Oysters, Black Radish, Chipolata Sausages (page 222)

hot

- Phyllo and Feta Wraps

- Cherry Tomato *Bruschetta*

- Truffled Whitefish Puffs

- Salmon-in-Blankets

- Plum-Glazed Stuffed Mushrooms

- Sausage and Bay Leaf Brochettes

- Shrimp Tapas

- Socca Blini, Olive "Caviar"

- Edam-Up Quesadillas (page 241)

- Eleven-Inch Parmesan Straws (page 236)

95

little radishes with whipped goat cheese and toasted cumin

**12 or more medium red radishes, with stems
    and leaves**
4 ounces fresh goat cheese
1 tablespoon cumin seeds

- Wash radishes and radish leaves well. Dry thoroughly. Cut leaves from radishes, leaving 1 inch of stem attached to each radish. Remove any spidery roots.
- Scatter radish leaves on large plate or platter. Cut radishes in half lengthwise and place on radish greens.
- Place goat cheese in food processor with 2 teaspoons cold water. Process until smooth, being careful not to overprocess. Mixture should be smooth and thick.
- Using a butter knife, spread cheese thickly on cut side of each radish, or pipe cheese through a pastry bag. Refrigerate until ready to use.
- In small nonstick skillet, cook cumin seeds over medium heat until they begin to darken and exude a fragrant aroma. Add ¼ teaspoon salt and mix well. Sprinkle each radish with cumin-salt mixture.

makes about 24 pieces

endive with sun-dried tomato and orange pâté

6 ounces sun-dried tomatoes in oil
3 medium oranges
4 medium Belgian endives

- Drain oil from sun-dried tomatoes and reserve. Place drained tomatoes in food processor.
- Grate rind of one orange so that you have ½ teaspoon grated zest. Add zest to tomatoes. Using a small sharp knife, cut rind and white pith from that orange and discard. Cut orange into large chunks and place in processor. Process tomatoes and orange chunks until thick and smooth. Add salt and freshly ground black pepper to taste. Add a little of the reserved oil to make the puree smoother but still thick. Transfer to small bowl.
- Wash endives and dry. Cut ½ inch from bottoms of endives and separate into leaves. Place leaves on platter or in flat wicker basket. Place ½ tablespoon tomato-orange pâté near the bottom of each leaf.
- Cut rind and pith from remaining 2 oranges and discard. Cut along membranes to release segments. Cut segments in half lengthwise and place 1 in each endive leaf.

makes about 32 pieces

prosciutto and melon batons

A signature antipasto from Laura Maioglio, proprietor of Barbetta, New York's oldest continuously family-run Italian restaurant.

1 ripe cantaloupe
½ pound thinly sliced prosciutto
24 grissini (long, thin Italian bread sticks) *

- Cut cantaloupe in half and scoop out seeds. With large part of melon baller, scoop flesh into 1-inch balls. Pat dry and reserve. Cut prosciutto into strips and wrap around melon balls.
- Insert 1 grissino into each melon ball to make a "lollipop." If melon is too firm, use a small knife to make a starter hole. If grissini are too thin, you might want to break them in half before inserting into melon.
- Garnish prosciutto with a grinding of black pepper and serve immediately.

makes 24 batons

> * Available in most supermarkets and specialty-food stores.

cocktail sandwiches:

smoked salmon–horseradish

8 ounces sliced smoked salmon
3 tablespoons prepared white horseradish
8 thin slices firm white bread *

- Place smoked salmon and horseradish in food processor. Process briefly to form a paste. You will have 1 heaping cup.
- Spread ¼ cup on each of 4 slices of bread. Top with another slice of bread and press firmly. Cut off crusts, making perfect squares. Cut each sandwich into 5 "fingers."

makes 20 sandwiches

   * Use a brand such as Pepperidge Farm or Arnold.

open-faced cucumber-feta

8 ounces feta cheese
1 seedless hothouse cucumber
6 thin slices pumpernickel bread *

- Place cheese and 2 tablespoons cold water in food processor. Blend until smooth.
- Peel cucumber and, using a thin-bladed sharp knife, cut into paper-thin rounds. Place in bowl.
- Spread cheese thickly on each slice of bread. Cover cheese with overlapping cucumber slices. Trim crusts. Cut each into 4 triangles. Dust with coarsely ground black pepper.

makes 24 sandwiches

   S T Y L E   N O T E : This looks dramatic on a black plate or lacquered tray.

   * I use Wild's Westphalian or Rubschlager.

cherry bombs

1¼ cups ricotta cheese
⅓ cup pickled jalapeño pepper slices
48 small cherry tomatoes

- Place ricotta in medium bowl. Drain jalapeños and dice to make 5 tablespoons. Add to ricotta with kosher salt and freshly ground white pepper to taste, and mix.
- Wash tomatoes, removing any stems. Dry well. Turn tomatoes so stem end faces down. Cut a small slice from "top" (which is actually bottom) of each tomato and save. Scoop out insides and discard.
- Using a small spoon or butter knife, fill each tomato with ricotta so that filling is rounded on top. Top with reserved tomato slice. Chill until ready to serve.

makes 48 bombs

S T Y L E N O T E: These tomatoes look great served in the tiny fluted paper cups usually used for candy.

celery bites

8 ounces cream cheese
2-ounce can rolled anchovies with capers in oil
1 large leafy bunch celery

- Place cream cheese in food processor. Drain anchovies and capers. Pat dry with paper towel. Process with cream cheese until smooth. Chill until ready to serve.
- Remove outer stalks from celery and save for another use. Separate remaining stalks and wash well. Peel about 8 of the narrower stalks so that they sit flat. Mince some of the celery leaves to make 2 heaping tablespoons. Add to cream cheese with a grinding of black pepper, then stir to combine.
- Scatter remaining celery leaves on platter. Cut peeled stalks into 1½-inch lengths. Using a small knife, fill celery with cheese mixture. Arrange on celery leaves.

makes about 32 pieces

smoked salmon kisses

1 pound smoked salmon, cut into 16 slices
1 teaspoon Asian sesame oil
1 bunch fresh chives

- Cut salmon slices in half to make 32 pieces.
- Finely mince half of the salmon using a large sharp knife. Place in small bowl. Add sesame oil and a grinding of black pepper. Finely chop enough chives to make 1 tablespoon. Add to minced salmon and mix gently.
- Place ½ tablespoon minced salmon in center of each of the remaining 16 pieces of salmon. Fold salmon over filling; turn and tuck ends underneath to make little packets. Tie each with a chive. If chives are not pliable, run under hot water, then quickly under cold water. Pat dry and tie in a knot around salmon packets.
- Serve on a platter, on a bed of chives, if desired.

makes 16 kisses

zucchini thimbles with goat cheese and chili oil

5 small zucchini (1 inch in diameter, 6 inches long)
5 ounces fresh goat cheese
2 tablespoons chili oil

- Wash zucchini and dry well. Cut off ends and reserve. Cut each zucchini into 5 ¾-inch-thick rounds. Using a melon baller, scoop center from each slice to form a "cup." Do not scoop through the bottom.
- Place cheese and ½ tablespoon water in food processor. Process until smooth.
- Spoon cheese into each zucchini cup, rounding it on top. Drizzle with chili oil and sprinkle lightly with salt.
- Cut reserved ends into small julienne strips. Use as a garnish on top of cheese.

makes 25 thimbles

STYLE NOTE: Beautiful on a yellow or orange ceramic plate.

an unusual hummus

Inspired by my globe-trotting sister-in-law, Gail Gold.

3 cups cooked chickpeas, or 2 15-ounce cans, drained
1½ tablespoons Asian sesame oil, plus more for drizzling (optional)
2 small cloves garlic, chopped

- Place chickpeas, sesame oil, and garlic in bowl of food processor. Begin to process, slowly adding about 6 tablespoons cold water to make a thick, smooth paste. Add salt and freshly ground black pepper to taste.
- Cover and refrigerate until ready to use. Spread thickly on large plate, making a flat well in center. Drizzle with a few more drops sesame oil, if desired. Serve with Pita Chips (see page 109) or Curry Crisps (see page 110).

makes about 2½ cups

singing clams

5-inch piece fresh ginger
1 large ripe avocado
24 littleneck clams on the half shell, with their juice *

- Peel ginger using a small sharp knife. Grate on large holes of box grater. Put grated ginger in paper towel and squeeze juice into bowl. You will have 1½ to 2 tablespoons juice.
- Cut avocado in half and remove pit. Peel avocado using a small sharp knife. Cut flesh into chunks and put in food processor with ginger juice. Puree until thick and smooth. Add salt and some of the clam juice. Process briefly.
- Place clams on platter or on bed of crushed ice. Top each with ½ tablespoon avocado puree.
- *Optional garnish:* Top with finely minced ginger or finely diced avocado.

makes 24 clams

* If necessary, have your fish store open the clams.

shrimp-in-a-snap:

wasabi-stuffed

**32 very large shrimp (about 2 pounds), cooked
   in their shells**
8 ounces cream cheese
2 tablespoons wasabi powder *

- You may buy shrimp already cooked from your
  fish store. To prepare your own, bring a large pot
  of salted water to a boil. Add uncooked shrimp.
  Lower heat to medium and cook for 3 to 4 minutes, until shrimp are pink. Place in colander
  under cold running water for 1 minute. Remove
  shells, leaving tails intact.
- Place cream cheese in food processor. In small
  bowl, mix wasabi with 1½ to 2 tablespoons cold
  water to form a thick paste. Add to food processor. Add ¼ teaspoon salt (or more to taste).
  Process until smooth.
- Split shrimp down the back, cutting almost all
  the way through. Using a small spoon or pastry
  bag, stuff each with 1½ teaspoons cream cheese.
  Press sides gently together.
- *Optional:* Serve with additional wasabi paste.

makes 32 shrimp

* Available in Asian markets and some specialty-
   food stores.

pickled pink

**32 very large shrimp (about 2 pounds), cooked
   in their shells**
1 bunch fresh cilantro
1 cup Japanese pickled ginger, * **with juice**

- You may buy shrimp already cooked or prepare
  as in previous recipe.
- Wash and dry cilantro. Split shrimp down the
  back, cutting almost all the way through. Fill
  with small pieces of pickled ginger and cilantro
  leaves. Drain remaining ginger and place juice in
  small ramekin for dunking.

makes 32 shrimp

* Available in Asian markets and some specialty-
   food stores.

1-2-3 dips for crudités or chips:

green peppercorn dip

1 cup light mayonnaise
2 tablespoons coarse-grain mustard
2 tablespoons green peppercorns in brine,
  drained

- Combine mayonnaise and mustard in small bowl. Crush peppercorns lightly with bottom of heavy saucepan. Add to mayonnaise mixture and stir until blended. Chill.

makes 1 heaping cup

za'atar pesto

½ cup za'atar *
6 tablespoons freshly grated Parmesan cheese
⅔ cup good-quality olive oil

- In small bowl, combine za'atar and Parmesan cheese. Add olive oil and mix with a spoon until blended. Transfer to jar and store in refrigerator.

makes 1 cup

  * Use za'atar imported from Lebanon or Israel, which has a greenish hue. Available in Middle Eastern markets.

dilled champagne cream

1½ cups nonfat sour cream, well chilled
¼ cup finely chopped fresh dill
2 tablespoons champagne vinegar

- In medium bowl, combine sour cream, dill, and vinegar. Add pinch of salt and freshly ground black pepper. Chill.

makes about 1½ cups

phyllo and feta wraps

1 pound feta cheese, in one piece
5 tablespoons unsalted butter, melted
6 sheets phyllo dough

- Preheat oven to 375°.
- Portion cheese into 24 "sticks" by cutting piece in half horizontally, then into rectangles that are 2½ inches long and ½ inch wide.
- Cut phyllo sheets into 4 equal pieces. Brush lightly with butter. Roll 1 piece of cheese in 1 piece of phyllo, tucking sides and flaps underneath. Brush with additional butter. Repeat until you have wrapped all the cheese. Place on baking sheet. Bake for 10 to 15 minutes, until golden brown. Serve on colorful platter.

makes 24 wraps

cherry tomato *bruschetta*

1 small loaf semolina bread
2 pints (4 cups) small cherry tomatoes
8 tablespoons garlic oil, store-bought or
**   homemade (see page 299)**

- Preheat oven to 375°.
- Cut bread into 16 to 20 ½-inch-thick slices. Place in oven and toast for about 5 minutes on each side, until golden and rather crisp. Place toasted bread on platter.
- Wash tomatoes and dry well, removing any stems. Cut tomatoes in half through stem ends.
- Heat 5 tablespoons oil in 12-inch nonstick skillet over high heat. Add tomatoes and cook, stirring often, until just softened, about 5 minutes. Add pinch of salt and freshly ground black pepper to taste.
- Spoon mixture onto toasted bread and drizzle with remaining oil. Sprinkle with coarse sea salt and arrange on rustic-looking platter.

makes 20 *bruschetta*

truffled whitefish puffs

1 sheet frozen puff pastry (8¾ ounces), thawed
8 ounces (1 cup) whitefish salad *
½ teaspoon white truffle oil **

- Preheat oven to 400°.
- Using a 2-inch round cookie cutter, cut 24 or more circles from the pastry. Place on baking sheet and bake for 10 to 12 minutes, until golden. Remove from oven. Let cool for 5 to 10 minutes.
- Place whitefish salad in small bowl. Add truffle oil and stir until thoroughly incorporated.
- Cut pastry puffs in half horizontally. Spoon 2 teaspoons whitefish salad on bottom piece and cover with top. Serve immediately on platter lined with lemon leaves or gold or silver doilies.

makes 24 puffs

   * Available in the deli section of most supermarkets.

  ** Available in specialty-food stores.

salmon-in-blankets

1 sheet frozen puff pastry (8¾ ounces), thawed
1 pound smoked salmon, cut into 16 slices
⅓ cup Creole mustard, * **plus more for dunking**

- Preheat oven to 400°.
- Roll pastry out so that it is ⅛ inch thick. Cut into 32 rectangles.
- Cut salmon into 32 pieces. Place ½ teaspoon mustard on each strip of salmon and roll up into a cylindrical shape. Then roll up salmon, like a traditional pig-in-a-blanket, in a piece of puff pastry. With the seam on the bottom, tuck sides underneath to make a tight little roll about 2½ inches long and ½ inch wide.
- Bake for 15 minutes, until golden brown and puffed. Arrange on oval platter with more mustard in small bowl for dunking. Serve hot.

makes 32 pieces

  * Use a brand such as Cajun's Choice from Louisiana Foods. You may also substitute coarse-grain mustard.

plum-glazed stuffed mushrooms

32 large white mushrooms
1 pound bulk pork sausage
½ cup or more Chinese plum sauce *

- Preheat oven to 375°.
- Scoop out stems from mushrooms and discard. Peel caps using your fingers.
- Fill each cap with 1 tablespoon sausage, packing it tightly and mounding it on top.
- Spread ¼ teaspoon plum sauce on each mound of sausage. Place on baking sheet and bake for 15 to 18 minutes.
- Meanwhile, heat remaining plum sauce in small saucepan until bubbling. Keep warm.
- Place mushrooms under broiler for 30 seconds. Arrange on plate. Serve with warm plum sauce in small shallow bowl.

makes 32 mushrooms

> * Available in supermarkets and Asian markets. I use China Bowl.

sausage and bay leaf brochettes

6 sweet Italian sausages (about 1 pound)
18 small fresh bay leaves or good-quality dried bay leaves *
1 large loaf Italian bread

- Preheat oven to 375°.
- Prick sausages several times with a fork. Cut into 3 pieces, about 1¼ inches each. If using dried bay leaves, soak in cold water for 5 minutes. Pat dry.
- Cut bread into 18 1-inch cubes, crust attached.
- Thread 18 small wooden skewers (4½ inches long) with a sausage, a bay leaf, and a bread cube. Place on baking sheet. Bake for 6 minutes, then turn over and bake for 6 minutes more. Arrange on wooden tray or interesting ceramic dish. Serve hot. Do not eat the bay leaves. They are used for flavor and decorative purposes only.

makes 18 brochettes

> * I use fresh bay leaves, available in many supermarkets, or dried California bay leaves from Spice Islands.

shrimp tapas

**1 pound (about 32) uncooked medium shrimp,
in their shells**
6 tablespoons unsalted butter
**2 heaping tablespoons chopped canned
chipotle peppers in adobo sauce**

- Peel shrimp, leaving shells intact.
- Melt butter in 12-inch nonstick skillet over
  medium heat. Do not let brown. Add chipotle
  peppers and shrimp, and increase heat to high.
- Stirring constantly, cook shrimp until just firm,
  about 5 minutes. Do not overcook. Sprinkle with
  salt and toss.
- Put shrimp and sauce on 8 small plates, tapas-
  style, or place on large platter. Serve with small
  wooden forks or toothpicks.

makes about 32 pieces

socca blini, olive "caviar"

Socca, an omnipresent snack food of Nice, is a
thin, flat pancake made from chickpea flour,
olive oil, salt, and water and traditionally prepared in a wood-fired oven. In this recipe, I use
the batter to form a kind of blin, or crepe, quickly
cooked in a skillet on top of the stove.

1 cup chickpea flour *
5 tablespoons extra-virgin olive oil
**¾ cup prepared black olive tapenade or
Eggplant "Caviar" (see page 116)**

- Sift flour into mixing bowl. Make a well. Whisk in
  ½ cup water to form a smooth, thick paste. Add
  another ½ cup water and 2 tablespoons olive oil,
  ¼ teaspoon coarse salt, and a grinding of black
  pepper. Stir until very smooth.
- In large nonstick skillet, heat remaining 3 tablespoons oil. When it begins to bubble, add table-
  spoonfuls of batter to make little pancakes.
  When batter has set, turn over and cook for 30
  seconds, or until golden.
- Remove to platter. Top each with about ½ tablespoon tapenade or "caviar." Serve warm or at
  room temperature.

makes about 24 blini

* Available in Middle Eastern markets and health
food stores.

107

By the Bowl

- Garlic Croûtes

- Pita Chips

- Curry Crisps

- Homemade Potato Chips (page 56)

- *flavored salts for cheese and crudités:* Paprika Salt; Curry Salt; Sesame Salt

- Sake Olives with Grapefruit

- *party nuts:* Shanghai Glazed Walnuts; Deviled Pecans

- Truffled White Bean Spread

- Chicken Liver and Sun-Dried Tomato Pâté

- An Unusual Pâté

- Fresh Cod Brandade #1

- Fresh Cod Brandade #2

- Eggplant Pâté with Tahina and Pomegranate Molasses

- Roasted Eggplant and Pesto Spread

- Eggplant "Caviar"

- *bar cheeses 1-2-3:* The World's Best Pimiento Spread; Roasted Garlic–Sapsago Spread; Pesto-Vermouth Spread

- Chicken Confit with Garlic and Thyme (page 247)

- Chicken Liver and Shiitake Pâté (page 55)

- Med-Rim Eggplant with Sun-Dried Tomatoes (page 199)

garlic croûtes

**1 long, narrow loaf Italian bread with sesame
   seeds (8 ounces)**
3 tablespoons good-quality olive oil
1 large clove garlic

- Preheat oven to 300°.
- Cut ends from bread and discard. Using a ser-
  rated knife, cut bread into slices ⅛ to ¼ inch
  thick. Distribute on 2 baking sheets. Using a pastry brush, lightly brush bread with olive oil.
- Bake for 25 minutes, until bread is lightly colored
  and crisp. Cut garlic clove in half. Rub toast
  lightly with garlic. Sprinkle very lightly with salt,
  if desired. Store in an airtight container.

makes about 36 croûtes

pita chips

3 large pita breads
**6 tablespoons garlic oil, store-bought or
   homemade (see page 299)**
6 tablespoons freshly grated Parmesan cheese

- Preheat oven to 300°.
- Split pita breads horizontally to make 6 rounds.
  Brush each with garlic oil, sprinkle with
  cheese, and cut into 8 triangles. Place on bak-
  ing sheet.
- Bake for 15 minutes, or until crisp and golden.
  Cool and store in airtight container for up to
  2 days.

makes 48 chips

curry crisps

8 8-inch flour tortillas
12 ounces sharp white cheddar cheese
4 teaspoons good-quality curry powder

- Preheat oven to 400°.
- Place tortillas on baking sheets. Grate cheese on large holes of box grater. Distribute 3 heaping tablespoons cheese right to the edge of each tortilla. Sprinkle with ¼ to ½ teaspoon curry powder. Sprinkle lightly with salt.
- Bake for 10 to 12 minutes, until golden and crisp. Cut each warm tortilla into 6 wedges or into irregular-shaped pieces, or leave them whole. Tortillas will crisp as they cool. Store in airtight container for up to 3 days.

makes 8 whole tortillas or about 48 crisps

flavored salts for cheese and crudités:

paprika salt

2 tablespoons sweet Hungarian paprika
2½ teaspoons salt

- Place in small bowl and stir. Store in tightly covered jar.

curry salt

2 tablespoons good-quality curry powder
2½ teaspoons salt

- Place in small bowl and stir. Store in tightly covered jar.

sesame salt

¼ cup sesame seeds
1 teaspoon salt

- Place sesame seeds in small nonstick skillet. Cook over medium heat until toasted and golden brown. Let cool completely. Place in spice or coffee grinder with salt. Briefly process until finely ground. Store in tightly covered jar.

sake olives
with grapefruit

**1¼ pounds unpitted green Spanish olives or
  green Alfonso olives, cracked**
1 medium grapefruit
¾ cup sake

- Wash olives in colander. Drain well and pat dry.
  Cut long strips of grapefruit rind with vegetable
  peeler.
- Place olives, sake, and strained juice of ½ grape-
  fruit in bowl. Add strips of grapefruit rind and
  2 teaspoons whole black peppercorns. Mix well.
- Transfer to jar so that liquid covers olives.
  Refrigerate for 2 to 3 days before using.

party nuts:

shanghai glazed walnuts

The beguiling interplay of sweet, salty, and bitter
makes a commonplace nut taste celebratory.
Splurge on good-quality jumbo walnuts from a
specialty-food store.

4 cups shelled walnuts, whole pieces or halves
½ cup sugar
Vegetable or peanut oil

- In medium saucepan, bring 8 cups water to a
  boil. Add walnuts, return to a boil, and cook for
  1 minute.
- Rinse nuts in colander under hot water. Drain
  well. Transfer to small bowl and add sugar. Toss
  well.
- In heavy skillet, heat 1-inch oil to 350°. Add half
  the walnuts and fry for 4 to 5 minutes, until
  crisp. With slotted spoon, remove nuts to sieve
  to drain. Sprinkle lightly with salt and mix gently
  to separate pieces.
- Repeat with remaining nuts. Place on sheets of
  waxed paper to cool.

makes 4 cups

deviled pecans

2 tablespoons unsalted butter
1 tablespoon Worcestershire sauce, plus more
  for drizzling
½ pound pecan halves

- Preheat oven to 350°.
- In nonstick skillet, melt butter and add Worcestershire sauce. Add pecans, pinch of salt, and freshly ground black pepper. Stir and cook over medium heat for a few minutes, until nuts are coated.
- Transfer to baking sheet and bake for 10 minutes, stirring often. Drain on paper towels. Sprinkle with salt, pepper, and additional Worcestershire sauce.

makes about 2 cups

truffled white bean spread

½ pound dried small white beans
¼ cup heavy cream
1½ tablespoons white truffle oil *

- Place beans in medium pot with water to cover by 1 inch. Bring to a boil and continue to boil for 2 minutes. Remove from heat. Cover and let sit for 1 hour.
- Drain beans in colander. Place beans in pot with 12 whole black peppercorns. Add fresh water to cover by 2 inches. Bring to a boil. Lower heat, cover, and simmer for 1 hour 20 minutes, or until beans are tender.
- Drain beans, saving 1 tablespoon cooking liquid. Place beans in food processor. Process until very smooth, adding cooking liquid. With motor running, slowly add cream and 1 tablespoon truffle oil.
- Transfer mixture to bowl. Stir in 1 teaspoon kosher salt and freshly ground white pepper to taste. Cover and chill until ready to use.
- Put mixture in large ramekin or shallow bowl. Drizzle with remaining ½ tablespoon truffle oil.

makes 2¾ cups

* Available in specialty-food stores.

chicken liver and
sun-dried tomato pâté

7- or 8-ounce jar sun-dried tomatoes in oil
1 pound fresh chicken livers
1 medium-large and 1 small onion

- Reserve one-third of the sun-dried tomatoes and 1 tablespoon of their oil for later use. Wash and thoroughly dry chicken livers.
- In large nonstick skillet, heat 2 to 3 tablespoons oil. Chop medium-large onion into small pieces and add to oil. Cook over medium-high heat for 1 minute, then add chicken livers.
- Cook livers over medium heat, stirring often, for about 10 minutes, or until firm and no longer pink. Transfer livers, onion, 2/3 of sun-dried tomatoes, and all juices to food processor and process until smooth, being careful not to overprocess.
- Peel small onion and grate on large holes of box grater so that you have 1 tablespoon onion juice. Add to chicken livers with salt to taste and lots of freshly ground black pepper. Process again briefly.
- Transfer pâté to ramekin. Cover with plastic wrap and chill 30 minutes.
- Process remaining sun-dried tomatoes and 1 tablespoon oil in food processor to form a smooth paste. Spread evenly over chilled pâté. Cover and chill until ready to use.

makes 1²/₃ cups

an unusual pâté

1 pound fresh chicken livers
4 ounces Italian Gorgonzola cheese, at room temperature
1 teaspoon cognac

- Wash chicken livers and drain well. Place livers in one layer in 10-inch nonstick skillet. Add enough cold water just to cover livers. Add a large pinch of kosher salt.
- Cut a round of waxed paper and place on livers. Bring just to a boil, then lower heat to medium. Poach livers until firm but a little pink in the center. Do not overcook. Remove from pan with slotted spoon. Let cool for 5 minutes.
- Meanwhile, cut rind from cheese, then cut cheese into ½-inch pieces. Place chicken livers and cheese in bowl of food processor. Process until incorporated. Add cognac and process until smooth.
- Transfer mixture to bowl. Add lots of freshly ground black pepper and a pinch of kosher salt, if desired. Cover and refrigerate until cold.
- Let come to room temperature before serving. Pack into ramekin or decorative dish to serve.

makes 1²/₃ cups

113

fresh cod brandade #1

1 pound thick cod fillets
1 large lemon
½ cup half-and-half

- Remove skin and any bones from fish. Place in large nonstick skillet in one layer. Put enough cold water in skillet to just reach top of fish. Cut a round of waxed paper and place on fish.
- Bring water to a boil. Lower heat to just above a simmer and cook for 10 to 15 minutes (depending on thickness of fish), until fish is opaque and firm.
- Remove pan from heat and let fish cool for 15 minutes in poaching liquid.
- Meanwhile, grate ½ teaspoon lemon zest. Cut lemon in half and squeeze 2 tablespoons juice.
- Drain fish well. Break into pieces and place in mortar. With pestle, gently crush fish until coarsely ground. Add lemon zest and juice and blend. Slowly add half-and-half, mashing with pestle until a coarse paste forms.
- Add kosher salt and freshly ground black pepper to taste. Cover and refrigerate until ready to use.

makes about 2 cups

fresh cod brandade #2

1 cup crème fraîche
2 small cloves garlic
2 pounds thick cod fillets

- Place crème fraîche in small bowl. Push garlic through garlic press into bowl and mix well. Cover and refrigerate until ready to use.
- Remove skin and any bones from fish. Place in large nonstick skillet in one layer. Put enough cold water in skillet to just reach top of fish. Cut a round of waxed paper and place on fish.
- Bring water to a boil. Lower heat to just above a simmer and cook for 10 to 15 minutes (depending on thickness of fish), until fish is opaque and firm.
- Remove pan from heat and let fish cool for 15 minutes in poaching liquid. Drain fish well, saving poaching liquid. Break fish into pieces and place in mortar. Gently crush with pestle until coarsely ground. Or you may pulse for a few seconds in food processor, but do not puree.
- Spoon in garlic crème fraîche, mixing well. Add 1 to 2 tablespoons poaching liquid. Add kosher salt and freshly ground black pepper to taste. Cover and refrigerate until ready to use.

makes about 3½ cups

eggplant pâté with tahina and pomegranate molasses

1 large eggplant (1½ pounds)
3 tablespoons tahina (sesame seed paste) *
2 tablespoons pomegranate molasses **

- Wash and dry eggplant. Place directly on open fire on top of stove. Or place on baking sheet and broil. Cook for a few minutes, turning several times so that skin blisters and chars. This will impart a lovely, smoky flavor to eggplant.
- Preheat oven to 400°.
- Place eggplant on baking sheet (if not already on one) and bake for 50 minutes, turning once halfway through.
- Remove from oven. Cut eggplant in half lengthwise and let cool for 10 minutes. Scoop out flesh and place in bowl of food processor.
- Add tahina and pomegranate molasses, and process until smooth, being careful not to overprocess. Transfer mixture to bowl. Stir in kosher salt and freshly ground black pepper to taste. Cover and refrigerate until cold.

makes 1²⁄₃ cups

* Available in jars in supermarkets and Middle Eastern markets.

** I use Cortas from Lebanon, available in Middle Eastern markets.

roasted eggplant and pesto spread

1 large eggplant (1½ pounds)
¼ cup pesto, homemade or prepared
1 large lemon

- Wash and dry eggplant. Place directly on open fire on top of stove. Or place on baking sheet and broil. Cook for a few minutes, turning several times so that skin blisters and chars. This will impart a lovely, smoky flavor to eggplant.
- Preheat oven to 400°.
- Place eggplant on baking sheet (if not already on one) and bake for 50 minutes, turning once halfway through.
- Remove from oven. Cut eggplant in half lengthwise and let cool for 10 minutes. Scoop out flesh and place in bowl of food processor.
- Add pesto to food processor. Grate lemon to get ½ teaspoon zest. Add to processor. Cut lemon in half and squeeze 2 tablespoons juice. Add to processor and process until fairly smooth.
- Transfer to bowl. Stir in kosher salt and freshly ground black pepper. Cover and refrigerate until cold.

makes 1²⁄₃ cups

eggplant "caviar"

1 medium eggplant (about 1 pound)
3 tablespoons prepared black olive tapenade
1 tablespoon freshly squeezed lemon juice

- Preheat oven to 400°.
- Put eggplant on baking sheet and prick with fork. Bake for 1 hour.
- Cut eggplant in half. Scoop out flesh and mash in bowl with tapenade and lemon juice. Add salt, if desired, and freshly ground black pepper to taste. Mix well and chill.

makes ¾ cup

bar cheeses 1-2-3:

the world's best pimiento spread

1 pound sharp English cheddar cheese
6½-ounce jar pimientos
⅔ cup light mayonnaise

- Cut rind off cheese. Cut cheese into small pieces and put in food processor. Add pimientos, including juice, and process until well blended.
- Add mayonnaise, ¼ teaspoon salt, and ⅛ teaspoon freshly ground white pepper. Process until as smooth as possible. Using a flexible rubber spatula, transfer to large ramekin or decorative bowl. Chill for at least 30 minutes before serving.

makes approximately 3½ cups

roasted garlic–sapsago spread

This distinctive pale jade dip will have people guessing what it is, then going back for more! The unusual flavor is from sapsago, a cone-shaped, pungent, low-fat grating cheese flavored with clover.

2 large heads garlic, unpeeled
6 ounces sapsago cheese
16 ounces cream cheese, softened

- Preheat oven to 400°.
- Cut ¼ inch from tops of garlic, exposing all the cloves. Wrap each head loosely in a 6-inch square of aluminum foil. Bake in pie tin for 1¼ hours.
- Remove garlic from foil. Let rest for 10 minutes, then squeeze out softened garlic pulp. You should have approximately 4 tablespoons.
- Grate sapsago cheese on medium holes of box grater. Place softened cream cheese in bowl of electric mixer. Add garlic pulp, grated cheese, and 2 tablespoons cold water. Beat on medium speed until ingredients are incorporated and cheese is light and fluffy. Spoon into bowl and chill for at least 30 minutes before serving.

makes 3 cups

pesto-vermouth spread

8 ounces cream cheese
6 tablespoons pesto, homemade or prepared
3 tablespoons dry vermouth

- Remove cream cheese from package and bring to room temperature.
- Break cream cheese into large pieces and place in food processor. Process, adding pesto 2 tablespoons at a time until incorporated. With motor running, add vermouth until mixture is smooth and creamy. Do not overprocess.
- Transfer contents to bowl. Stir in a pinch of kosher salt and a grinding of black pepper.
- Pack mixture into small bowl or ramekin. Cover with waxed paper or plastic wrap. Refrigerate for several hours. This cheese improves with age and will keep for up to 1 week.

makes 1⅓ cups

Finger Food

cold

- Tartines
- Crispy Oatcakes with Cheese and Fruit
- A Rainbow of Cheese Truffles
- Two-Tone Mussels
- Star Anise Tea Eggs
- Smoked Salmon Roulades
- Drunken Chicken (page 52), Flavored Salts (page 110)
- Brie Croustades with Black Caviar (page 222)
- Wrinkled Potatoes with Salmon Caviar (page 227)

hot

- Little Roquefort Biscuits
- Asparagettes
- Provolone-Pesto Pizza
- Blue-Cheese-and-Broccoli-Stuffed Mushrooms
- Thai Chicken Skewers
- Silver-Dollar Corn Cakes with Bacon and Crème Fraîche
- "Smoked" Carnitas
- Rib Bits
- Hot and Crispy Swiss Truffles (page 267)
- Shiitake-Scallion Satés (page 44)

tartines

1 narrow loaf crusty French or Italian bread
**1 pound triple-cream cheese with edible rind
(Saint Andre, Boursault, Brillat-Savarin, or
Explorateur), at room temperature**
**Choice of toppings: finely chopped toasted
pecans, *herbes de Provence,* coarsely cracked
coriander seeds, fresh raspberries or *fraises
des bois* (wild strawberries), shaved truffles,
a few drops truffle oil or Armagnac, sweet
butter or truffle paste**

- Slice bread horizontally as if you were making a
  big sandwich. Cut each half into 1-inch-wide
  strips. You will have about 20 pieces. Place on
  baking sheet and place 8 inches from broiler.
  Toast until golden, but do not let brown.
- Slather cheese, rind and all, on each slice. Top
  with pecans, *herbes de Provence,* coriander,
  berries, shaved truffles, truffle oil, or Armagnac.
  Or you may first spread bread with butter or
  truffle paste and then slather on cheese.
- *Optional:* As a dessert, drizzle tartines with an
  exquisitely flavored honey, such as wild thyme or
  wildflower.

makes about 20 tartines

> S T Y L E   N O T E : Arrange on a beautiful
> platter or in a shallow basket lined with fresh
> leaves that have been washed and dried.

crispy oatcakes with cheese and fruit

Serve these fabulous "biscuits" with champagne
or room-temperature cheese and fresh fruit at
the end of a meal, instead of dessert.

crispy oatcakes

3 cups old-fashioned rolled oats
**1 stick salted butter, plus 1 tablespoon for
greasing the pan**
⅔ cup nonfat sweetened condensed milk

- Preheat oven to 325°.
- Put oats in food processor and process until they
  are the consistency of flour. Put in bowl of electric mixer. Cut 1 stick butter into small pieces and
  add to bowl along with condensed milk. Blend
  well. Using a flexible metal spatula, spread in
  buttered 10-inch tart pan with removable bottom.
- Bake for 25 to 30 minutes, until golden. Release
  from pan and cut into 16 to 20 thick wedges.
- Reduce oven temperature to 275°. Place wedges
  on baking sheet and bake for 12 minutes, until
  golden all over. Let cool. Store in airtight tin.

makes 16 to 20 oatcakes

great fruit and cheese combinations:

- Aged Parmigiano-Reggiano and Medjool dates

- Pont l'Evêque and Bosc pears

- Cabrales and guava paste

- Gorgonzola dolce and fresh figs

- Saint Andre and purple globe grapes

- Aged goat cheese and mangoes

- Mimolette and Macoun apples

- Ripe Camembert and Asian pears

- Vella dry jack and dried pears

- Fresh goat cheese and ripe plums

- Stilton and champagne grapes

- Chaource and fresh strawberries

- Pecorino Romano and sweet red cherries

- Taleggio and Forelle pears

- Farmhouse cheddar and green apples

- Cambazola and fresh peaches

a rainbow of cheese truffles

Here's a great use for leftover cheese. Serve these marble-size morsels just at room temperature, and they'll have a most unusual texture. I present them rolled in a rainbow of assorted coatings.

½ pound unsalted butter, at room temperature
2 cups (6 ounces) shredded cheese: sharp cheddar, aged Gouda, fontina, or other
Choice of coatings: fine fresh bread crumbs made from black bread; sweet Hungarian paprika or mild chili powder; poppy seeds; finely chopped fresh parsley; cumin seeds, toasted and pulverized; toasted sesame seeds; dried mint leaves

- Cut butter into pieces and cream in bowl of electric mixer. Add cheese and blend. Add salt and freshly ground black pepper to taste. Chill until firm but still pliable.
- Shape into ¾-inch balls. Roll thoroughly in any of the coatings. I like to use 4 or 5 different types to create a colorful effect. Chill until 20 minutes prior to serving.

makes about 34 truffles

STYLE NOTE: I arrange them in rows (alternating colors) in a candy box or Japanese bento box, or present them on a doily on a small silver tray.

two-tone mussels

2 pounds (about 42) small fresh mussels
½ cup prepared pesto *
¼ cup sour cream

- Scrub mussels well. Discard any that are open. Put mussels in medium pot with cold water barely to cover. Cover and cook over high heat for 10 minutes, frequently shaking pot back and forth. Be careful not to overcook.
- Remove mussels with slotted spoon and discard any that have not opened. Boil mussel broth over high heat until reduced to ½ cup. Strain through a double layer of cheesecloth or a coffee filter. Taste for salt, let cool, and refrigerate until cold.
- Meanwhile, remove top shell from each mussel and set aside. Place mussels on the half shell on large platter. Cover and refrigerate until well chilled. Spoon ½ teaspoon pesto over each mussel. Using a butter knife, put ¼ teaspoon sour cream in the pointed area of each shell. Chill in the refrigerator.
- When ready to serve, spoon a little reduced broth over each mussel. Mussels can be eaten directly from bottom shells or served with reserved top shells to use as spoons.

makes about 42 mussels

> S T Y L E   N O T E: These mussels look great on a silver or white ceramic tray. Provide a small bowl for empty shells.

> * I use Contadina, available in many supermarkets in the dairy case.

star anise tea eggs

12 medium or large eggs
6 tablespoons loose black tea leaves
3 tablespoons star anise, in pieces *

- Place eggs in large saucepan and cover with cold water. Bring to a boil, lower heat, and cook for 10 minutes, or until eggs are hard-boiled. Chill under cold running water.
- Tap each egg lightly on flat surface to make a web of small cracks all over the shell. Place eggs in large saucepan. Add tea, star anise, and 2 tablespoons salt. Cover with cold water.
- Bring to a boil. Reduce to a simmer and cook, with cover askew, for about 2 hours. Let eggs cool in liquid.
- Peel eggs. Cut in half widthwise and place flat side down on large white plate or platter.

makes 24 pieces

> * Available in Asian markets, specialty-food stores, and spice stores.

smoked salmon roulades

1 pound smoked salmon, cut into 8 slices
1 cup chive cream cheese
6 kirby cucumbers (1 inch diameter)

- Lay salmon slices flat. Spread each slice thickly with 2 tablespoons cream cheese. Roll up jelly roll–style into even, 1-inch-thick rolls. Wrap each tightly in plastic wrap, twisting ends to make compact package. Refrigerate for at least 1 hour to firm the roulades.
- Wash cucumbers and dry well. Trim ends and cut into ¼-inch-thick rounds.
- Unwrap roulades. Using a sharp knife, cut each into ¼-inch-thick rounds. Place 1 round on each cucumber.

makes about 32 roulades

S T Y L E N O T E: Arrange on a large, round, brightly colored plate.

little roquefort biscuits

8 ounces imported Roquefort cheese, at room temperature
1 stick unsalted butter
1⅓ to 1½ cups packed self-rising flour

- Preheat oven to 350°.
- Crumble Roquefort into bowl of electric mixer. Add butter, cut into small pieces, and mix for 1 minute until well blended. Add a grinding of black pepper, flour, and 1 to 2 tablespoons cold water. Mix on medium speed until dough comes away from sides of bowl. Do not overmix. Dough should be firm and not at all sticky. Add a little flour if necessary.
- Lightly dust a flat surface with flour and with your hands roll dough into a 1-inch-diameter log. Slice into ½-inch-thick rounds.
- Place rounds on ungreased baking sheet and bake for 20 minutes. Serve warm. These also freeze well and reheat beautifully.

makes 22 to 24 biscuits

S T Y L E N O T E: Arrange in a shallow basket lined with a linen napkin.

asparagettes

36 medium-thin fresh asparagus
12 sheets (12 by 17 inches) phyllo dough
½ cup basil or rosemary oil *

- Cut stems from asparagus, leaving a 3-inch-long piece from the tip down.
- Bring large saucepan of salted water to a boil. Add asparagus and cook for 3 to 4 minutes, until bright green and just beginning to get tender. Drain immediately in colander under cold running water. Pat dry. You may prepare up to this point and refrigerate.
- Preheat oven to 375°.
- Cut each sheet of phyllo into 6 rectangles. Using a pastry brush, brush 36 rectangles with oil. Place a rectangle without oil on top of each oiled rectangle.
- Place 1 asparagus stalk (make sure it is very dry) on the edge of each phyllo stack and roll up tightly, brushing with oil as you go. The result should look like a big cigarette.
- Brush with more oil and sprinkle lightly with salt. Place on baking sheet.
- Bake for 15 minutes, turning twice during baking. Remove from oven when pastry is crisp and golden.

makes 36 pieces

S T Y L E   N O T E: Arrange side by side on a platter or like the spokes of a wheel on a large round plate.

* I use Consorzio or all-natural Boyajian, available in most supermarkets and specialty-food stores.

provolone-pesto pizza

1 pound frozen bread dough
6 ounces provolone cheese
⅔ cup prepared pesto

- Thaw bread dough according to package directions.
- Preheat oven to 400°.
- Roll out dough to fit 12-inch tart pan with removable bottom. Spray pan with nonstick vegetable spray and fit dough into pan, making sure it covers the bottom. Press down with fingers and prick 8 times with a fork.
- Remove rind from cheese. Grate cheese on large holes of box grater and reserve.
- Bake crust for 15 minutes. Spread pesto evenly over crust and add a grinding of black pepper. Cover with grated cheese.
- Quickly return to oven and bake for 10 minutes, until cheese is melted and bubbly. Cut into thin wedges. Serve immediately.

makes 10 to 12 wedges

S T Y L E   N O T E: Looks great on a wooden board.

123

blue-cheese-and-broccoli-stuffed mushrooms

1 bunch broccoli
5 ounces Saga blue cheese
24 large white mushrooms

- Remove and discard bottom third of broccoli. You should have about ½ pound tops and stems.
- Bring small pot of salted water to a boil. Add broccoli and cook for 8 to 10 minutes, until tender but still bright green. Drain in colander under cold running water. Dry well. Coarsely chop and place in bowl of food processor.
- Remove rind from cheese and add to processor. Process until a smooth paste forms. Add salt and freshly ground black pepper to taste. Transfer to bowl, cover, and refrigerate until ready to use.
- Preheat oven to 375°.
- Remove stems and scoop out centers of mushrooms. Peel mushrooms using a small knife or your fingers. Fill with broccoli-cheese mixture, mounding on top. Place on baking sheet and bake for 10 to 12 minutes, until hot.

makes 24 mushrooms

S T Y L E N O T E: These look great on a brightly colored red or purple plate.

thai chicken skewers

1 pound skinless boneless chicken breasts
1¾ cups light coconut milk
1½ teaspoons Thai red curry paste *

- Remove "tenders" from breasts and set aside. Cut remaining chicken into long strips, cutting on the bias across the breasts. You will have approximately 16 strips of chicken about 4½ inches long and ½ inch wide, including the tenders.
- Thread each piece of chicken on an 8-inch bamboo skewer, weaving the skewer in and out in several places. Place skewers in large shallow casserole or baking dish.
- In small bowl, combine coconut milk, red curry paste, and 1 teaspoon salt. Pour over chicken skewers. Cover and refrigerate for 1 to 1½ hours.
- Preheat broiler.
- Remove skewers from marinade. Pat each very dry using paper towels. Place marinade in small saucepan. Bring to a boil, lower heat to medium, and cook, whisking frequently, for 10 minutes, until sauce is thickened and reduced to ¾ cup. Keep hot.
- Place skewers on baking sheet and broil for 5 minutes, turning after 2 or 3 minutes.
- Place cooked skewers on a round tray in a pinwheel fashion. Pour the hot sauce over the chicken but not the skewers.

makes 16 pieces

* I use Thai Kitchen, available in many supermarkets.

silver-dollar corn cakes with bacon and crème fraîche

8 slices bacon
2 cups stone-ground yellow cornmeal
½ cup crème fraîche

- Preheat oven to 400°.
- Cut bacon into ¼-inch pieces. Place in large non-stick skillet and cook over low heat until bacon is done, but not crisp, and much of the fat has been rendered. Remove with slotted spoon, leaving bacon fat in pan.
- Bring 2¼ cups water to a boil. Place cornmeal in medium bowl. Add boiling water, bacon, 1 teaspoon salt, and lots of freshly ground white and black pepper. Stir well. The mixture will be thick.
- Heat bacon fat until hot. Take heaping tablespoons of cornmeal mixture and flatten into small pancakes about 1½ inches in diameter. Cook in hot fat over medium-high heat for several minutes, until crisp. Turn and cook on other side until crisp. You may need to do this in batches. Hold corn cakes on baking sheet in hot oven until all are cooked. Top each with small dollop of crème fraîche, and, if you wish, additional crisp bacon bits.

makes about 30 cakes

*[handwritten] *1 use 2 c boiling H2O*
*[handwritten] *2 ALLOW MIXTURE TO SIT*
[handwritten] mix 2 eggs & ¼ c cream
[handwritten] blend - Add to cornmeal

"smoked" carnitas

1½ pounds smoked pork butt *
½ cup tequila
1 cup jarred _salsa verde_ **

- Remove plastic and netting from pork. Cut into 1-inch cubes. Sprinkle very lightly with salt and freshly ground black pepper.
- Preheat oven to 300°.
- Transfer pork to baking sheet. Bake for 2 hours, occasionally pouring off fat. Turn once or twice during baking.
- Using slotted spoon, transfer pork to large platter. Serve with separate bowls of tequila and _salsa verde_ for dunking.

makes about 50 pieces

* I use Freirich, available in most supermarkets and butcher shops.

** A green salsa made with tomatillas, found in most supermarkets.

rib bits

16 individual pork spareribs
1 cup unsulfured molasses
1¼ cups balsamic vinegar

- Using a cleaver, cut each rib into 2 short pieces, or have your butcher do it. You will have 32 pieces about 2¾ inches long.
- Place in large shallow casserole. Combine molasses and vinegar in small bowl. Add 1 teaspoon salt and freshly ground black pepper. Pour over ribs. Cover and refrigerate for 2 hours, turning every 30 minutes.
- Preheat oven to 375°.
- Remove ribs from marinade. Transfer marinade to small saucepan. Place ribs on 1 or 2 baking sheets. Bake for 40 minutes. Turn and bake for 35 minutes more.
- Meanwhile, bring marinade to a boil. Lower heat and simmer until reduced to a syrup, about 10 to 15 minutes. Add salt and pepper, if desired.
- Remove ribs from baking sheet, discarding all the fat. Using a pastry brush, paint each rib with reduced marinade. Place on platter and serve with lots of napkins.

makes 32 bits

Small Forks

cold

- A Duet of Cured Salmons (page 223)

- Plugged Honeydew with Prosciutto (page 137)

- Herring Salad with Dill Havarti (page 257)

- Carrots Moroccaine (page 201)

- Roasted Eggplant Wedges, Cilantro Dressing (page 172)

- Asparagus Tonnato (page 40)

- Sturgeon with Chive Flowers and Lemon Oil (page 15)

- Roasted Yellow Peppers, Caper–Golden raisin Emulsion (page 183)

- Roasted Pepper Salad with Anchovies and Crushed Almonds (page 34)

warm

- Potato "Tortilla" (page 224)

- Mozzarella Bagna Cauda (page 166)

hot

- Sage Shrimp and Crispy Pancetta (page 40)

- Shiitake-Scallion Satés (page 44)

- Wine and Cheese Fondue (page 37)

- Sautéed Shrimp on Red and Green Pepper Confit (page 132)

winter

spring

menus:

summer

fall

sit-down dinners

A sit-down dinner is the

most noble mode of entertainment, providing the best opportunity for meaningful conversation (as opposed to cocktail chitchat), nourishing the soul (with, one hopes, sensational food), and stimulating the mind (with a seductive selection of wines).

Entertaining is not always about big numbers. The great gastronome Brillat-Savarin believed that the ideal number for a seated dinner party was six. I like the intimacy of four. Menus in this chapter are for four or six, and all can be doubled or tripled to fit your needs. But beware of dinners for twelve that tend to fragment into three or four smaller groups.

Small, frequent dinner parties suit my lifestyle, and you should size yours according to your ability to express a personal level of hospitality.

As host, you control the evening's three most important elements: timing and flow, food and style of service, and the comfort of your guests.

Some dos and don'ts:

Don't overextend the cocktail "hour," or your evening will lose focus. It should be no longer than thirty minutes from the time your last guest arrives, or one hour total.

Don't serve too many kinds of hors d'oeuvres, or you'll befuddle the appetite. I try to limit my assortment to three. Select them from Chapter 5 or go with my suggestions accompanying each menu. For more ideas, see "Sips and Bits" (page 77).

Do maintain interest by varying your style of service. If some dishes are plated in the kitchen, pass others at the table. Passing can be done by you, by a waiter hired for the evening, or by the guests themselves.

Don't have food on the table when people sit down.

Do serve bread with the main course, but avoid it for the first course, or people will bulk up and nod off early.

Do inject a surprise to liven things up. Champagne Sorbet (see page 225) or a trou normand (a swig of Calvados) at mid-meal, a spectacular piece of cheese with fruit before dessert, or two separate dessert courses all give the evening a lift. My most effective surprise came between courses when I served a lemon sorbet spiked with minced jalapeño peppers. The effect was electrifying!

Do offer second helpings.

Do keep it seasonal. Use ingredients at their peak, when they're most flavorful and you need do little to coax out their inherent goodness. The following menus also speak to the seasons with regard to their "weight": lighter in summer, with some room-temperature make-ahead dishes and desserts meant to refresh; more substantial in winter, with full-bodied, hotter foods.

Don't invite guests to another room for dessert and coffee. You'll dissolve the "social glue" that's holding your party together. Even worse, some guests will take this as an invitation to leave, and the evening will collapse. On the other hand, this is a great way to end an evening early.

Shrimp and Monkfish

Sautéed Shrimp on Red and Green Pepper Confit

Olive Oil Biscuits, Hot from the Oven

Herb-Mustard Monkfish Wrapped in Bacon

Rice Pilaf with Lima Beans and Dill

Julienne Carrots with Madeira

Lingonberry Mousse

Concentrate on the simple techniques behind each recipe, and you will have splendid results. This menu boasts the colors and flavors of the season and would make a lovely all-fish dinner for Christmas Eve.

menu notes
Prepare the dessert early in the day. Prepare the pepper confit and shrimp one hour before serving. Bake the biscuits while you finish assembling the shrimp dish, then put the fish in the oven immediately after removing the biscuits. Vegetable accompaniments can be prepared ahead and reheated.

suggested hors d' oeuvres
To make this an all-fish feast, begin with Fresh Cod Brandade (see page 114) and a favorite store-bought or homemade cracker (see pages 109 and 110).

grapenote
For this menu's earthy flavors, try a southern Italian white such as Greco di Tufo or Falerno from Villa Matilde, or try a Sicilian Vermentino (there's a lovely inexpensive one called Aragosta and a better one called Soletta at twice the price). A white Côtes du Rhône, such as Domaine de Becassonne, would also be appropriate.

sautéed shrimp
on red and green
pepper confit

**2 large red and 2 large green bell peppers
(½ pound each)**
**¾ cup garlic oil, store-bought or homemade
(see page 299)**
**48 uncooked medium-large shrimp, in the shell
(about 1¾ pounds)**

- Wash and dry peppers. Cut in half lengthwise and remove seeds. Cut into ¼-inch-wide strips and then into ¼-inch cubes. Try to make them as uniform as possible. You will have about 4 heaping cups diced peppers.

- Place peppers in large saucepan or pot so that they are in one layer. Pour ½ cup garlic oil over peppers. Add about 1 cup cold water, so that the peppers are just covered. Sprinkle with 1 teaspoon salt and freshly ground black pepper. Bring to a boil, lower heat, and simmer over low heat for 40 minutes, until peppers are soft but still retain their shape. Set aside.

- Meanwhile, peel shrimp. Save shells for making stock, or discard. Place shrimp in bowl and cover with remaining ¼ cup garlic oil. Let sit for 30 minutes to 1 hour.

- When ready to serve, heat large nonstick skillet until very hot. Add shrimp and oil, and cook over medium heat, stirring frequently, until shrimp are just pink. Sprinkle with salt and stir.

- Gently heat pepper confit. Mound confit with some of its liquid in center of 6 large flat soup plates. Flatten slightly to form a circle. Arrange 8 shrimp evenly on the peppers.

- *Optional:* Drizzle with additional garlic oil or red pepper juice. To make red pepper juice, cut 1 large red bell pepper in half and remove seeds. Put through a professional juicer and add a pinch of salt. Use immediately.

serves 6

olive oil biscuits, hot from the oven

2 cups self-rising flour
¾ cup milk
½ cup extra-virgin olive oil

- Preheat oven to 400°.
- In medium bowl, combine flour and ¼ teaspoon salt. Make a well in the center and add milk and 7 tablespoons olive oil. Stir until blended. Do not overwork, or biscuits will be tough.
- On lightly floured surface, roll dough out to a ⅓-inch thickness. Cut into 1½-inch rounds with a plain or fluted cookie cutter, and place on baking sheet.
- Bake for 10 minutes, until biscuits just begin to turn golden. Using a pastry brush, brush tops with remaining 1 tablespoon olive oil and sprinkle lightly with salt.

makes about 20 biscuits

herb-mustard monkfish wrapped in bacon

6 7-ounce monkfish fillets
¾ cup herb or imported Dijon mustard
12 slices applewood-smoked or other good-quality bacon

- Trim all membranes and any dark spots from fish. Sprinkle with salt and freshly ground black pepper. Rub each fillet with 2 tablespoons mustard to coat completely.
- Wrap 2 slices bacon around each fillet, securing them tightly with toothpicks. Edges of slices should touch each other, not overlap, so that bacon completely envelops fish.
- Wrap each fillet tightly with plastic wrap, twisting the ends as if making a thick sausage. Refrigerate for 1 hour.
- Preheat oven to 375°.
- Unwrap fish and place on baking sheet. Bake for 25 minutes. Place under broiler for 30 seconds to crisp bacon.
- Drizzle some pan juices over fish and serve immediately.

serves 6

133

rice pilaf with
lima beans and dill

2 cups basmati or other long-grain rice
2 cups fresh or frozen small lima beans
1 bunch fresh dill

- In medium pot, put 4 cups water, 1 teaspoon salt, and rice. Bring to a boil, stirring once. Cover pot and reduce heat to low. Cook for 18 to 20 minutes, until all the water is absorbed.
- Meanwhile, cook lima beans in salted water until quite tender but not falling apart. The length of time will depend on whether you are using fresh or frozen beans.
- Wash dill and dry thoroughly. Finely chop to make ⅓ cup.
- Remove rice from heat and let stand, covered, for 5 minutes. Add cooked beans and chopped dill. Add salt and freshly ground black pepper to taste. Mix gently with a fork, fluffing rice as you mix.

serves 6 or more

julienne carrots
with madeira

1½ pounds fresh carrots
6 tablespoons plus 2 teaspoons Madeira
2 tablespoons unsalted butter, chilled

- Peel carrots. Cut into 2 inch by ⅛ inch julienne or into small sticks. You will have approximately 4 cups.
- In medium heavy saucepan place carrots, 6 tablespoons Madeira, and 1 tablespoon butter. Add ½ teaspoon salt. Bring to a boil. Cook over medium heat, covered, for 15 minutes, or until carrots are tender.
- Remove carrots with slotted spoon and place in bowl. Add 2 teaspoons Madeira to pan and cook liquid over high heat for a few seconds. Whisk in 1 tablespoon cold butter and swirl to melt.
- Return carrots to saucepan and heat gently.

serves 6

lingonberry mousse

¼ cup farina
2 10-ounce jars lingonberries in sugar *
1 cup heavy cream, well chilled

- In medium saucepan, bring 1½ cups water and ¼ teaspoon salt to a boil. Add farina slowly, stirring constantly with wooden spoon. Cook over medium heat for 3 minutes, stirring constantly to prevent sticking. Farina should be very smooth and thick. Remove from heat.
- Add 1½ cups lingonberries and 2 tablespoons heavy cream, stirring thoroughly. Chill for at least 1 hour, or until cold.
- Whip remaining heavy cream until thick and reserve. In bowl of electric mixer, beat lingonberry-farina mixture until thick and fluffy. Add all but 3 tablespoons whipped cream and mix briefly to create a mousselike texture.
- Spoon into 6 wineglasses. Top each with ½ tablespoon whipped cream and chill until ready to serve.
- To serve, spoon ½ teaspoon lingonberries on top of each little mound of whipped cream.

serves 6

* You need only 15 to 16 ounces for the recipe, but 10-ounce jars are easier to find. I use the Felix brand from Sweden (specifically called Original Wild Swedish Lingonberries in Sugar), available in many specialty-food stores. Spread leftover berries on hot buttered toast for a 1-2-3 morning treat.

135

Salmon

Plugged Honeydew with Prosciutto

Salmon Roasted in Butter

Lentils in Red Wine with Roasted Garlic

Braised Endives with Bay Leaves

White Chocolate Custard

"There is nothing simpler and few things better" than salmon roasted in butter, says friend and fellow author Mark Bittman. Inspired by the sheer simplicity of his preparation, this wintry dinner supports the fish in its starring role.

During the bistro craze of the 1980s, salmon with lentils became the sine qua non of trendiness — a nod to simplicity, an unpretentious antidote to the fussiness of nouvelle cuisine.

menu notes
The dessert can be made the day before. Marinate the melon and endives early in the day. Make the endives several hours before dinner; reheat briefly or serve at room temperature. The lentils also can be made ahead and reheated.

suggested hors d'oeuvres
Begin with a trio of crudités and two "bowls" — Eggplant "Caviar" (see page 116) and Truffled White Bean Spread (see page 112).

grapenote
Begin with an Italian white: Vernaccia di San Gimignano or a big, rich Soave Classico such as the one from Gini. Stay with this right through the main course or switch to a light red. Interesting choices are Valpolicella Superiore from Palazzo delle Torre; Barbera from Michele Chiarlo; Pinot Noir from Talus in California; or a new Pinot from Louis Latour, Domaine de Valmoissine from Provence.

plugged honeydew
with prosciutto

1 large ripe honeydew melon (about 3½ pounds)
2 cups white port
6 to 8 ounces very thinly sliced good-quality prosciutto

- Using a small sharp knife, cut a triangular-shaped plug from the stem end of the melon. Pour 1 cup port into melon. Replace plug and let marinate for 4 to 6 hours, turning melon occasionally.
- Remove plug. Drain all liquid through fine-mesh sieve into small saucepan. Add remaining 1 cup port and bring to a boil. Reduce liquid to ⅔ cup of syrup.
- Cut melon in half and remove seeds. Using a melon baller, scoop out small melon balls and place in bowl, collecting any of the juices. Add a pinch of salt and a grinding of black pepper. Stir.
- Mound melon balls evenly on 6 large flat plates. Drizzle with reduced port. Drape prosciutto over melon and serve. Pass the pepper mill.

serves 6

salmon roasted
in butter

4 tablespoons unsalted butter
3-pound center-cut salmon fillet, skin on
1 cup coarsely chopped fresh Italian parsley

- Preheat oven to 475°.
- Make sure your fishmonger has scaled the fish. With small tweezers, remove any remaining bones.
- Melt butter in small saucepan. Pour into heavy shallow baking pan large enough to accommodate fish. Place salmon flesh side down in butter. Roast for 8 minutes. Carefully turn fish using 2 spatulas and roast for about 6 to 8 minutes (or longer), depending on thickness of fish.
- Sprinkle fish with salt and freshly ground black pepper. Cut into 4 portions using a very sharp knife. Garnish with parsley and a little of the browned butter from the pan. Serve immediately.

serves 6

137

lentils in red wine
with roasted garlic

1 very large head plus 1 large clove garlic
1 cup green lentils (preferably French) *
1¾ cups dry red wine

- Well ahead of mealtime, preheat oven to 400°.
- Wrap whole head of garlic in aluminum foil, place in pie tin, and bake for 1 hour. Remove from oven.
- Meanwhile, in medium heavy pot with cover, put lentils, 4 cups water, 1¼ cups wine, ½ teaspoon salt, and 10 whole black peppercorns. Push remaining 1 clove garlic through garlic press into pot. Bring to a boil. Cover pot, lower heat, and let simmer until lentils are tender, about 40 to 50 minutes.
- In small nonreactive saucepan, put remaining ½ cup wine. Reduce over medium heat to ¼ cup. Cut head of roasted garlic in half to expose all the cloves and squeeze pulp into reduced wine. (You will have approximately 3 tablespoons garlic pulp.) Mix well.
- Drain lentils in colander, reserving ½ cup cooking water. Transfer lentils to bowl. Add reduced wine with garlic. Mix gently, adding salt and freshly ground black pepper to taste. Moisten with a little of the cooking liquid and serve immediately.

serves 6

* The best come from an area of France called Le Puy and are known as lentilles du Puy. They are available in many supermarkets and specialty-food stores.

braised endives
with bay leaves

6 medium Belgian endives
½ cup extra-virgin olive oil
12 fresh bay leaves or good-quality dried bay leaves *

- Remove any dark outer leaves from endives and discard. Place in shallow baking dish with cover. Pour olive oil over endives. Place bay leaves under, in between, and on top of endives. Cover. Marinate for several hours at room temperature or overnight in refrigerator.
- Preheat oven to 275°.
- Sprinkle endives lightly with salt. Cover and bake for 1½ hours, shaking several times during baking.
- Serve immediately or reheat briefly in hot (475°) oven before serving. Add salt and freshly ground black pepper to taste. Braised endives prepared in this way also are delicious served at room temperature or chilled.
- Decorate with bay leaves.

serves 6

* Use fresh bay leaves, available in many supermarket produce sections, or dried California bay leaves from Spice Islands.

white chocolate custard

2 cups heavy cream
8 ounces white chocolate
3 extra-large egg yolks

- Preheat oven to 325°.
- Heat cream in medium heavy pot. Chop white chocolate into small pieces and add to cream. Stir constantly over low heat until chocolate is completely melted and mixture is smooth.
- Beat egg yolks in bowl of electric mixer until pale yellow, about 3 to 4 minutes. Pour hot cream mixture over eggs a little at a time, beating constantly until all the cream is incorporated.
- Pour into 6 5-ounce ramekins. Place ramekins in deep baking dish and carefully add boiling water so that it comes almost all the way up the sides of the ramekins. Bake for 25 to 30 minutes, or until barely set.
- Remove ramekins from water bath. Let cool, then refrigerate for several hours until cold.

serves 6

Roast Duck

Pear, Endive, and Boursin Salad

Roast Duck with Pomegranate-Rosemary Jus

Small Potatoes

Brussels Sprout–Caraway Puree

Pithiviers of Apricots and Almond Paste

Great home-cooked duck is a rarity these days. This stunning dinner for eight has a celebratory air, and so will your kitchen. The aromas of rosemary and roasted duck will have your guests drooling as they walk through your door.

If you really want to impress your guests, serve Honey Ice Cream (see page 163) alongside dessert.

menu notes

Prepare the dessert early in the day or several hours before dinner. The salad dressing, duck stock, and brussels sprout puree can be made the day before. The ducks and potatoes are cooked at the same temperature and share space and time in the oven.

suggested hors d'oeuvres

Prosciutto and Melon Batons (see page 97) and Silver-Dollar Corn Cakes with Bacon and Crème Fraîche (see page 125).

grapenote

With the salad, a light acidic red wine from the Loire makes a terrific match: a Sancerre Rouge, Bourgueil, or Chinon. The duck requires a serious Rhône, such as a Gigondas (Cros de la Mure or Domaine les Goubert) or a St. Joseph (Pierre Gonon). With dessert, a sweet wine is an elegant touch: Hungarian Tokay or a sweet Muscat from Samos.

pear, endive, and boursin salad

**1 5.2-ounce package Boursin cheese with garlic
and fine herbs, well chilled**
8 medium Belgian endives
4 medium-large ripe green or red pears

- Break cheese into several pieces and place in bowl of food processor. With the motor running, slowly add ½ to ⅔ cup cold water and process until smooth, thick, and creamy. Taste and add a little salt if needed. If using immediately, set aside at room temperature while you prepare salad. If using later, cover and refrigerate. Let come to room temperature before using. If it's too thick, add a little water.
- *To prepare salad:* Immediately before serving, wash endives and pears and dry well. Cut endives on the bias into slightly less than ⅛-inch-thick slices. Place in mounds in center of 8 large plates.
- Cut pears in half through the stems and remove seeds. Cut each pear half into ⅛-inch-thick slices.
- Drizzle several tablespoons of dressing over each mound of endives. Shingle pear slices on top. Drizzle with ½ tablespoon dressing.

serves 8

roast duck with pomegranate-rosemary jus

2 5½-pound ducks
2 large bunches fresh rosemary
2 large pomegranates

- Remove entire wings and all the giblets from ducks. Discard livers, save to sauté with dinner,* or save for another use.
- *To make stock:* Place wings and giblets (except livers) in medium pot. Cover with cold water. Add 1 large branch rosemary, 1 teaspoon whole black peppercorns, and 1 teaspoon salt. Bring to a boil. Skim off any foam that rises to the top. Lower heat and simmer for 45 minutes. Strain broth through fine-mesh sieve into clean pot. You will have approximately 3 cups. Bring to a boil. Lower heat and cook until reduced to 2 cups. Reserve.
- Preheat oven to 375°.
- Scatter 1½ bunches rosemary on bottom of heavy shallow roasting pan. Mince enough remaining rosemary to make 1 tablespoon and set aside.
- Prick ducks all over with a fork. Rub skin with salt and freshly ground black pepper. Place ducks on

rosemary and roast for about 2 hours. Skin will be crispy and duck meat juicy and tender.

- *Note:* After 1 hour of cooking, remove about ½ cup duck fat to use for making Small Potatoes (see the next recipe).
- While ducks are cooking, cut 1 pomegranate in half through the "equator." With hand juicer, squeeze pomegranate halves to get about ½ cup juice. Remove seeds from remaining pomegranate and save. Add any collected juices to ½ cup juice. Set aside.
- When ducks are finished, transfer rosemary to serving platter and place ducks on large cutting board to rest while you prepare sauce.
- Drain off fat from roasting pan and place pan on top of stove. Add reserved duck broth and reserved pomegranate juice. Cook over high heat, scraping up brown bits with spatula. Cook until sauce is syrupy and reduced to about 1⅓ cups. Season with salt and pepper. Pour through fine-mesh sieve into small pot. Keep hot.
- Cut ducks into 6 or 8 pieces. Place on rosemary on serving platter. Scatter with pomegranate seeds. Pour warm sauce around duck pieces, drizzling a little on top. Serve immediately with 1 tablespoon minced rosemary.

serves 8

> *
> If serving duck livers, season with salt and pepper and cook on each side in nonstick skillet with a little duck fat. Livers should be firm but still a little pink inside.

small potatoes

2 pounds (28 to 30) small, thin-skinned white potatoes
½ cup duck fat, melted *
3 medium cloves garlic

- Preheat oven to 375°.
- Peel potatoes and cut in half lengthwise. Place in saucepan and cover with cold water. Add 1 teaspoon salt. Bring to a rolling boil. Lower heat to medium and cook for 10 minutes.
- Drain potatoes in colander. Place on baking sheet in one layer. Pour 6 tablespoons duck fat over potatoes. Slice 2 cloves garlic paper-thin. Toss potatoes with garlic, duck fat, and a sprinkling of coarse salt and freshly ground black pepper. Turn potatoes so that cut side is down.
- Bake for 30 minutes, turning potatoes several times using a metal spatula, until crisp and golden.
- Meanwhile, heat remaining 2 tablespoons duck fat in skillet. Mince remaining garlic and add to duck fat. Heat gently for 1 to 2 minutes. Do not let garlic take on any color.
- Transfer potatoes with fat to platter. Pour garlicky duck fat in skillet over potatoes. Sprinkle with coarse sea salt and freshly ground black pepper. Toss gently and serve.

serves 8

> *
> Use rendered duck fat from previous recipe or buy it from D'Artagnan, (800) DARTAGN.

brussels sprout–
caraway puree

**3 10-ounce packages fresh brussels sprouts
(about 2 pounds)**
1½ tablespoons caraway seeds
6 tablespoons unsalted butter

- Trim ends from brussels sprouts. Wash well and drain. Place in medium pot with cold water to cover. Add 1 teaspoon salt and bring to a boil. Lower heat to medium and cook until tender, about 25 minutes depending on size.
- Meanwhile, chop caraway seeds coarsely, using a large heavy chef's knife. Toast in small nonstick skillet over very low heat for 1 to 2 minutes, until fragrant. Set aside.
- Melt butter in small saucepan and cook until light golden brown.
- When brussels sprouts are tender, drain in colander, saving 1 cup cooking water.
- Place brussels sprouts, cooking water, melted butter, and all but 1½ teaspoons chopped caraway seeds in food processor and process until very smooth. Add salt and freshly ground black pepper to taste.
- Serve immediately or reheat in saucepan, adding a little water or additional butter if needed. Sprinkle with remaining caraway seeds.

serves 8 (makes 4½ cups)

pithiviers of apricots
and almond paste

1½ pounds good-quality dried apricots
2 sheets frozen puff pastry (17¼ ounces)
4 ounces almond paste

- Place apricots and 2 cups water in medium heavy pot and let soak for 1 hour.
- Bring water to a boil. Cover pot and lower heat to medium. Cook for 45 minutes, stirring several times.
- Remove cover, add ¼ cup water, and cook for 1 to 2 minutes more, or until water has evaporated. Apricots will be soft and lightly caramelized. Transfer to bowl with any remaining juices. You will have approximately 3 cups apricot compote. Let cool completely.
- Meanwhile, thaw pastry according to package directions.
- Preheat oven to 400°.
- Roll out both sheets of pastry so that you can cut out 2 12-inch circles. Spread apricot compote on 1 pastry circle, leaving a 1-inch border. Break up almond paste into small pieces and evenly disperse over apricots. Top with second pastry circle, adhering top and bottom together with a little cold water around the rim of the bottom circle. Press edges together firmly and trim with a sharp knife to form a perfect circle.
- Transfer to baking sheet and bake for 30 minutes. Let cool completely. Cut into wedges and serve.

serves 8

143

Stuffed Veal Chops

Turnip and Potato Soup, Salt Pork "Croutons"

Stuffed Veal Chops with Manchego Cheese and Green Olives

Sautéed Spinach with "Burnt" Almonds

Roasted Pearl Onions, Sherry Vinegar Glaze

Strawberries Catalan

This is a Catalan-inspired indulgence with big, bold tastes. Ingredients familiar to the cuisine of northeast Spain, such as sherry vinegar and Manchego cheese, are now available in America.

Meant to appease guests with voracious appetites in ardent quest of flavor, this meal is made with the greatest of ease. Excellent choices for urbane company, these recipes can be doubled or tripled.

menu notes
Prepare the soup early in the day; reheat and crisp the croutons before serving. The veal chops can be stuffed an hour before dinner and refrigerated. The onions can be made in advance and reheated. Serve with a round loaf of crusty bread.

suggested hors d'oeuvre
Serve a platter of Roasted Yellow Peppers, Caper–Golden Raisin Emulsion (see page 183) with a stack of little plates and small forks, tapas-style.

grapenote
With the soup, serve a chilled fino sherry: Try Jarana from Emilio Lustau. Move on to a Rioja from the excellent 1994 vintage: Some names to look for are Viña Ardanza, Marques de Grinon, and Remelluri. Finish with a dessert-type sherry from Emilio Lustau: Capataz Andres, which is a blend of Oloroso and Pedro Ximénez.

turnip and potato soup, salt pork "croutons"

4 medium-large white turnips (about 1½ pounds)
2 large, waxy white potatoes (about ¾ pound)
6-ounce piece smoked salt pork

- Peel turnips and potatoes. Cut into large pieces and put in saucepan with cover. Add 4 cups cold water, making sure vegetables are just covered. Add a 2-ounce piece salt pork and 1 teaspoon kosher salt. Bring to a boil. Lower heat to medium and cook, with cover askew, for 50 minutes, until potatoes and turnips are very soft. Remove salt pork and set aside.
- Place vegetables and liquid in food processor. (You may need to do this in 2 batches.) Process until very smooth and return to saucepan. Set aside.
- Cut cooked salt pork and remaining 4-ounce piece salt pork into ¼-inch cubes. Place in nonstick skillet and cook until pork is crisp and fat is rendered, about 15 minutes.
- Add 2 tablespoons fat (or more to taste), to soup and reheat, adding salt if necessary.
- To serve, transfer hot soup to 4 flat soup plates. Garnish with crisped salt pork and coarsely ground black or white pepper (or a combination of both).

serves 4 (makes 5 cups)

stuffed veal chops with manchego cheese and green olives

4 10-ounce 1-inch-thick veal rib chops
8 ounces Manchego cheese*
½ cup coarsely chopped pimiento-stuffed green olives (3-ounce jar, drained)

- Preheat broiler.
- With a sharp knife, cut a horizontal pocket in each chop. Season chops lightly on each side with salt and freshly ground black pepper.
- Remove rind from cheese. Cut cheese carefully into ¼-inch cubes and put in bowl. Pat chopped olives dry and add to cheese. Add pepper and toss.
- Fill chops with cheese-olive mixture. Broil for about 3 minutes per side, until chops are medium-rare. Serve immediately.
- *Optional garnish:* Top with extra cubed cheese and chopped olives.

serves 4

   * You may substitute another firm Spanish cheese such as Idiazábal.

sautéed spinach
with "burnt" almonds

2 pounds fresh curly spinach
½ cup (1 ounce) sliced almonds, with skins
3 tablespoons garlic oil, store-bought or
    homemade (see page 299)

- Remove stems from spinach and discard. Wash leaves carefully in colander. Drain but do not pat dry.
- In small nonstick skillet, cook almonds over medium heat, shaking pan back and forth, until they begin to darken. Add a large pinch of salt. Set aside.
- In very large pot, heat garlic oil. Add spinach, with water clinging to leaves, and toss over medium-high heat until it wilts and softens. Do not overcook, as you want it to stay bright green. Add salt and freshly ground black pepper to taste.
- Transfer to platter. Scatter toasted almonds on top. Serve immediately.

serves 4 or more

roasted pearl onions,
sherry vinegar glaze

1¼ pounds (about 60) white or red pearl onions
1 cup sherry vinegar
3 tablespoons honey

- Preheat oven to 350°.
- Bring medium pot of water to a boil. Add unpeeled onions and boil for 3 minutes. Rinse onions in colander under cold running water. Trim root ends using a small sharp knife, then peel.
- In small bowl, mix together vinegar, honey, 2 tablespoons water, ¼ teaspoon salt, and freshly ground black pepper.
- Place onions in shallow casserole large enough to hold them in one layer. Pour vinegar-honey mixture over onions.
- Roast until tender, about 1 hour 20 minutes. Shake pan often during roasting so that onions are evenly glazed. Most of the liquid will evaporate, and onions will be dark golden brown.
- If too much liquid remains, use slotted spoon to transfer onions to shallow bowl and reduce liquid to ¼ cup. Pour over hot roasted onions.

serves 4 or more

strawberries catalan

2 pints large ripe strawberries
1 cup heavy cream, well chilled
½ cup dark brown sugar

- Preheat broiler.
- Wash and stem berries and pat dry. Cut in half lengthwise. Place berries cut side down in shallow casserole or decorative dish large enough to hold them in one layer.
- Whip cream until very stiff and thick. Spread evenly over berries.
- Press sugar through coarse-mesh sieve and scatter evenly over whipped cream. Place under broiler until sugar melts and caramelizes and cream just begins to bubble. Serve immediately.

serves 4

147

Beef Shank

Truffled Consommé with Vermicelli

Beef Shank Italienne

Polenta-Peas-Parmesan

Baked Fennel with Garlic Bread Crumbs

Gianduia Torta

Though quite suave, this menu is without pretense and can be prepared successfully by anyone with a love and understanding of good food. Its blockbuster Italian dishes begin with a classic soup enhanced by truffle oil and end with a beloved Italian treat known as *gianduia* — a sinful and sumptuous confection of chocolate and hazelnuts.

In between, satisfaction is guaranteed with slow-cooked beef shank braised to a melting texture. *Contorni*, or vegetable side dishes, of sturdy baked fennel and pea-strewn polenta merge into a powerful union under the meat's heady sauce, redolent of Sicily.

This would be a perfect menu for Father's Day, if only it were celebrated in winter.

menu notes

You can reduce the broth for the soup early in the day, adding the truffle oil and pasta at the last minute. The beef shank is best made the day before. The fennel is prepped and baked ten minutes before serving. The dessert can also be made the previous day, but let it come to room temperature before serving.

suggested hors d'oeuvre

In the Italian spirit of this meal, begin with Sage Shrimp and Crispy Pancetta (see page 40), served with toothpicks or small plates.

grapenote

Italian all the way. Start with a young Spanna or Gattinara, then open a luxurious Super-Tuscan such as Lavischio or Sassoalloro from Biondi Santi, or Logaiolo from Aiola. Still wonderful but less expensive would be a good Chianti Classico from the 1990 or 1995 vintage. With dessert, sip a small glass of Frangelico.

truffled consommé with vermicelli

6 cups beef broth, homemade or low-sodium canned
4 ounces vermicelli pasta
1 to 1½ teaspoons truffle oil *

- Place broth in medium saucepan. Add ½ teaspoon whole black peppercorns. Bring to a boil, lower heat to medium, and cook until broth is reduced to 5 cups. This should take about 10 to 15 minutes.
- Meanwhile, bring large pot of salted water to a boil. Break vermicelli in half and add to boiling water. Cook until al dente. Drain immediately, making sure that all the water has been shaken off.
- Add pasta to broth and reheat. Turn off heat and add truffle oil to taste. Add salt if necessary.
- Ladle into flat soup bowls, evenly dividing pasta among bowls. Serve immediately.

serves 6

> * Available in specialty-food stores.

beef shank italienne

3 pounds (net weight) beef shin meat, cut into 2½-inch pieces *
2½ cups dry marsala
3 14½-ounce cans stewed tomatoes with oregano and basil **

- Place meat in shallow casserole in one layer. Pour 1 cup marsala over meat and marinate for 1 hour at room temperature.
- Meanwhile, drain tomatoes in large coarse-mesh sieve, pressing down hard to release all the juices. You will have approximately 2¼ cups tomato liquid. Set aside for later use.
- Drain meat. Season with salt and freshly ground black pepper. Place in casserole or pot with cover in one layer. Spread drained tomatoes on top of meat. Add 1 cup marsala. Bring to a boil. Lower heat to a simmer and cover. Cook for 3 hours.
- Meanwhile, put tomato liquid and remaining ½ cup marsala in small saucepan and reduce until very thick. You will have about ¾ cup.
- Using slotted spoon, transfer meat to platter. Raise temperature under juices in pot and reduce liquid until syrupy. Add salt and pepper to taste. Pour juices over meat and drizzle with tomato-marsala sauce. Serve immediately. Also delicious reheated the next day.

serves 6

> * I have bought 1½-inch thick slices of beef shin with the marrow bone at my supermarket. Using a small sharp knife, you can cut around the marrow bone and cut the shin meat into pieces along the natural muscle lines of the meat. This cut of meat is also known as beef soup meat shank.
>
> ** I use Redpack.

149

polenta-peas-parmesan

**2¾ cups (about 1 pound) Italian polenta or
stone-ground yellow cornmeal**
**10 ounces fresh or thawed frozen green peas,
cooked al dente**
**6 ounces (about 1¾ cups) freshly grated
Parmigiano-Reggiano cheese**

- In large pot, bring 8 cups water and 1 teaspoon
salt to a boil. Lower heat and add polenta or
cornmeal in a slow steady stream, whisking constantly with a wire whisk. Continue to cook over
low heat for 8 minutes. Add peas, stir with
wooden spoon, and cook for 1 minute. Add 1 cup
grated cheese and stir. Cook for 1 minute more.
Add salt and freshly ground black pepper to
taste.
- Pour into shallow casserole or large soufflé
dish. Sprinkle with remaining cheese. Place under
broiler for 1 minute, until cheese turns golden
brown. Or, if serving later, cover casserole and set
aside. Reheat in 400° oven, covered, for 10 minutes, then place under broiler until cheese turns
golden.

serves 6

baked fennel
with garlic bread crumbs

**3 medium fennel bulbs (about ¾ pound each),
with lots of fronds**
**3 tablespoons garlic oil, store-bought or home-
made (see page 299), plus more for drizzling**
1½ cups fresh bread crumbs *

- Trim several inches from stalks of fennel bulbs,
leaving 2 inches of green stems. Save trimmed
stems with fronds. Cut each fennel bulb in half
lengthwise through the root.
- Place fennel halves in large pot with salted
water to cover. Bring to a boil, lower heat to
medium, cover pot, and cook for 20 minutes.
- Preheat oven to 400°.
- In large nonstick skillet, heat 3 tablespoons garlic oil. Add bread crumbs and cook over low heat
until crumbs absorb oil, begin to turn light
brown, and are toasted. Add salt and freshly
ground black pepper to taste.
- Finely chop feathery fennel fronds from reserved
stems so that you have 3 tablespoons. Add to
toasted bread crumbs and stir.
- When fennel is done, drain well. Place fennel cut
side up in shallow baking dish. Pack crumbs well
onto each fennel half, covering cut surface thoroughly. Drizzle garlic oil over fennel and bake for
10 minutes. Serve hot or at room temperature.

serves 6

* A good-quality white bread such as Pepperidge
Farm will do. Place 5 or 6 slices in bowl of food
processor and process until you have fine crumbs.
Do not use dried bread crumbs.

gianduia torta

2½ cups shelled hazelnuts, with skins
1½ cups heavy cream
1 pound semisweet chocolate chips

- Place hazelnuts in large nonstick skillet and toast over medium heat for 5 minutes, until nuts begin to brown and smell faintly nutty. Shake pan back and forth to distribute nuts. Rub nuts in a towel to remove as many of the blistered skins as possible.
- Place scant cup warm nuts in bowl of food processor. Process until smooth paste forms, adding 1 to 2 teaspoons water to make this easier. You will have approximately ¾ cup hazelnut paste.
- Heat 1 cup cream in small heavy saucepan until it almost comes to a boil. Lower heat. Add chocolate chips and stir constantly with wooden spoon until chocolate is completely melted and is smooth and glossy. Add a pinch of salt. Keeping heat low, add hazelnut paste and stir thoroughly. Remove from heat. Fold in ¾ cup toasted hazelnuts.
- Line 8½-inch springform pan with a round of waxed paper or parchment paper. Spray with nonstick vegetable spray. Pour in chocolate mixture. Finely chop remaining ¾ cup nuts and scatter on top. Let cool completely, then refrigerate for several hours.
- Let sit at room temperature for 30 minutes before serving. Cut with sharp knife warmed in hot water and dried. Whip remaining ½ cup heavy cream and serve with torte.

serves 8

Teriyaki Salmon

Littleneck Clams in Cilantro Broth

Teriyaki Salmon with Scallions

Wasabi Mashed Potatoes

Snow Peas and Baby Corn

Ginger-Poached Pineapple

A menu can embody a culture. It can be a road to knowledge, a memory, or a fantasy.

This menu is a bit of all these things, summoning a strong sense of place and taste, and is sturdy enough to weather a blustery day in spring.

For optimal results, use impeccable ingredients. Littlenecks, small hard-shell clams, should measure no more than one inch from side to side; Manila clams, where more prevalent, are just as good. Highly prized and tender, littlenecks are expensive but worth the price, requiring only cleaning with a stiff brush and steaming in an aromatic broth.

The salmon should be thick and richly marbled, cut from the center of the fish.

The rest of the menu gains momentum with stronger flavors: a resounding punch of Japanese horseradish in wasabi-laced potatoes, and a dessert with a sharp note of ginger.

Finish with a pot of hot green tea.

menu notes
Prepare the dessert the day before or the morning of your dinner. The rest of the meal is done in forty-five minutes.

suggested hors d'oeuvres
Star Anise Tea Eggs (see page 121), Plum-Glazed Stuffed Mushrooms (see page 106), or Thai Chicken Skewers (see page 124).

grapenote
To set the mood, begin with ice-cold sake served in white-wine glasses. Then switch to a full-bodied Chardonnay (Lindemans Padthway) or a surprise dry Gewürztraminer from Bargetto Winery (located in California's Santa Cruz Mountains) or Amity Vineyards (Oregon).

littleneck clams
in cilantro broth

4 dozen littleneck clams
½ cup unsalted whipped butter, well chilled
    and cut into pieces
2 large bunches fresh cilantro, coarsely chopped
    (1 cup leaves, plus more for garnish)

- Scrub clams well. Place in large heavy pot with tight-fitting cover. Add ½ cup water, butter, ½ teaspoon whole black peppercorns, 1 teaspoon salt, and 1 cup cilantro.
- Bring mixture to a boil. Cover pot and cook over high heat for 6 to 8 minutes, shaking pot back and forth to cook clams evenly. Remove from heat the minute clams open.
- Transfer clams to 4 large flat soup plates and pour broth over them. Garnish with remaining cilantro, finely chopped. Serve immediately.

serves 4

teriyaki salmon
with scallions

4 6-ounce center-cut salmon fillets, skin on
1 cup teriyaki sauce
3 bunches scallions

- Remove any bones from salmon and discard. Place salmon in bowl or shallow casserole. Cover with teriyaki sauce. Marinate for 5 minutes.
- Meanwhile, trim roots from scallions. Trim 2 bunches of scallions so that each scallion has only 1 inch of green on top. Place trimmed scallions in nonstick skillet with enough salted water to cover. Bring to a boil, lower heat, and cook until scallions are soft, about 5 minutes. Keep warm.
- Remove salmon from marinade. Reserve marinade. Press ½ teaspoon butcher-grind black pepper into skinless side of each salmon fillet. Heat 1 very large or 2 smaller nonstick skillets until very hot. Put salmon skin side up in pan(s) and cook over medium-high heat for 3 minutes. Turn over and cook 2 more minutes.
- Meanwhile, finely dice remaining scallions so that you have ½ cup. Add to reserved marinade. Add marinade and ¼ cup water to salmon. Heat for 1 to 2 minutes, until salmon is cooked as desired. Serve immediately with boiled scallions.

serves 4

153

wasabi
mashed potatoes

2 pounds Yukon Gold potatoes
2 tablespoons wasabi powder *
1 stick unsalted butter

- Wash potatoes and scrub well. Place unpeeled potatoes in large pot of salted boiling water. Cover pot. Lower heat and cook for 30 to 40 minutes, until potatoes are very tender. Drain in colander, saving ¼ cup cooking water.
- Peel potatoes quickly and place in large bowl. Mash with potato masher until smooth and creamy.
- In small cup, dissolve wasabi powder in 4 tablespoons cold water. Stir until smooth. Add to mashed potatoes.
- Cut butter into small pieces. Using a wire whisk, incorporate butter and potatoes, along with a few tablespoons potato cooking water, so that potatoes are smooth and fluffy. Add salt to taste and stir well. Serve immediately, or reheat gently.

serves 4 or more (makes 4½ cups)

* Available in Asian markets and some specialty-food stores.

snow peas
and baby corn

1½ pounds fresh snow peas
15-ounce can whole sweet baby corn *
2 tablespoons roasted peanut oil **

- Wash snow peas under cold water. Pat dry. Trim ends using a sharp knife. Remove strings. Set aside.
- Place baby corn in colander and rinse well under cold water. Pat dry. Using a small sharp knife, cut corn in half lengthwise. Leave whole the pieces of corn that are either small or very thin.
- Bring large pot of water to a boil. Place snow peas and halved baby corn in steamer basket and place basket in pot. Cover and cook over boiling water for 8 minutes. Snow peas will be tender but still bright green.
- Transfer snow peas and corn to shallow bowl or platter. Add roasted peanut oil and toss well. Add ¼ teaspoon (or more) butcher-grind black pepper and fine sea salt to taste. Toss again. Serve hot.

serves 4

* Available in the Asian section of most supermarkets and in specialty-food stores.

** I use Loriva, available in supermarkets and specialty-food stores. If unavailable, substitute 1 tablespoon roasted sesame oil.

ginger-poached pineapple

1 ripe medium pineapple
½ cup sugar
5- to 6-inch piece fresh ginger (1 tablespoon
 juice * and 12 thin slices)

- Peel pineapple with a small sharp knife. Cut into 4 wedges. Cut hard, woody core from each wedge. Cut each wedge crosswise into 3 thick pieces. Set aside.
- In heavy pot large enough to accommodate pineapple in one layer, put 1 cup water, 1 table-spoon ginger juice, and 12 slices peeled ginger. Bring to a boil and cook for 1 minute.
- Add pineapple in one layer. Bring to a boil again. Cover pot and lower heat. Simmer for 10 minutes. Turn pineapple over and simmer for 10 minutes more.
- Using slotted spoon, transfer pineapple to shallow bowl. Reduce liquid in pot over high heat until syrupy, being careful not to burn it. Pour over pineapple.
- Cool and then refrigerate until very cold.

serves 4

*
To make ginger juice, peel a 3½-inch piece of ginger with a small sharp knife. Grate on large holes of box grater. Put grated ginger in paper towel and squeeze juice from ginger. You will have approximately 1 tablespoon juice.

Halibut

Mussels in Hard Cider and Cream

Steamed Halibut with Leek Fondue

Potatoes Boulangère

Roasted Beet Puree with Allspice, Fried Beets

Oranges and Grapefruit in Black Currant Syrup, Black Currant Granita

When cooking with only three ingredients, each must be strongly expressed, and like the primary colors in a painting, the harmony among them can result in a richly layered experience.

One of my favorite paintings, *Harmony in Red* by Henri Matisse, depicts a brilliant red dining room punctuated by swirls of blue and bright flashes of yellow. I've often imagined what artful meals might logically grace the table in this exuberant painting.

What follows is one possible menu — my dinner for Matisse, equally colorful, with bright flashes of brilliant flavors.

menu notes

Prepare this menu in reverse order, beginning with the dessert, which needs hours to freeze. The beets can be roasted and then pureed several hours in advance.

The potatoes will require an hour and twenty minutes to bake. The leeks can be prepared an hour or so before cooking the fish (which should be cooked just before serving). Prepare the mussels at the last minute. Serve the meal with slices of a crusty baguette. Small forks and soupspoons should accompany the mussels. With dessert, offer Crispy Oatcakes (see page 119), if desired.

suggested hors d'oeuvres

Roasted Garlic–Sapsago Spread (see page 117), served with black bread, and Asparagettes (see page 123).

grapenote

A Sauvignon Blanc that has spent some time in wood is the right white for the mussels. Try one from Kenwood, Hogue Cellars, or Shenandoah Vineyards. With the main course, step up to a big, rich Chardonnay: Raymond, St. Francis, or Beckmen. With dessert, a Kir Royale (champagne and crème de cassis) is both delicious and celebratory.

mussels in hard cider and cream

3 pounds medium fresh mussels, in their shells
1¼ cups heavy cream
1½ cups hard apple cider *

- Scrub mussels and rinse under cold water. Pat dry. Discard any that are not tightly closed.
- Put cream and cider in large pot with cover. Add ½ teaspoon salt and freshly ground black pepper. Bring to a boil for 1 minute. Reduce heat to medium and cook for 2 minutes, until liquid is slightly reduced.
- Add mussels and cover pot. Increase heat to high. Cook mussels for 8 to 10 minutes, shaking pot back and forth.
- Remove cover. Using a slotted spoon, divide mussels among 6 warm flat soup plates.
- Reduce liquid in pan over high heat for 1 minute. Pour over mussels. Serve immediately.

serves 6

    *
I use Cider Jack Hard Cider, available in many supermarkets.

steamed halibut with leek fondue

1¼ pounds leeks
7 tablespoons unsalted butter
6 1-inch-thick halibut steaks (about 12 ounces each)

- Remove all the dark green parts from leeks. Discard. Wash leeks well, making sure to remove any dirt between the leaves. Pat dry.
- Slice only the white parts of leeks paper-thin. Melt butter in medium pot. Add leeks, 6 tablespoons water, ¼ teaspoon salt, and a pinch of freshly ground white pepper. Bring to a quick boil, then lower heat to a simmer. Cover and cook for 25 minutes.
- Add ¼ cup water, cover, and cook for 10 minutes more. Leeks should be very soft and form a fondue, which means "melted." Set aside.
- Season halibut steaks lightly with salt and white pepper. Place in large flat steamer, or steam in 2 large nonstick skillets in ½ inch water. Steam over medium heat for 10 to 12 minutes, until fish is opaque. Be careful not to overcook.
- Gently reheat leek fondue. Add salt to taste. Pour over hot fish. Serve immediately. Pass a pepper mill filled with whole white peppercorns.

serves 6

157

potatoes boulangère

2 pounds (4 large) Idaho potatoes
3 ounces (about ¾ cup) freshly grated
Parmesan cheese
2 cups chicken broth, homemade or low-sodium
canned

- Preheat oven to 375°.
- Cut a round of parchment paper to fit the bottom of an 8½-inch springform pan.
- Peel potatoes and slice into paper-thin rounds.
- Sprinkle 2 tablespoons grated cheese onto paper in pan. Top with one-quarter of the potatoes, placed in one layer with slices overlapping. Sprinkle with 2 tablespoons grated cheese and freshly ground black pepper.
- Repeat 3 more times. You will have 4 layers of potatoes in all. Before adding remaining grated cheese, pour chicken broth over potatoes. Press down with spatula. Sprinkle with remaining grated cheese.
- Place pan on baking sheet. Bake for 1 hour 20 minutes. Potatoes will be tender and will have absorbed the broth. Cheese will be golden brown on top.
- Remove from springform, cut into wedges, and serve immediately.

serves 6

roasted beet puree
with allspice, fried beets

2½ pounds (5 large) beets, plus 2 large beets
for julienne (optional)
2½ tablespoons vegetable oil, plus 1 cup oil
for frying (optional)
2 teaspoons allspice berries

- Preheat oven to 400°.
- Trim 2½ pounds beets, but do not peel. Wash well. Rub beets with a little vegetable oil and place in heavy pie tin. Add ¼ cup water and bake for 2 hours. Beets will be soft.
- Peel beets with a sharp knife. Cut into large chunks and place in food processor. Add 2 tablespoons oil and process until smooth. Transfer contents to saucepan. Add salt and freshly ground black pepper to taste. Reheat when ready to serve.
- Crush allspice berries with the flat edge of a chef's knife until coarsely ground. Sprinkle hot beet puree with allspice. Serve immediately.
- *Optional garnish:* Peel 2 large beets. Cut into ¹⁄₁₆-inch-thick slices, then cut slices into thin julienne. Heat 1 cup oil in small saucepan until very hot. Add julienne beets and cook until crisp, about 3 minutes. Remove from oil with slotted spoon and drain on paper towels. Sprinkle with salt. Serve on hot puree.

serves 6 (makes 3 heaping cups)

oranges and grapefruit in black currant syrup, black currant granita

8 large oranges
3 large grapefruit
1¼ cups black currant syrup *

- Grate rind of 1 orange so that you have ½ teaspoon grated zest. Repeat with 1 grapefruit so that you have ½ teaspoon grated zest. Set zests aside.
- Using a small sharp knife, cut rind from oranges and grapefruit, being sure to collect any juices. (You will need ⅓ cup juices to make the granita.) Cut along membranes to release segments, being careful to keep segments intact. Again, collect any juices. Place segments in bowl. Cover and refrigerate until ready to serve.
- *To make granita:* Place ⅞ cup black currant syrup and 1¼ cups water in shallow metal pan. Add orange and grapefruit zest and ⅓ cup juices. Stir well and place in freezer. Stir with a fork every 45 minutes, breaking up ice to create a slushy frozen consistency. This will take about 2½ hours.
- *To serve dessert:* Place citrus segments in 6 large balloon-shaped wineglasses. Drizzle 1 tablespoon black currant syrup in each glass over fruit. Using an ice cream scoop, place granita on top. Serve immediately.

serves 6

* I use Cassis Vedrenne syrup from France, available in many specialty-food stores. Do not use cassis liqueur.

159

Spring Chicken

Asparagus and Shrimp Potage

Spring Chicken with Watercress À L'Ami Louis

Potato Puree with Goat Cheese and Truffle Oil

Haricots Verts à la Crème

Honey Ice Cream Quenelles

Rhubarb Compote with Toasted Almond Streusel, Brown Sugar Syrup

For most home cooks, "French" means "frightening" and "fussy." But these fundamentally simple recipes combine to create an elegant menu that's unmistakably French.

The potage, or soup, can be made early in the day. The roast chicken, inspired by the ultimate Parisian bistro, À L'Ami Louis, is utterly easy and pure in taste, balanced by lots of peppery watercress (which needs only washing).

My favorite mashed potatoes play a gastronomic arpeggio on the palate, issuing forth a cascade of flavors that linger as a harmonious chord. If truffle oil is unavailable or beyond your budget, use Garlic Oil (see page 299).

Slow-cooked rhubarb, the garden's harbinger of spring, reveals the fruit's inherent acidity, balanced by sugar and toasted nuts. It will bring sweet words of praise when accompanied by honey ice cream.

Making your own ice cream may sound ambitious, but it's a snap if you do it a day ahead, and it provides a glorious sense of achievement.

menu notes
Prepare the soup and ice cream the day before. The potatoes and compote can be made several hours before serving. The chicken and *haricots verts* are best cooked right before serving. A freshly made baguette makes a great accompaniment.

suggested hors d'oeuvres
Smoked Salmon Roulades (see page 122) and crudités with Dilled Champagne Cream (see page 103).

grapenote
Stay French. A white Bordeaux that's seen a little bit of wood can go all the way through this meal. Three good choices are Château Lamothe, Château Le Sartre, and Château Carbonnieux. For dessert, try one of my favorites: Muscat de Beaumes de Venise from the Rhône. A half bottle is all you need. Serve it slightly chilled.

asparagus and shrimp potage

1¼ pounds uncooked medium shrimp, in their shells
1½ bunches (about 6 large) leeks
2¼ pounds medium-thick fresh asparagus

- Peel shrimp, remove tails, and refrigerate. Place shrimp shells and tails in medium pot with 4 cups cold water (or just enough to cover).
- Wash leeks well. Chop green parts so that you have 1 cup. Add to pot with shrimp shells. Add ½ teaspoon whole black peppercorns. Bring to a boil. Lower heat and simmer, with cover askew, for 45 minutes. Strain broth through fine-mesh sieve into clean bowl. You will have about 3 cups broth. Set aside.
- Finely chop white part of leeks so that you have 1 cup. Snap off woody bottoms of asparagus and discard. Scrape asparagus lightly with vegetable peeler and cut into 1-inch lengths.
- Place reserved broth and chopped leeks (white parts) in medium pot. Bring to a boil. Lower heat to medium and cook for 5 minutes. Add asparagus and cook for about 15 minutes, until tender. Do not overcook, or asparagus will turn an unpleasant color.
- Transfer to blender in batches. Puree each batch until very smooth. This will take several minutes. Pass through coarse-mesh sieve into bowl. Add 1 ½ teaspoons salt and freshly ground black pepper. Return to pot.
- Bring pot of salted water to a boil. Lower heat and add shrimp. Cook for just under 1 minute. Drain in colander. Cut into ¼-inch pieces.
- Gently heat soup. Ladle into large flat soup plates. Place a mound of diced shrimp in center of soup and serve immediately.

serves 6 (makes 6 cups)

161

spring chicken with watercress à l'ami louis

2 4-pound roasting chickens
8 tablespoons unsalted butter
2 bunches fresh watercress, trimmed

- Preheat oven to 400°.
- Place giblets (except liver) inside chicken cavities. Truss with string and place in roasting pan just large enough to hold both chickens.
- Rub each chicken with 1 tablespoon butter and sprinkle lightly with salt. Roast, basting every 15 minutes, for 1¼ to 1½ hours. Chickens are done if juices run clear when thigh is pricked with a toothpick.
- Remove pan from oven. Pour any juices from chicken cavities into roasting pan. Discard giblets. Transfer chickens to platter to rest.
- Add remaining 6 tablespoons butter and ½ cup water to roasting pan. Cook over high heat until sauce thickens. Add salt and freshly ground black pepper to taste.
- Carve chickens as desired. Pour sauce over chicken pieces and garnish with watercress.

serves 6 or more

potato puree with goat cheese and truffle oil

5 large russet potatoes (about 2½ pounds)
6 ounces fresh goat cheese, crumbled
2 tablespoons truffle oil,* plus more for drizzling (optional)

- Wash potatoes well and peel. Cut into halves or quarters depending on size. Cover with cold salted water by 1 inch. Bring to a boil, lower heat, and cook, partially covered, for 30 to 35 minutes, or until tender. Drain potatoes, saving cooking water. Boil potato water until reduced to 1¼ cups.
- Mash potatoes well with potato masher or put through ricer. For extra creamy potatoes, press through a sieve. Slowly add enough reduced potato water to make desired consistency and then add the goat cheese. Mix until smooth. Add salt and freshly ground white pepper to taste. Add truffle oil and reheat gently before serving. Drizzle with a little extra truffle oil, if desired.

serves 6 (makes about 4½ cups)

*Available in specialty-food stores.

haricots verts
à la crème

2 ounces shallots
1 cup heavy cream
**1¾ pounds *haricots verts* or very thin green
 beans**

- Peel shallots and chop very fine. You will have
 about ⅓ cup. Place heavy cream in small saucepan. Add shallots, a pinch of salt, and a pinch of
 freshly ground white pepper.
- Bring just to a boil. Lower heat to a simmer and
 cook for 20 to 25 minutes, or until cream thickens and is reduced to ¾ cup.
- Meanwhile, trim ends of green beans. Bring
 large pot of salted water to a boil. Add beans
 and cook for 10 minutes, until tender but still
 bright green.
- Drain beans in colander and return to pot. Spoon
 cream sauce over beans and mix well. Add salt
 and white pepper to taste. Serve immediately or
 reheat gently before serving.

serves 6

honey ice cream
quenelles

3 cups light cream
4 extra-large egg yolks
½ cup aromatic honey, plus more for drizzling

- In medium saucepan, heat cream until small
 bubbles appear around edges. Remove from heat.
 In large bowl, whisk egg yolks and honey until
 blended. Gradually beat in hot cream. Pour mixture back into saucepan and cook, stirring constantly, until slightly thickened. Do not boil.
- Strain mixture into bowl. Let cool. Cover and
 chill overnight. Freeze in ice cream maker according to manufacturer's directions.
- If ice cream becomes too hard, place in refrigerator for 30 minutes before serving. When serving,
 shape into quenelles using an oval ice cream
 scoop or 2 large spoons. Drizzle with additional
 honey.

serves 6 (makes about 4 cups)

rhubarb compote with toasted almond streusel, brown sugar syrup

2 pounds fresh rhubarb
1 cup (5 ounces) shelled almonds, with skins
1½ cups packed dark brown sugar

- Preheat oven to 350°.
- Remove any rhubarb leaves. Wash stalks and cut into 3½-inch pieces. If stalks are 1 inch or more thick, cut in half lengthwise. Place rhubarb pieces in shallow 3-quart nonreactive casserole. Rhubarb should be tightly packed in two layers. Sprinkle on ¼ cup water.
- Place almonds in medium nonstick skillet and cook over medium heat until you smell a faint nutty odor. Shake pan occasionally to distribute nuts. Let cool. Place almonds in bowl of food processor and process until finely ground.
- In small bowl, combine grounds nuts and 1 cup sugar. Sprinkle over rhubarb to cover completely.
- Bake for 1½ hours. Place under broiler for 30 to 60 seconds to brown.

- Meanwhile, prepare brown sugar syrup. In small nonstick skillet, put remaining ½ cup sugar and ½ cup cold water. Stir to dissolve sugar. Bring to a boil, lower heat to medium-high, and cook for about 10 minutes, until liquid is reduced to ½ cup. Let cool.
- Remove rhubarb from oven. Let cool for 10 to 15 minutes. Serve warm or at room temperature.
- To serve, use a spatula or large spoon to distribute compote among 6 large plates. Pour a little brown sugar syrup around compote.

serves 6

Veal Roast

Mozzarella Bagna Cauda

Veal Roast with Fresh Thyme and Honey Mustard Jus

Braised Escarole and Orzo

Slow-Cooked Baby Carrots

Cantaloupe in Sweet Vermouth, Crushed Amaretti

This menu of sophisticated Italian flavors is perfect for your most discriminating guests. The dishes provide a combination of tastes that create a sumptuous meal — from a pungent, warm anchovy sauce for fresh mozzarella cheese to a doubly sweet dessert of cantaloupe in sweet vermouth.

The main course recipe demonstrates how long, gentle cooking coaxes the maximum flavor from many foods. The veal roast is juicy and tender from slow cooking in moist heat, which also allows the fragrant thyme to impregnate the flesh. The slow-cooked escarole becomes a silky counterpoint for the orzo. Carrots and garlic cooked in a long hot bath become an intensely flavored side dish.

Time is on your side, as simple ingredients transform themselves into a special dinner. All you have to do is wait.

menu notes

Marinate the veal for at least two hours before cooking. The side dishes can be prepared while the veal in is the oven. The fruit for dessert should be marinated for several hours.

Be sure to use fresh mozzarella for the first course, which should be prepared fifteen to twenty minutes before your guests sit down.

Serve this meal with whole-grain and sourdough rolls.

suggested hors d'oeuvres

Asparagettes (see page 123) and Two-Tone Mussels (see page 121).

grapenote

First choice would be a highly extracted Alsatian white, such as Zind-Humbrecht Pinot d'Alsace (well worth the cost). For something less expensive, try a fairly woody Chardonnay from California: Estancia or Lambert Bridge. With dessert, try a bottle of off-dry Asti Spumante, an undervalued sparkler that doesn't get enough respect.

165

mozzarella bagna cauda

3 large firm, ripe beefsteak tomatoes
1 pound fresh mozzarella cheese
1 2-ounce can rolled anchovies with capers in oil

- Preheat oven to 500°.
- Cut tops and bottoms off tomatoes. Set aside.
- Cut each tomato horizontally into 2 thick slices. Place tomato slices on baking sheet.
- Cut mozzarella into 6 thick slices. Place on tomato slices and trim edges as necessary so that cheese does not hang over edges of tomatoes. Bake for 5 to 7 minutes, until cheese begins to melt.
- Meanwhile, put anchovies, capers, and oil in small nonstick skillet. Add 2 tablespoons water and warm over very low heat until anchovies begin to melt. Stir with wooden spoon. Keep warm.
- Cut reserved ends of tomatoes into tiny dice. Remove tomatoes from oven. Place 1 tomato slice in center of each of 6 large plates. Drizzle with anchovy mixture and scatter minced tomato on plate. Sprinkle with freshly ground black pepper. Serve warm or at room temperature.

serves 6

veal roast with fresh thyme and honey mustard jus

3½-pound veal roast (shoulder and neck meat)
½ cup good-quality honey mustard
2 large bunches fresh thyme

- Place veal in shallow dish. In small bowl, combine honey mustard and 2 tablespoons thyme leaves. Rub mustard-thyme mixture over entire surface of veal roast. Cover and marinate in refrigerator for 2 hours.
- Preheat oven to 325°.
- Place remaining thyme and thyme branches in large casserole with cover. Scrape marinade off veal roast and save.
- In large nonstick skillet, brown veal quickly on all sides. Sprinkle with salt and freshly ground black pepper. Place in casserole on thyme branches. Add ½ cup water and reserved marinade to warm skillet. Bring to a boil. Pour over veal roast.
- Cover casserole and bake for 2½ hours. Check every 30 minutes to make sure all the liquid hasn't evaporated. You want to cook the roast in moist heat. Add a little water if necessary.
- Remove roast. Internal temperature should be at least 185°. Flesh should be soft when pierced with the tip of a long thin knife. Let sit for 5 minutes, then carve into thick slices. Meat will be very moist and tender. Serve with pan juices.

serves 6 or more

166

braised escarole and orzo

1 large head escarole (1½ pounds)
6 tablespoons unsalted butter
12 ounces (1¾ cups) orzo

- Wash escarole thoroughly and cut into 1-inch pieces. Place in colander. Sprinkle on 1 table-spoon salt and toss well. Place heavy object on escarole and let drain for 30 minutes. Wash salt from escarole and dry thoroughly.
- Melt 5 tablespoons butter in large pot. Add esca-role and cook over medium heat for at least 20 minutes, until very soft and lightly browned.
- Meanwhile, melt remaining 1 tablespoon butter in medium pot. Add orzo and stir constantly with wooden spoon until golden brown and lightly toasted, about 2 to 3 minutes. Add 8 cups water and ½ teaspoon salt. Bring to a boil. Lower heat and cook for 10 to 12 minutes, until orzo is tender. Do not overcook.
- Drain orzo, saving ½ cup cooking liquid. Add orzo to pot with escarole and toss well, adding a little cooking water if necessary. Add salt and freshly ground black pepper to taste. Serve hot.

serves 6 or more (makes 6 heaping cups)

slow-cooked baby carrots

1½ pounds fresh baby carrots, peeled
12 small cloves garlic
¼ cup extra-virgin olive oil

- In large nonstick skillet or shallow casserole dish with cover, place carrots in one layer.
- Cut garlic cloves in half. Add to carrots. Add oil and 1½ cups water (or more to cover carrots).
- Add ½ teaspoon salt and ½ teaspoon cracked black pepper. Bring to a boil. Lower heat to a sim-mer and place cover askew. Cook over low heat for 50 minutes to 1 hour, until carrots are tender.
- Remove carrots and garlic with slotted spoon. Reduce pan juices until thick and syrupy and pour over carrots. Serve immediately.

serves 6

167

cantaloupe in sweet vermouth, crushed amaretti

1 large ripe cantaloupe (2½ to 3 pounds)
1 cup sweet vermouth
4 ounces amaretti cookies

- Cut cantaloupe in half and remove seeds. Using a melon baller, scoop out as many melon balls as possible, being careful to avoid the rind.
- Place balls in bowl with any accumulated juices. Add a pinch of salt and sweet vermouth. Cover and refrigerate for 1 to 2 hours.
- Meanwhile, place cookies between two pieces of waxed paper and crush with rolling pin until they are a coarse powder.
- Divide melon balls and juices among 6 large wine goblets. Scatter crushed amaretti on top. Serve with long spoons.

serves 6

Rack of Lamb Harissa

Fennel Salad with Warm Ricotta Salata, Lemon Oil

Rack of Lamb Harissa, Braised Shallots

Couscous el Souk

Roasted Eggplant Wedges, Cilantro Dressing

Strawberry-Arrack Sharbat, Strawberry Salad

Your guests will love the decidedly Mediterranean yet unfamiliar aromatics of this meal. The unusual interplay of hot and cold temperatures, as well as hot and spicy flavors, will keep the taste buds, and the conversation, stimulated.

Harissa, a chili-based condiment found in Morocco, Algeria, and Tunisia, adds a fiery note to lamb, which is then tempered by the sweetness of braised shallots. Couscous is perfumed with stick cinnamon and tinted musky yellow by turmeric.

The menu ends with a sensational combination of strawberries and licorice-scented arrack, frozen into a *sharbat*, or sorbet. *Sharbat* is the first known iced dessert, which originally began as a drink. It was introduced by the Chinese to the Persians and Arabs, who introduced it to the Italians, who introduced it to the French.

menu notes

Prepare the *sharbat* the day before or early in the day. The eggplant can be made several hours ahead and served at room temperature. The fennel for the salad can be preboiled and assembled, and the cheese cooked at the last minute. Prepare the couscous immediately before serving.

Serve the first course on individual plates. The main course is lovely on large platters. This menu is easily doubled.

suggested hors d'oeuvres

An Unusual Hummus (see page 101) and Pita Chips (see page 109). A bowl of three varieties of olives (oil-cured, Kalamata, and cracked green) would also be nice.

grapenote

Bertani's new Due Uve, a blend of Sauvignon Blanc and Pinot Grigio, is a lovely choice for the salad. For the lamb, splurge on a hot-blooded Château Musar from Lebanon, an Australian Shiraz (Penfolds or Richard Hamilton), or a South African Pinotage such as Rooiberg Cellars.

169

fennel salad with warm *ricotta salata*, lemon oil

2 large fennel bulbs (about 1¼ pounds each)
5 tablespoons lemon oil *
6-ounce piece *ricotta salata* **

- Remove fennel fronds and set aside. Cut all but 1 inch of stalks off fennel bulbs and discard. Remove any dark spots from bulbs. Cut each bulb lengthwise through root end into very thin slices. Some of the slices will fall apart, which is fine.
- Bring medium pot of salted water to a boil. Add fennel and cook for 3 minutes. Fennel will be slightly tender but will still have some crunch.
- Drain fennel in colander. Transfer to bowl and toss well with 4 tablespoons lemon oil and sea salt and freshly ground black pepper to taste. Set aside.
- Preheat oven to 450°.

- Grease heavy pie tin with remaining 1 tablespoon lemon oil. Slice cheese into 4 slices. Place in pie tin. Bake for 6 to 8 minutes, until cheese browns and crisps around edges.
- To serve, mound fennel salad in center of 4 large plates. Finely chop fennel fronds and lightly scatter over and around fennel. Top each with warm cheese. Serve immediately.

serves 4

   * I use Colavita Limonolio or Zeta (Land of Canaan) Natural Oils from Israel, or Boyajian, available in some supermarkets and specialty-food stores.

  ** A pure white, lightly salted sheep's milk cheese pressed into a block. It has a sweet, milky flavor and is available in many supermarkets, specialty-food stores, and Italian markets.

rack of lamb harissa, braised shallots

1 pound large shallots

4 4-chop racks of lamb, chine bones and fat removed, then Frenched (about 12 ounces each after trimming) *

2 tablespoons harissa, ** **plus more for serving (optional)**

- Peel 8 shallots (about ½ pound). Grate on large holes of box grater so that you get grated shallots and shallot juice. Coat lamb racks with shallots and juice. Plate, cover with plastic wrap, and refrigerate for 3 to 4 hours.
- Preheat oven to 450°.
- Scrape shallots from lamb and pat dry. Rub lamb racks with harissa and sprinkle lightly with salt. Place in heavy shallow roasting pan and roast for 22 to 25 minutes for rare to medium-rare.
- While lamb racks are cooking, melt lamb fat in large nonstick skillet so that you have about 3 tablespoons. Peel remaining shallots and cut each in half lengthwise through root end. Add to skillet and sauté over low heat for 10 to 12 minutes, until lightly caramelized. Add salt and freshly ground black pepper to taste.

- Remove lamb from oven. Let sit for several minutes before carving. Cut racks into single chops or into double chops. Serve 4 single chops or 2 double chops per person, with several sautéed shallots and an extra dab of harissa, if desired.

serves 4

* Have butcher give you the trimmed lamb fat.

** A spicy North African condiment made from chili peppers. Available in small cans or tubes in Middle Eastern markets.

couscous el souk

2 3½-inch-long cinnamon sticks
1 teaspoon ground turmeric
2 cups (about 11 ounces) fine couscous

- Place 3½ cups water, cinnamon sticks, ¾ teaspoon turmeric, 1 teaspoon salt, and ⅛ teaspoon each freshly ground white and black pepper in medium pot with cover. Bring almost to a boil, lower heat to medium, cover, and cook for 5 minutes.
- Remove cover and add couscous. Continue to cook for 2 to 3 minutes, stirring constantly, until most of the liquid is absorbed. Fluff with a fork. Remove from heat, replace cover, and let sit for 5 to 6 minutes.
- Fluff with a fork again and add salt to taste. Mound hot couscous on platter in pyramid shape. Cut cinnamon sticks in half lengthwise and place equidistantly on sloping sides of couscous. Sprinkle with remaining ¼ teaspoon turmeric. Serve immediately.

serves 4 or more

roasted eggplant wedges, cilantro dressing

1 large eggplant (about 1 pound)
6 tablespoons garlic oil, store-bought or homemade (see page 299)
1 large bunch fresh cilantro

- Wash eggplant and dry. Cut green top from eggplant and discard. Cut eggplant lengthwise into 8 wedges; if very wide, cut into 10 wedges. Cut each wedge in half width-wise. You will have 16 or 20 pieces.
- Put eggplant in bowl. Drizzle with 1 tablespoon garlic oil. Add ½ teaspoon salt and freshly ground black pepper. Toss well and marinate for 1 hour.
- Preheat oven to 500°.
- Place eggplant in one layer on baking sheet. Bake for 20 minutes. Turn eggplant and bake for 10 minutes more. Eggplant will be soft and browned but still retain its shape.
- While eggplant is baking, make dressing. Place remaining 5 tablespoons garlic oil, 3 tablespoons cold water, and ½ cup packed cilantro leaves in bowl of food processor. Process until smooth and thick. Add salt and pepper to taste.
- Transfer eggplant to platter and pour dressing over. Serve hot or at room temperature. This can be made several hours ahead of time and reheated, covered, in 500° oven for 5 minutes. Garnish with fresh cilantro leaves.

serves 4

strawberry-arrack *sharbat*, strawberry salad

¾ cup plus 2 tablespoons sugar
4 pints ripe strawberries
¼ cup arrack,* plus more for serving (optional)

- In small saucepan, bring ¾ cup sugar and ¾ cup water to a boil. Cook for 2 minutes, or until sugar is completely dissolved. Let cool.
- Wash 2 pints strawberries and dry well. Remove stems and leaves. Cut berries in half. Place in bowl of food processor and process until very smooth. You should have about 3 cups puree.
- Add sugar syrup and arrack, then process until incorporated. Chill well. Pour mixture into ice cream maker and freeze according to manufacturer's directions.
- Meanwhile, wash remaining 2 pints berries. Remove stems and leaves from all but 4 berries, which you will use as garnish. Cut berries in half and place in bowl. Mix with remaining 2 tablespoons sugar. Refrigerate until ready to serve.
- To serve, place sugared berries in large wine goblets or decorative dessert dishes. Sprinkle berries with a little arrack, if desired. Top with a scoop of *sharbat*. Garnish each with a whole berry.

serves 4 or more

* A licorice-flavored liqueur from Israel. You may substitute anisette, or ouzo, or raki — from Italy, Greece, and Turkey, respectively.

173

Solo Verdure

Tiny Seashells with Arugula, Garlicky Pepper Oil

Big Portobellos Filled with Creamed Spinach and Pernod

Almond-Crusted Baked Tomatoes

White Beans and Celery with Gorgonzola

Orange-Orzata Italian Ices, Angel Food Toast

Solo verdure means "vegetarian" in Italian. In fact, this healthy style of eating has become so popular in Italy that the American word has crept into Italian culture, making one either a *vegetariano* or *vegetariana*. You may not claim to be one, but this is a welcome way to eat during the warm-weather months.

Vegetarian meals, even in summer, need a bit of heft to make you feel as though a proper dinner has been served. This particular menu, inspired by Italy, relies on impeccable ingredients — peppery arugula and superripe (but not too soft) tomatoes — and on a good amount of cheese, nuts, pasta, and beans as sources of protein.

Dessert, a sticky nod to the sweet summers of childhood, offers a fat-free counterpoint to an otherwise rich meal.

menu notes
About three hours before dinner, cook the beans, prepare the filling for the mushrooms, and freeze the ices. The rest of the meal can be prepared less than half an hour before serving. The cooked beans need to be reheated and the cheese added close to service. All the dishes can be served warm or at room temperature. The dessert should be ice-cold.

suggested hors d'oeuvre
Roasted Eggplant and Pesto Spread (see page 174) with crudités or Garlic Croûtes (see page 109).

grapenote
Good summer whites include Pinot Grigio (try Villa Frattina), Sauvignon Blanc (try Spottswoode), and Chenin Blanc (try Pine Ridge), all of which go nicely with this menu. For dessert, experience a flavor blast with Quady Essencia.

tiny seashells with arugula, garlicky pepper oil

1 pound tiny seashell pasta
4 large bunches arugula
⅔ cup garlic oil, store-bought or homemade (page 299)

- Bring large pot of salted water to a boil. Add pasta and cook for 10 to 12 minutes, until al dente.
- Meanwhile, wash and dry arugula. Cut leaves into ½-inch pieces; discard stems. You will have about 4 cups packed leaves. Place in large bowl.
- Drain pasta in colander, saving ½ cup cooking water.
- Add garlic oil and hot pasta to arugula and toss. Add 1 teaspoon butcher-grind black pepper and enough hot cooking water to coat pasta. Add salt to taste. Toss again.
- Serve from large platter or in individual flat soup plates. Delicious warm or at room temperature.

serves 6

big portobellos filled with creamed spinach and pernod

12 large portobello mushrooms (3 to 4 ounces each)
3 9-ounce packages frozen creamed spinach, thawed (about 3 cups)
3 to 4 tablespoons Pernod

- Preheat oven to 400°.
- Remove stems from mushrooms. Trim bottoms of stems and finely chop. Place in small saucepan with water to cover. Bring to a boil and cook for 1 minute. Drain in fine-mesh sieve.
- Place creamed spinach in medium bowl. Add cooked mushrooms, Pernod, and freshly ground black pepper. Mix thoroughly.
- Wipe mushroom caps with wet paper towels. Place stem side up on baking sheet. Mound creamed spinach mixture into each mushroom.
- Add several tablespoons water to baking sheet. Bake for 8 to 10 minutes, until mushrooms are soft but still retain their shape. Serve immediately.

serves 6

almond-crusted baked tomatoes

6 medium-large ripe tomatoes
½ cup sliced almonds, with skins
¾ cup freshly grated Parmigiano-Reggiano
 cheese

- Preheat oven to 425°.
- Cut stem ends off tomatoes and scoop out ½ inch of tomato flesh. Salt insides of tomatoes and turn them upside down on paper towels to drain.
- Place almonds in small nonstick skillet and toast over medium heat, tossing occasionally, until golden. Let cool for 5 minutes. Place almonds in bowl of food processor and process until finely ground. Add cheese and freshly ground black pepper, and pulse to mix.
- Fill tomato cavities with almond-cheese mixture, mounding it on top. Place tomatoes on baking sheet with a few tablespoons water. Bake for 10 to 15 minutes, until tomatoes are soft and stuffing is crusted. Serve warm or at room temperature.

serves 6

white beans and celery with gorgonzola

¾ pound dried small white beans
1 leafy bunch celery
6 ounces Italian Gorgonzola cheese, cut into
 small pieces

- Bring large pot of salted water to a boil. Add beans and boil for 2 minutes. Remove from heat, cover pot, and let sit for 1 hour.
- Drain beans and return to pot. Cover with fresh water. Add ½ teaspoon whole black peppercorns. Bring to a boil and skim off any foam. Lower heat and cook for 1½ hours with cover askew.
- Pick off 1 cup packed celery leaves and set aside. Finely chop enough celery to make 3 cups. Add chopped celery to beans and cook for 30 minutes, or until beans are tender and celery is soft.
- Drain beans in colander, saving ½ cup cooking liquid. Place beans in bowl. Add cheese and some of the cooking liquid, then toss to coat beans. Add salt to taste. Tear celery leaves and add to beans. Stir well and serve hot, warm, or at room temperature.

serves 6

orange-*orzata* italian ices, angel food toast

10 large juice oranges
²/₃ cup *orzata* (almond syrup) *
10- to 12-ounce angel food cake, store-bought
    or homemade

- Grate enough orange rind to make 2 teaspoons grated zest. Cut oranges in half and squeeze 2¼ to 2½ cups juice.
- Place orange zest and juice in shallow metal pan. Pour in ⅓ cup *orzata* and stir. Place in freezer. Every 30 minutes, scrape up slush with fork to make crystals. Continue process until mixture freezes completely, about 2½ to 3 hours.
- When ready to serve, preheat oven to 400°.
- Cut cake into ¾-inch-thick slices. Place on ungreased baking sheet and toast on each side for 6 minutes, until lightly browned and slightly dried. Set aside until ready to assemble dessert.

- *To assemble dessert*: Place 2 overlapping slices of toasted angel food cake in center of 6 large plates. Drizzle approximately 1 tablespoon *orzata* over cake.
- Cut rind and pith from remaining oranges and cut along membranes to release segments. Scatter segments and accumulated juice over cake.
- Remove ices from freezer. Place large scoops on cake. (You may also process ices in food processor for a smoother texture.) Serve immediately.

serves 6

* Available at specialty-food stores, especially those featuring Italian imports. Also known as orgeat.

177

Swordfish Swords

Watermelon, Feta, and Black Olive Salad

Swordfish Swords with Pomegranate Molasses

Cucumbers in Yogurt Dressing

Bulgur with Pine Nuts and Cilantro

Figs and Halvah, Honey Syrup

After my recipe for watermelon salad appeared in the *New York Times* in 1997, it was widely copied. This pairing of sweet watermelon and salty feta is a common snack in Turkish and Israeli cafés, and that part of the world, "the other Mediterranean," is the flavor source of this summer menu.

Marinating swordfish in good olive oil yields a velvety texture. Combining slightly charred fish with sour-sweet pomegranate molasses makes this dish surprisingly right for red wine.

Dessert is an unorthodox coupling of fleshy black figs with paper-thin slices of earthy halvah, resembling shards of Parmesan cheese.

menu notes

This is almost a no-cooking menu. Marinating the fish and letting the yogurt drain requires time but not your attention. The fish needs less than ten minutes of cooking, the bulgur fifteen minutes, and the honey syrup only one minute!

suggested hors d'oeuvres

Pita Chips (see page 109) with Za'atar Pesto (see page 103), and Carrots Moroccaine (see page 201).

grapenote

A juicy-fruit pink is the perfect mate for the unusual salad. Charles Melton Rosé of Virginia from the Barossa Valley in Australia may be hard to find, but it possesses an intense bouquet of watermelon. You may happily substitute Joseph Phelps Vin du Mistral Grenache Rosé. With the main course, try a fruity Merlot — Stonehedge, Bogle, or Hahn from California, or Villa Pillo from Tuscany.

watermelon, feta, and black olive salad

2½-pound piece ripe watermelon
½ pound feta cheese, in one piece
2 cups oil-cured black olives

- Remove rind and seeds from watermelon and discard. Cut watermelon into slices about ¼ inch thick. Overlap slices on large platter.
- Cut feta cheese into very thin slices, about ⅛ inch thick. Distribute over watermelon.
- Scatter black olives over cheese. Let come to room temperature before serving.

serves 6

swordfish swords with pomegranate molasses

3½ pounds swordfish, cut into 2 or 3 1¼-inch-thick steaks
½ cup olive oil, plus more for drizzling
½ cup pomegranate molasses,* plus more for serving (optional)

- You will need 6 12-inch-long metal skewers.
- Cut swordfish into 48 large chunks. Thread each skewer with 8 pieces of swordfish.
- Place skewers on platter. Coat thoroughly with olive oil. Sprinkle lightly with sea salt and freshly ground white pepper. Marinate for 1 hour at room temperature.
- Heat a charcoal fire or gas grill, or preheat the broiler.
- Cook swordfish skewers on all sides until lightly charred but moist inside.
- Serve 1 "sword" per person. Drizzle each with about 1 tablespoon (or more) pomegranate molasses and some olive oil. You may also pass extra pomegranate molasses in a small pitcher.

serves 6

*Available in most Middle Eastern markets. Cortas, from Lebanon, is a good brand.

179

cucumbers in yogurt dressing

2 cups plain yogurt
3 medium-large cucumbers (about 2 pounds)
1 medium clove garlic

- Line fine-mesh sieve with coffee filter and place over bowl. Place yogurt in filter and let drain for 45 minutes to 1 hour, until 1⅓ cups yogurt remains. Yogurt will be fairly thick.
- Meanwhile, peel cucumbers. Cut in half lengthwise. Using a small spoon, scrape out seeds and discard. Cut cucumber into ¼-inch-thick slices. They will be crescent-shaped. Place cucumbers in colander, sprinkle with 1 tablespoon kosher salt, and let sit for 15 minutes. Wash thoroughly with cold water. Squeeze dry, then dry with paper towels.
- Place thickened yogurt in medium-large bowl. Push garlic through press and stir into yogurt. Add cucumbers and mix thoroughly, also adding a liberal grinding of black pepper. Cover and refrigerate for 1 to 2 hours, or until cold.

serves 6

bulgur with pine nuts and cilantro

2 cups (¾ pound) coarse bulgur wheat
½ cup pine nuts
1 bunch fresh cilantro

- In medium pot, bring 7 cups water and 1 teaspoon salt to a boil. Add bulgur, stirring constantly. Reduce heat to medium. Cook for 15 minutes, stirring frequently, until tender.
- Meanwhile, put pine nuts in small nonstick skillet and cook over low heat for several minutes, shaking pan constantly. Be careful not to burn. You want pine nuts to turn golden.
- Wash cilantro and dry well. Cut leaves into julienne strips so that you have 6 tablespoons.
- Drain bulgur in colander. Place in bowl or on platter. Add salt and freshly ground black pepper to taste. Top with toasted pine nuts and julienne cilantro.

serves 6 (makes 5 cups)

sable with dill cream (page 16),

toasted bagels with salt-cured tomatoes and ricotta cheese (page 16),

amrus (mango smoothie) (page 85)

roasted pepper salad with anchovies and crushed almonds (page 34),

TWO PASTAS: penne pasta à la vodka (page 34),

chicken-stuffed ravioli with fresh sage butter (page 35)

swordfish champignon with fresh asparagus (page 195),
corn off the cob (page 196)

chilled asparagus bisque with crabmeat (page 236),
eleven-inch parmesan straws (page 236)

pistachio-crusted salmon (page 237),
very lemony mashed potatoes (page 238),
spring vegetables à la vapeur (page 237)

sautéed shrimp on red and green pepper confit (page 132),
olive oil biscuits, hot from the oven (page 133)

seared tuna with coconut milk and wasabi (page 44),
macadamia rice with basil (page 45), orange-cucumber salsa (page 45)

red snapper in champagne sauce (page 228),
jasmine rice with edible flowers (page 229),
broccoli-ginger puree (page 228)

roast duck with pomegranate-rosemary jus (pages 141–42)

sweet garlic-fennel soup (page 204), cornish hens stuffed with pancetta and sage (page 205),
chopped broccoli rabe and roasted red onions (page 206),
crispy potatoes with italian parsley (page 206)

THANKSGIVING: oyster bisque (page 252), turkey ballottine with fresh sage and garlic jus (pages 252–53), wild rice with five-hour onions (page 254), roasted acorn squash and carrot puree (page 254), cranberry conserve (page 255)

fennel salad with warm *ricotta salata*, lemon oil (page 170),

rack of lamb harissa, braised shallots (page 171), couscous el souk (page 172),

roasted eggplant wedges, cilantro dressing (page 172)

tournedos balsamico (page 191),
potato galette, rosemary salt (page 192)

figs and halvah,
honey syrup

½ cup honey
18 large fresh black figs
½ pound pistachio halvah, in one piece

- Put honey and 2 tablespoons water in small saucepan. Cook over high heat for 1 minute, stirring constantly. Keep warm.
- Wash figs and cut in half lengthwise. On each of 6 large plates, arrange 5 fig halves in a circle, cut side up. Place 6th fig half skin side up in center of circle.
- Cut halvah into paper-thin slices using a long, thin-bladed, sharp knife.
- Drizzle 1½ tablespoons honey syrup over and around figs. Scatter a few slices of halvah around and on top of figs.

serves 6

Bluefish

Roasted Yellow Peppers, Caper—Golden Raisin Emulsion

Bluefish on a Bed of Red Onions and Purple Sage

Potatoes Cooked in Aromatic Tomato Sauce

Warm Salad of Wilted Kale and Bacon

Lemon Sorbetto with Rosemary, Sweet Gremolata

There are changeable days in late summer, when flirtatious weather reminds us of time's passage. As summer fades, a weighty menu like this one becomes more appropriate.

Perfect for serving out-of-doors while your guests ignore their need for sweaters, this menu offers taste-intense riffs on simple ingredients. Yellow peppers, charred and softened, shine brightly under an unusual dressing of salty capers and sweet golden raisins, an idea inspired by chef/wizard Jean-Georges Vongerichten.

Bluefish is treated like meat, with strong accents of red onions that caramelize and purple sage that provides a reverberating flavor. Distilled white vinegar revs up wilted kale.

Dessert gives you a good reason to trim your rosemary hedge — and gives your guests a chance to to say wow!

menu notes

Prepare the *sorbetto* earlier in the day — or, at the last moment, draft your guests into churning an old-fashioned ice cream maker (with layers of ice and rock salt) out-of-doors. The kale can be washed and cut, the peppers prepared, and the potatoes cooked several hours before dinner. The bluefish and salad need to be made right before you eat — twenty-five minutes and fifteen minutes, respectively.

suggested hors d'oeuvre

Truffled White Bean Spread (see page 112) with Garlic Croûtes (see page 109).

grapenote

It's lovely to start summer meals with a Rosé. For the peppers, you need a dry, crisp one from the south of France: L'Estandon, Domaine de la Citadelle, Domaine de Monpertuis, and Domaine de Fondréche are all possible matches. With the fish, try a young red Burgundy such as a 1996 Bourgogne Rouge from LeRoy, although a high-acidity Sauvignon Blanc could work as well. A shot of *limoncello* would be a sexy accompaniment to dessert.

roasted yellow peppers, caper–golden raisin emulsion

6 large yellow bell peppers (about 3 pounds)
⅓ cup large capers, drained
½ heaping cup golden raisins

- Preheat broiler.
- Wash peppers and dry. Wash capers and drain.
- Place peppers on baking sheet and broil for several minutes on all sides to blacken completely. Transfer peppers to paper bag, tie tightly, and steam for 5 to 10 minutes.
- Place raisins and capers in blender or bowl of food processor. Process until smooth, adding 4 tablespoons cold water. Add freshly ground black pepper and a pinch of salt, if needed. You will have a heaping ½ cup dressing.
- Remove peppers from bag and scrape off all the blackened skin. Do not rinse peppers, as you want to collect any sweet juices. Cut each into quarters lengthwise, removing the core, seeds, and any coarse membranes.
- Mix peppers with dressing and any collected juices. Divide among 6 large plates, flattening peppers to cover interior surface of plate. Do not refrigerate. This can be prepared several hours before serving.

serves 6

bluefish on a bed of red onions and purple sage

2½-pound center-cut bluefish fillet, skin on and scaled
1 large bunch fresh sage, preferably purple
1 pound medium red onions

- Preheat oven to 500°.
- Using a thin-bladed sharp knife, remove dark flesh from middle of fillet.
- Wash sage leaves and dry. Remove stems. Fill channel in bluefish (where you have removed dark flesh) with sage leaves, packing them tightly. Save some sage leaves for garnish. Season fish with salt and freshly ground black pepper.
- Peel onions and slice into very thin rounds. Scatter onions in center of baking sheet. Place fish skin side up on onions, tucking them under fish. Add ¼ cup water to sheet.
- Roast for 22 to 25 minutes, depending on thickness of fish. Skin will become slightly crisp.
- Turn fish over onto cutting board and cut into 6 portions. Top with roasted onions. Finely julienne reserved sage leaves and sprinkle over fish. Serve with pan juices.

serves 6

183

potatoes cooked in aromatic tomato sauce

1½ pounds medium russet potatoes
2 14½-ounce cans stewed tomatoes with
**   oregano and basil** *
¼ cup garlic oil, store-bought or homemade
**   (see page 299)**

- Peel potatoes and cut into quarters lengthwise. Cut each quarter crosswise into ⅓-inch-thick pieces.
- Put potatoes in skillet large enough to hold them in one layer. Add tomatoes and all their liquid. Drizzle 2 tablespoons garlic oil over tomatoes and add a liberal grinding of black pepper.
- Bring to a boil. Lower heat and cover skillet. Cook over low heat for about 50 minutes, or until potatoes are tender.
- Remove potatoes with slotted spoon. Reduce pan juices a little over high heat and pour over potatoes. Drizzle with remaining oil. Serve immediately or reheat later in covered pan over low heat.

serves 6

* I use Redpack.

warm salad of wilted kale and bacon

1 large bunch kale (about 1 pound)
9 slices bacon, cut into 1-inch pieces
6 tablespoons distilled white vinegar

- Separate kale leaves from stems and discard stems. Wash leaves well and chop coarsely. You will have approximately 12 cups packed leaves.
- In large pot, cook bacon slowly until it just begins to crisp and its fat is rendered. Add kale and turn up heat. Add vinegar and cook for 4 minutes over high heat, stirring constantly, until kale is wilted and cooked. Add salt and freshly ground black pepper to taste and an extra splash of vinegar, if desired.
- Serve immediately.

serves 6

lemon *sorbetto* with rosemary, sweet gremolata

6 large lemons
1 small bunch fresh rosemary
1½ cups plus 2 tablespoons sugar

- Grate rind of enough lemons to get 2 heaping tablespoons grated zest. Set 1 tablespoon zest aside to make sweet gremolata. Cut lemons in half and squeeze 1 cup juice.
- Wash rosemary and dry. Finely mince enough to make 1 tablespoon. Reserve remaining rosemary for making sweet gremolata.
- Place 1½ cups water, 1½ cups sugar, and 2 sprigs rosemary in small saucepan. Heat until boiling, reduce heat, and simmer for 1 to 2 minutes, until liquid is clear. Let cool. Remove rosemary.
- Mix syrup with lemon juice and zest and finely minced rosemary. Chill until very cold. Place in ice cream maker (electric is preferable) and freeze according to manufacturer's directions.
- Right before serving, make sweet gremolata. In a small bowl, thoroughly mix 1 tablespoon reserved zemon zest, 2 tablespoons sugar, and 1 teaspoon finely minced rosemary.
- Serve *sorbetto*, sprinkled with sweet gremolata, in wineglasses.

serves 6 (makes 3 cups)

185

Chicken Vatel

Crab au Vinaigre

Chicken Vatel

Saffron Rice and Brie

Sautéed Cherry Tomatoes

Real Peach Melba

This chicken recipe was Escoffier's solution to the legendary Vatel's conundrum: what to do when one's professional honor hangs in the balance?

Vatel, a great but perhaps hysterical seventeenth-century chef, fell on his sword to save face when the fish for a royal banquet didn't arrive in time. Escoffier, a more coolheaded chef, would have replaced fish fillets with crumbed chicken breasts, "the flesh crushed with a pestle" and cooked in clarified butter — chicken masquerading as sole.

"Never lose your head when faced with great difficulty," he said; "that must be the motto of every *chef de cuisine.*" The age of creativity had begun. Escoffier called his dish "Filets de Sole Monseigneur," but I've renamed it Chicken Vatel.

I feel a certain kinship with Escoffier, who not only exclaimed, "Keep it simple," but who also had a particular passion for menu making.

This summery menu looks rich but "eats light."

Escoffier immortalized such women as Nellie Melba in enduring recipes, and he also made it acceptable for women to eat in fine public dining rooms.

menu notes

Reduce the vinegar for the crab ahead of time, but make the dish just before serving. The dessert can be made a day ahead or early in the same day. The chicken and cherry tomatoes should be cooked right before service. The rice can be made earlier and reheated. The clarified butter may also be prepared ahead of time.

suggested hors d'oeuvres

Crudités with Green Peppercorn Dip (see page 103) and Truffled Whitefish Puffs (see page 105).

grapenote

The classic menu for a classic white Burgundy — Meursault or Chassagne-Montrachet (look for one from Verget) — or a less expensive Bourgogne Blanc from Les Belles Roches. A fun accompaniment to dessert would be a sparkling *pêche* (Peach Gala from Clinton Vineyards) or a demi-sec champagne with a little peach liqueur added.

crab au vinaigre

1 pound fresh jumbo lump crabmeat
½ cup apple cider vinegar
5 tablespoons unsalted butter, well chilled

- Place crab in bowl and carefully pick through to remove any shells or cartilage. Try to keep the lumps intact.
- In small heavy pan bring vinegar to a boil. Lower heat and cook until reduced by one-half. Set aside to cool.
- Preheat broiler.
- In large nonstick skillet, melt 2 tablespoons butter. Add crab and cook over low heat until heated through. Do not overcook. Add freshly ground white pepper.
- Remove crab with slotted spoon, leaving all the liquid in pan, and add reduced vinegar. Distribute crab among 4 small shallow casseroles, crème brûlée dishes, or large scallop shells.
- Bring liquid in pan to a boil. Lower heat and whisk in 2 tablespoons cold butter. Sauce will thicken. Pour evenly over crab. Top with remaining 1 tablespoon butter, cut into thin slices. Place under broiler for 30 seconds to brown lightly. Serve immediately.

serves 4

chicken vatel

7 tablespoons unsalted butter
4 large skinless boneless chicken breast halves
2 cups fresh white bread crumbs *

- *To clarify butter:* Melt butter in small heavy saucepan over very low heat. Remove pan from heat and let stand for 5 minutes. Skim foam. Let stand for 5 minutes more and slowly pour clear butter into small bowl, leaving behind milky solids in bottom of pan. You will have about 6 tablespoons clarified butter.
- Remove tenderloins from chicken breasts and save for another use. Season bread crumbs with ½ teaspoon salt and a pinch of freshly ground white pepper.
- Brush both sides of chicken breast with clarified butter, using a pastry brush. Dredge chicken in bread crumbs, coating both sides. Using the side of your hand, pound crumbs into breasts. Let sit for 10 minutes.
- In large nonstick skillet, heat remaining clarified butter. Add chicken and cook over medium heat for 5 minutes, until golden brown. Turn over and cook for 4 to 5 minutes more, until chicken is cooked through but still moist and crust is golden. Do not overcook. Serve immediately.

serves 4

* Make crumbs in a blender or food processor using good-quality soft white bread. Do not use dried crumbs.

187

saffron rice and brie

½ teaspoon saffron threads
1 cup extra-long-grain rice
4 ounces ripe Brie cheese

- Bring 2¼ cups water to a boil in medium pot. Add ½ teaspoon salt and saffron. Stir. Add rice, cover, and lower heat to a simmer. Cook slowly for 20 minutes, until water is absorbed. Rice should still be moist.
- Cut rind off cheese and cut cheese into small pieces. Add to pot with hot rice and stir with wooden spoon until cheese melts. Add salt and freshly ground black pepper to taste.
- When ready to serve, pack hot rice into 4 timbales or custard cups to make a thick round form. Turn out and serve immediately. Or make timbales and reheat, covered, in 350° oven for 10 minutes.

serves 4

sautéed cherry tomatoes

24 cherry tomatoes
2 tablespoons olive oil
3 tablespoons minced shallots

- Wash tomatoes, remove stems, and dry well.
- In large nonstick skillet, heat olive oil and add shallots. Cook over low heat for 1 minute.
- Add tomatoes and cook over high heat for 5 to 6 minutes, or until tomatoes are soft but not browned.
- Add salt and freshly ground black pepper to taste. Stir and serve immediately.

serves 4

real peach melba

4 large ripe peaches
1 pint good-quality vanilla ice cream, plus more
for rosettes (optional)
10-ounce package frozen raspberries in syrup

- Place peaches in large heavy pot with water to cover. Bring to a boil, lower heat, cover, and cook until barely soft. Remove peaches with slotted spoon and peel. Let cool, then refrigerate.
- Soften ice cream and spoon into 4 custard cups or timbales. Refreeze.
- *To make raspberry puree:* Thaw berries, then process in food processor or blender until smooth. Pass through fine-mesh sieve to remove seeds. You will have 1 cup raspberry puree.
- Turn ice cream out onto chilled dessert plates or into very large wine goblets. Cut peaches in half and remove pits. Place 2 peach halves on ice cream. Cover with raspberry puree.
- If desired, put additional soft ice cream in pastry bag and squeeze rosettes onto raspberry puree. Serve immediately.

serves 4

Tournedos Balsamico

Roasted Tomato and Onion Soup

Tournedos Balsamico

Potato Galette, Rosemary Salt

Fried Green Beans

Fresh Cherries on Ice, Sweet Lemon Mascarpone

Pignoli Crunch

Here is a meat-and-potatoes meal dressed for summer. This sumptuous dinner menu is so easy to prepare that you might set the table for twelve instead of six. The room-temperature soup soars with intense tomato flavor; the tournedos can be cooked indoors or out; the potatoes as a paper-thin galette are ethereal. Even the green beans, quickly fried, absorb only a bit of oil and taste unusually light.

The evocative palette of this meal (balsamic vinegar, tomatoes, rosemary, mascarpone, pignoli) will have your guests proclaiming, "Next year in Tuscany!"

menu notes

Prepare the soup, Pignoli Crunch, sweet mascarpone, rosemary salt, and vinegar reduction early in the day while the kitchen is cool. Marinate the meat for at least two hours before cooking. The potatoes can be made an hour before your guests arrive, then reheated briefly. The tournedos and beans should be prepared right before service. All these dishes taste delicious warm or at room temperature, instead of hot.

If you are using your grill, you can make 1-2-3 *bruschetta* to eat right through the meal: Cut thick slices of peasant bread, grill or toast on both sides, rub with a cut clove of garlic, and anoint with extra-virgin olive oil and sea salt.

suggested hors d'oeuvres

Asparagus Tonnato (see page 40); and Plugged Honeydew with Prosciutto (see page 137)

grapenote

Suave Italian flavors need suave Italian wines. With the soup, try a Chiaretto Bardolino from Cavalchina, a Rosé from Regaleali (Sicily), or a Rosato (Salice Salentino) from Albarosso. The main course calls for a big red: Vino Nobile di Montepulciano or a Rosso di Montalcino. Sip a small glass of Vin Santo with the Pignoli Crunch.

roasted tomato and onion soup

4 large ripe tomatoes (about 2 pounds)
8 medium onions (about 2 pounds), unpeeled
3 tablespoons extra-virgin olive oil, plus more for drizzling

- Preheat oven to 250°.
- Bring large pot of water to a boil. Make a small x in bottom of each tomato using a small sharp knife. Plunge tomatoes in water for 1 minute. Drain in colander and peel. Cut tomatoes in half and place cut side down on large baking sheet.
- Place whole unpeeled onions on baking sheet. Drizzle 1 tablespoon olive oil over tomatoes and onions, using your hands to coat them well. Sprinkle tomatoes with salt. Roast for 3 hours. Slip onions from their skins.
- Place tomatoes and 5 peeled onions in bowl of food processor. Process until very smooth. Add ½ to ⅔ cup water and remaining 2 tablespoons olive oil, and process again.
- Transfer to bowl. Add salt and freshly ground black pepper to taste. If not serving right away, you may need to add water, as soup will thicken. Serve at room temperature.
- To serve, ladle soup into 6 flat soup plates. Cut remaining peeled onions in half lengthwise. Place 1 half in center of soup and drizzle with olive oil.

serves 6 (makes about 5 cups)

tournedos balsamico

6 10-ounce 1-inch-thick beef tenderloin fillets
½ cup extra-virgin olive oil, plus more for grilling
2 tablespoons plus ½ cup balsamic vinegar

- Place meat in shallow casserole. Pour olive oil and 2 tablespoons vinegar over fillets. Marinate for 2 hours, turning fillets after 1 hour.
- Remove fillets from marinade. Sprinkle salt on both sides. On one side of each fillet, press 1 tablespoon butcher-grind black pepper.
- Coat grill pan very lightly with olive oil. Heat pan until very hot and cook fillets on each side for about 3 to 4 minutes for medium-rare.
- Meanwhile, place remaining ½ cup balsamic vinegar in small saucepan and cook over medium heat until reduced to ¼ cup.
- When fillets are done, transfer to warm plates. Drizzle each with a little reduced vinegar. Serve immediately.

serves 6

191

potato galette, rosemary salt

2 teaspoons ground rosemary *
1½ pounds medium russet potatoes
6 tablespoons unsalted butter, softened

- Preheat oven to 400°.
- Mix ground rosemary with ½ teaspoon salt. Set aside.
- Peel potatoes. Using a very sharp knife, slice into very thin rounds, about ¹⁄₁₆-inch thick or thinner if possible. (You may also do this with a mandolin.)
- Melt 4 tablespoons butter in small saucepan. Toss with potatoes, adding salt and freshly ground black pepper.
- Spread remaining butter in bottom of 2 heavy pie tins. Place 1 potato slice in center, then make tightly overlapping concentric circles to completely cover bottom of 1 tin. Repeat for other tin.
- Place flat inflammable object (small pan, pot cover, another pie tin) on top of potatoes. Bake for 25 minutes. Remove weights with spatula and bake for 6 to 8 minutes more. Galettes should be golden brown and crispy.
- Sprinkle galettes with rosemary salt. Cut each into three pie-shaped wedges and serve immediately. Or place in 400° oven for a few minutes to warm before serving.

serves 6

* Grind dried rosemary in a spice grinder or purchase ground.

fried green beans

1½ pounds young green beans
1½ cups all-purpose flour
1 cup or more olive oil

- Trim ends of green beans. Bring large pot of salted water to a boil. Add beans and cook for 1 minute. Drain under cold water. Pat dry.
- Mix flour with 1 tablespoon salt and freshly ground black pepper. Roll beans in flour, shaking off excess.
- Heat olive oil in nonstick skillet and fry beans until crisp. Remove from oil with slotted spoon and drain on paper towels. You will need to do this in several batches. Sprinkle with salt. Serve immediately.

serves 6

fresh cherries on ice, sweet lemon mascarpone

8 ounces mascarpone
**6 tablespoons lemon-flavored confectioners'
    sugar, plus more for serving**
2½ pounds fresh cherries with stems

- In bowl of electric mixer, whip mascarpone and sugar until light and fluffy. You will have 1 heaping cup. Set aside until ready to serve. Make sure it is at room temperature before serving.
- Wash cherries well and dry. Do not remove stems. Fill large platter with crushed ice. Distribute cherries evenly on ice. Serve with bowl of sweet lemon mascarpone for dipping.
- *Alternative presentation:* Chill cherries until very cold. Serve a scoop of sweet lemon mascarpone in center of 6 large plates. Surround with cherries. Dust plate with additional lemon-flavored confectioners' sugar pushed through fine-mesh sieve.

serves 6

pignoli crunch

¾ cup pignoli (pine nuts)
1½ cups sugar
1 teaspoon ground cloves

- In small nonstick skillet, lightly toast pignoli over low heat, tossing periodically, until golden. Set aside.
- In larger nonstick skillet, put sugar and cloves. Over medium heat, melt sugar, stirring constantly, until it forms a dark brown caramel. When all the sugar is melted and there are no lumps remaining, stir in pignoli to distribute evenly.
- Spray baking sheet with nonstick vegetable spray or line with parchment paper. Immediately pour mixture onto sheet.
- Let cool until hard. Break into pieces to serve.

serves 6 or more

Swordfish Champignon

Tony May's Iced Tomatoes

Swordfish Champignon with Fresh Asparagus

Corn off the Cob

Wild Rice with Walnut Oil and Scallions

Tart Lemon Mousse

This menu signals a change in the weather, using summer's last voluptuous tomatoes. Iced Tomatoes, a recipe from Tony May, owner of New York's prestigious San Domenico, respects the mature fruit's simple goodness.

Next come juicy swordfish steaks, supporting a thatch of freshly cooked asparagus under a blanket of molten Champignon cheese (also known as mushroom Brie), each distinct component melding into one.

Corn, cut fresh from the cob, takes no time to cook in just a bit of salted water with fresh thyme and a julienne of red pepper. The corn tastes buttery when paired with thyme.

A sturdy side dish of wild rice with walnut oil and scallions is an earthy partner to the luxurious rich cheese (imported from Germany) flecked with bits of fungi.

The slow melt of frozen lemon mousse symbolizes the last gasp of summer.

menu notes

Prepare the dessert no more than three hours before serving. The wild rice requires fifty to fifty-five minutes of cooking but practically no prep. The remainder of the menu takes less than thirty minutes and also requires little prep. This menu can be easily doubled.

suggested hors d'oeuvres

Zucchini Thimbles with Goat Cheese and Chili Oil (see page 100) and Two-Tone Mussels (see page 121). Or serve a platter of Mozzarella Bagna Cauda (see page 166) alongside the Iced Tomatoes.

grapenote

Begin with a full-flavored California Rosé from Heitz (made from Grignolino) or a Sanford Vin Gris (made entirely from Pinot Noir). The next course calls for a lovely Sauvignon Blanc: Sancerre or Pouilly-Fumé from the Loire Valley.

tony may's iced tomatoes

4 large, very ripe tomatoes
1 small bunch fresh oregano
¼ cup garlic oil, store-bought or homemade
   (see page 299), plus more for drizzling
   (optional)

- Bring large pot of salted water to a boil. Make a small x with a sharp knife on bottom of each tomato. Drop in boiling water. Cook for 1 minute. Remove immediately with slotted spoon. Plunge tomatoes into bowl of very cold water. Place in colander and, under cool running water, remove tomato skins with your fingers or a small sharp knife.
- Cut each tomato into 12 thin wedges. Place in large bowl.
- Pick leaves from oregano to make about ¼ cup. Scatter over tomatoes.
- In small bowl, whisk together garlic oil and ½ teaspoon kosher salt. Spoon over tomatoes. Let sit for 30 minutes. When ready to serve, place 6 crushed ice cubes on tomatoes. Garnish with large sprigs of oregano. Drizzle with additional garlic oil, if desired.

serves 4

swordfish champignon with fresh asparagus

8 ounces Champignon cheese (mushroom Brie)
12 ounces medium-thick fresh asparagus
4 6-ounce ¾-inch-thick swordfish steaks

- Cut rind off cheese with a sharp knife. Cut cheese into small pieces and place in small heavy saucepan with 1 tablespoon water. Over very low heat, melt cheese slowly, stirring often with wooden spoon.
- Trim asparagus so that they are ¼ inch longer than swordfish steaks. Cook asparagus in 2 inches salted water for 5 to 6 minutes, until tender. Be careful not to overcook.
- Meanwhile, season swordfish lightly with salt and freshly ground black pepper. Cook in 12-inch nonstick skillet for 3 to 4 minutes on each side, until outside is lightly caramelized and inside is translucent and moist.
- Drain asparagus. Top each swordfish steak with a mound of hot asparagus and cover with 3 tablespoons of melted cheese sauce. Serve immediately.

serves 4

195

corn off the cob

5 large ears yellow sweet corn
1 large red bell pepper
1 small bunch fresh thyme

- Remove husks and silky threads from corn.
- Using a sharp knife, cut corn kernels from cobs, cutting very close to cobs. You will have about 4½ to 5 cups corn. Place in large nonstick skillet.
- Cut red pepper into fine julienne strips about 2½ inches long and ⅛ inch wide. Add to skillet along with ½ cup water. Bring to a boil, lower heat immediately, and cook until corn is tender, about 5 minutes. Add a little more water if needed. Stir frequently.
- Remove leaves from thyme to make 1½ table-spoons. Add to corn mixture along with salt and freshly ground black pepper. Cook for 1 minute more. Almost all the liquid will have evaporated. Serve immediately. Garnish with tiny thyme sprigs.

serves 4

wild rice
with walnut oil
and scallions

1 cup wild rice
1 large bunch scallions
2 tablespoons walnut oil, plus more for driz-zling (optional)

- In medium heavy saucepan, bring 6 cups salted water to a boil.
- Wash rice in colander and add to boiling water. Lower heat, cover, and cook for 50 to 55 minutes, or until rice is tender. (Time will vary depending on type and age of rice.)
- Meanwhile, trim all but 1 inch of green tops from scallions and reserve. Remove roots and cut scallions in half lengthwise, then across into ¼-inch pieces. You will have ½ cup chopped scallions.
- Heat oil in small nonstick skillet. Add scallions and cook over low heat for 15 minutes, or until scallions are very soft but not brown. Set aside.
- Drain rice in colander and transfer to bowl. Add scallions to rice and toss. Add salt and a generous amount of freshly ground black pepper.
- Finely chop reserved green tops of scallions to make ¼ cup. Sprinkle on rice. If desired, drizzle a little walnut oil over rice. Serve hot.

serves 4 (makes 2¾ cups)

tart lemon mousse

2 large lemons
**6 extra-large egg yolks and 4 extra-large egg
    whites**
½ cup sugar

- Grate rind of lemons so that you have 1 tablespoon grated zest. Squeeze lemons to get ⅓
  cup juice.
- In large mixing bowl, beat egg yolks vigorously
  with wire whisk or electric beater until pale yellow. Gradually add sugar, beating constantly.
  Continue beating until mixture is light and
  fluffy.
- Add zest and juice to beaten yolks.
- Transfer mixture to top section of double
  boiler. Beat over simmering water for 10 minutes, or until mixture is the consistency of a
  soft pudding. Remove from heat and reserve.
- In clean bowl, beat egg whites with a pinch of
  salt until very stiff. Gently fold whites into custard to incorporate thoroughly. Spoon into 4
  wineglasses or decorative dessert cups.
- Refrigerate until 15 minutes before serving.
  Place in freezer for 15 minutes, then serve.

serves 4

197

Lemon-Za'atar Chicken

Med-Rim Eggplant with Sun-Dried Tomatoes

Lemon-Za'atar Chicken

Whole Wheat Couscous with Grilled Scallions

Carrots Moroccaine

Spiced Oranges in Cardamom Syrup

Chickpea Flour Cookies

Za'atar, a spice mixture redolent of antiquity, offers the dominant flavor cue in this menu. An intoxicating blend of dried hyssop, sumac, and sesame seeds, it is at once ancient and trendy, an unidentifiable flavor wallop for lemon-kissed chicken.

This guest-friendly dinner, punctuated by geographically appropriate ingredients such as cumin, chili oil, cilantro, and cardamom, culminates with an original cookie recipe made from roasted chickpea flour.

As every dish tastes delicious hot or at room temperature, these recipes can be expanded to serve sixteen or more as the basis for a great Mediterranean buffet (see page 278).

menu notes

Although the chicken can be served at all temperatures, if you're serving it hot, cook it right before serving. Serve with stacks of warm pita bread.

suggested hors d'oeuvre

Phyllo and Feta Wraps (see page 104).

grapenote

This lusty meal calls for ripe, Rhône-style reds — and not necessarily from the Rhône, either. A Syrah from Michel Picard and L'Epayrié from the Languedoc, or Cline Vineyards, and Edmunds St. John from California are good choices. L'Enfant Terrible, a Mourvèdre from the latter winery, would also be delicious.

med-rim eggplant
with sun-dried tomatoes

1 very large or 2 medium eggplants (1½ pounds)
¾ packed cup sun-dried tomatoes in oil
1 bunch fresh cilantro

- Preheat broiler.
- Place eggplant on baking sheet and put under broiler so skin chars and blisters. Turn several times with tongs during this process, which should take about 5 minutes. This can also be done on top of the stove directly over a gas flame.
- Preheat oven to 400°. Bake eggplant for 1 hour.
- Meanwhile, drain sun-dried tomatoes in sieve over small bowl. Save ¼ cup oil. Cut tomatoes into tiny squares (smaller than ¼ inch) and set aside. Chop cilantro leaves so that you have ¼ cup. Set aside.
- Cut eggplant in half lengthwise and scoop out all the flesh. Place on large cutting board and, using a large knife or potato masher, chop flesh until you have a coarse paste. Transfer to a bowl.
- Add all but 2 tablespoons chopped tomatoes. Add 2 tablespoons oil and mix well. Add ½ teaspoon kosher salt and freshly ground black pepper. Mix well again.
- Line 4 6-ounce ramekins or custard cups with plastic wrap so that the plastic hangs over the cups. Pack eggplant mixture tightly into cups, covering tops with plastic wrap. Refrigerate for several hours, or until very cold.
- Unmold each cup in center of large plate. Garnish with remaining 2 tablespoons chopped tomatoes, remaining 2 tablespoons oil, and chopped cilantro leaves.

serves 4

199

lemon-za'atar chicken

1 large roasting chicken (4 to 4½ pounds)
½ cup za'atar *
4 lemons

- Cut chicken into 4 portions — 2 breast and 2 leg-thigh pieces. Remove chicken wings for later use. Remove and save giblets (except liver, which you may reserve for another recipe).
- Place chicken in shallow casserole. Sprinkle with za'atar. Grate the rind of 2 lemons and sprinkle over chicken. Cut these lemons in half and squeeze juice over chicken. Add freshly ground black pepper and mix well. Cover and refrigerate for at least 3 hours.
- Meanwhile, make chicken stock. Place giblets and chicken wings in medium pot. Cover with 2 cups cold water. Add ¼ teaspoon kosher salt and ¼ teaspoon whole black peppercorns. Bring to a rapid boil. Lower heat and simmer, uncovered, for 30 minutes, skimming often.
- Strain through fine-mesh sieve into small saucepan. Over low heat, reduce to about ¾ cup broth. Set aside.
- Preheat oven to 375°.
- Place chicken pieces on baking sheet or in shallow broiler pan. Sprinkle lightly with salt. Bake for 45 minutes. Transfer chicken to platter.
- Add a little chicken broth to baking sheet and scrape up all the browned bits and juices. Add to saucepan containing broth. Cook over high heat until a bit syrupy. Add salt to taste and pour over the chicken. Serve immediately with remaining 2 lemons cut into wedges.

serves 4

* Za'atar is available at Middle Eastern markets and by mail order from Adriana's Caravan (800-316-0820) or Greater Galilee Gourmet (800-290-1391). Purchase the greenest blend you can find, generally imported from Jordan or Israel.

whole wheat couscous with grilled scallions

2 bunches scallions
3 tablespoons unsalted butter
1½ cups (about 10 ounces) whole wheat couscous

- Cut green tops from scallions and reserve. Slice white parts of scallions very thin. You should have about 1⅓ cups.
- Melt 2 tablespoons butter in medium saucepan and add sliced scallions. Cook over medium heat until scallions are soft but still translucent. You do not want them to brown.
- Add couscous and stir over medium heat for 1 minute. Add 3 cups boiling water and stir. Bring to a boil, lower heat, and cover. Simmer for 3 minutes. Remove from heat and let stand for 5 minutes, until water is absorbed.
- Meanwhile, melt remaining 1 tablespoon butter and toss with green tops of scallions. Heat cast-iron grill pan until very hot. Add scallions and cook, turning several times, until they begin to soften and grill marks are emblazoned on greens. This will take several minutes.
- Remove cover from couscous. Add salt and freshly ground black pepper to taste. Fluff couscous with a fork. Place on large platter and top with grilled scallions. Serve immediately.

serves 4 or more

carrots moroccaine

1 pound long, slender fresh carrots, preferably organic
1½ tablespoons chili oil *
1¼ teaspoons good-quality ground cumin, plus more for serving (optional)

- Trim and peel carrots. Cut them in half lengthwise and then in half crosswise. Cut slender bottom halves crosswise into ¼-inch cubes. Cut thicker top halves in half again lengthwise, then cut crosswise to make ¼-inch cubes. Place in pot with just enough water to cover. Bring to a boil, then lower heat and cook until tender, about 10 minutes, being careful not to overcook.
- In medium nonstick skillet, combine chili oil, cumin, and ½ teaspoon kosher salt. Cook over low heat for 1 minute. Remove from heat.
- When carrots are tender, drain in colander, saving 2 tablespoons cooking liquid. Add carrots and cooking liquid to skillet. Heat quickly, stirring to coat carrots thoroughly with oil mixture. Add additional salt or cumin, if desired. This is delicious served hot or at room temperature.

serves 4

* Available in supermarkets and specialty-food stores. I use Chile Oil Olé from The Brown Adobe, (800) 392-2041.

201

spiced oranges in cardamom syrup

4 large oranges (2½ pounds)
1 cup sugar
24 green cardamom pods,* plus more for
  garnish (optional)

- With a small sharp knife, cut off stem ends of oranges so that they can sit without wobbling. Trim off rind, including all the white pith. Cut pith from 4 large strips of rind and discard.
- Place oranges in medium pot. Add 8 cups cold water, 4 strips orange rind, sugar, cardamom, and 12 whole white peppercorns. Bring to a boil. Lower heat to medium-low, cover, and cook for 20 minutes.
- Transfer oranges with slotted spoon to deep bowl with flat bottom. Bring liquid in pot to a boil and cook over high heat for about 20 minutes, until reduced to 2 cups. Pour over oranges through fine-mesh sieve. Remove rind and cut into very fine julienne. Scatter over oranges. Let cool before serving.
- *Optional garnish:* Lightly toast additional cardamom pods and scatter over oranges.

serves 4

> * Available in Middle Eastern markets and specialty-food stores.

chickpea flour cookies

2 sticks unsalted butter, at room temperature
1¼ cups or more confectioners' sugar
2 cups roasted chickpea flour,* plus more for
  sprinkling board

- Preheat oven to 300°.
- In bowl of electric mixer, beat butter until light and fluffy. Add 1 cup sugar and mix thoroughly. Stir in chickpea flour and a pinch of salt. Continue to mix until dough forms a smooth ball. Wrap in plastic and refrigerate for 15 minutes.
- Sprinkle pastry board lightly with chickpea flour. Using a rolling pin, roll dough out to ¼-inch thickness. Cut into desired shapes using cookie cutter, preferably one with fluted edge. Rounds, squares, or diamond shapes are nice.
- Place cookies on ungreased baking sheet. Bake for 25 minutes, or until golden. Let cool on sheet.
- Sprinkle with remaining ¼ cup (or more if needed) confectioners' sugar pushed through a sieve, covering cookies heavily. Transfer to platter.

makes 36 cookies

> * Available in Middle Eastern markets and specialty-food stores. You may also use plain, or unroasted, chickpea flour.

Cornish Hens

Sweet Garlic-Fennel Soup

Cornish Hens Stuffed with Pancetta and Sage

Chopped Broccoli Rabe and Roasted Red Onions

Crispy Potatoes with Italian Parsley

Chocolate Zabaglione

The attraction of modern Italian food, and of this menu, lies in the quality and variety of its components.

Herbs are, if you'll excuse the expression, the spice of life and can bring specific parts of the world immediately to mind. In this case, rosemary, flat-leaf parsley, and fennel fronds scream Italy and make lusty flavor pals for other equally rousing ingredients: garlic, broccoli rabe, red onions, and pancetta.

This dinner is best served family-style: soup, piping hot, from a large tureen; halved birds and accompaniments from large platters.

Zabaglione, an otherwise traditional dessert, is jazzed up with coffee liqueur and cocoa to make a resounding chocolate finale.

A coda in many Italian meals is a bowl of fresh fruit. Try a seasonal mélange of globe grapes, Forelle pears, and figs.

menu notes

The success of this menu relies on slow-cooking techniques. Garlic cloves and fennel sweeten in long-simmering cream to become a wondrous soup that can be made early in the day and reheated. While the hens are crisping in the oven, the giblets simmer into a stock. The roasted onions also can be prepared hours before service or alongside the hens. (Just put them in the oven fifteen minutes before.) Both the potatoes and the broccoli rabe are prepared on top of the stove. For best results, prepare the dessert just before serving.

suggested hors d'oeuvres

Cherry Tomato *Bruschetta* (page 104), Celery Bites (page 99), and An Unusual Pâté (page 113).

grapenote

This Italian leitmotif calls for Italian wines: a crisp Gavi to accompany the soup and a wonderfully full, ripe red for the main course. Two interesting choices are from southern Tuscany, Morellino di Scansano and Ciabatta, both table wines tasting of bright cherry fruit.

203

sweet garlic-fennel soup

2 large heads garlic (¼ pound)
2 cups heavy cream
2 large fennel bulbs (1 pound each)

- Peel garlic cloves. Place in medium pot with cover. Add heavy cream and bring just to a boil. Lower heat, cover, and simmer for 40 minutes, until cloves are very soft.
- Meanwhile, using a small sharp knife, remove wispy fronds from fennel bulbs and reserve for later use. Keep fronds refrigerated, wrapped in a moist paper towel.
- Cut each fennel bulb, including darker stalks, into ½-inch pieces. Place in colander and wash thoroughly to remove dirt. Drain well.
- After 40 minutes, remove cover from garlic cream. Add fennel and 3 cups water. Bring just to a boil, lower heat, and cover. Simmer for 40 minutes, until fennel is very soft.

- Transfer to blender or food processor and puree in several batches until very smooth. Return to pot. Add 1 teaspoon salt and finely ground white pepper to taste. Heat for several minutes until soup thickens a bit.
- Finely chop fennel fronds and scatter on soup. Serve hot or reheat before serving.

serves 6 to 8 (makes about 8 cups)

cornish hens stuffed with pancetta and sage

6 Cornish hens (1¼ pounds each)
¾ pound pancetta, cut into ¼-inch-thick slices
2 large bunches fresh sage

- Preheat oven to 375°.
- Remove giblets from hens, discarding livers or saving them for another use. Cut off wing tips and set aside. Wash hens thoroughly and pat dry with paper towels.
- Cut pancetta into ¼-inch cubes. Put in bowl.
- Remove leaves from sage, saving some whole sprigs for garnish and stock. Finely mince leaves, using a chef's knife or scissors. Add 6 tablespoons minced sage and several grindings of black pepper to pancetta. Mix well. Set aside ¼ cup.
- Fill cavity of each bird with remaining pancetta mixture until well packed. Rub salt into skin of each hen, then truss with kitchen string. Place in large shallow roasting pan and bake for 40 minutes.

- Meanwhile, prepare stock. Place giblets and wing tips in medium saucepan. Add reserved ¼ cup pancetta mixture, several leaves of sage, ½ teaspoon whole black peppercorns, and enough cold water to cover. Bring to a boil, skimming any foam. Cook over medium-low heat for 30 minutes. Strain stock into clean saucepan and continue cooking until reduced to 1¼ cups.
- Transfer hens to large platter. Serve whole or halved. Add stock to roasting pan and, scraping up browned bits, cook over high heat for 1 minute, or until sauce is a bit syrupy. Pour over hens. Serve immediately, garnished with remaining sage leaves.

serves 6

chopped broccoli rabe
and roasted red onions

4 large red onions (6 ounces each), unpeeled
3 tablespoons unsalted butter
2 large bunches broccoli rabe (1 pound each)

- Preheat oven to 375°.
- Peel 1 red onion and cut into very small dice (⅛ to ¼ inch). You will have approximately 1½ cups diced onion. Set aside.
- Cut remaining 3 unpeeled onions in half horizontally through the center. Spread 1 tablespoon butter on bottom of sturdy pie tin or other metal pan large enough to hold onion halves in one layer. Place onions cut side down in pan. Roast for 30 minutes. Press down with spatula to release any juices and carefully turn onions over. Roast for 25 minutes more.
- Meanwhile, trim ¼ inch from stems of broccoli rabe and discard. Wash broccoli rabe thoroughly, but do not dry. Cut stems into ¼-inch pieces and leafy parts into ½-inch pieces.
- In very large pot, melt remaining 2 tablespoons butter. Add diced onion and cook over medium heat for 5 minutes, until onion is soft but not brown.
- Add chopped broccoli rabe, 1 teaspoon salt, and ¼ cup water. Cook over high heat for 10 minutes, stirring frequently. Reduce heat to medium, cover, and cook for 10 minutes more. Uncover and cook for 1 minute to let any moisture evaporate. Broccoli rabe should be tender.
- Transfer broccoli rabe to platter and surround with roasted onion halves. Serve hot or at room temperature.

serves 6 (makes 6 cups)

crispy potatoes
with italian parsley

2 pounds small red new potatoes
3 tablespoons unsalted butter or chicken fat
1 small bunch fresh Italian parsley

- Peel potatoes. Quarter them and rinse several times under cold running water. Dry thoroughly with kitchen towel.
- Heat butter or fat in large skillet. Add potatoes and cook over medium-high heat until thoroughly browned on one side, about 10 minutes. Shake pan several times, but do not turn potatoes.
- After one side is browned, turn potatoes and cook for 5 minutes. Repeat this process twice more until potatoes are crisp on the outside and tender when pierced with the tip of a small sharp knife. Total cooking time will be about 25 minutes. Be careful not to let potatoes turn dark brown.
- Transfer potatoes to bowl. Coarsely chop parsley or snip with scissors so that you have ¼ cup. Toss with potatoes, adding salt and freshly ground black pepper to taste.
- Garnish with additional parsley, if desired. Serve immediately.

serves 6

chocolate zabaglione

12 extra-large eggs
10 tablespoons Kahlúa
½ cup good-quality unsweetened cocoa
 powder, * **plus more for sprinkling**

- Separate eggs. Cover whites and refrigerate. Save for another use, such as Cocoa Clouds, page 225.
- Bring large pot of water to a boil. Place large bowl over boiling water, making sure it doesn't touch water. Remove bowl.
- Place egg yolks and Kahlúa in bowl. Using a wire whisk, whip until blended. Place bowl over boiling water and immediately lower heat to medium. Whisking constantly, whip air into yolk mixture and cook for about 4 minutes, until yolks begin to thicken.
- Add cocoa powder a little at a time, still whisking constantly. Slowly add approximately ½ cup hot water (I use the water in the pot), continuing to whisk over medium to medium-high heat for about 5 minutes. Small bubbles will begin to appear, and mixture will thicken like pudding. Whisk vigorously until mixture is thick, dark, and very smooth.
- Spoon immediately into 6 small wineglasses or martini glasses. Serve warm or at room temperature, dusted with a little cocoa powder put through a sieve.

serves 6

 * I use Ghirardelli or Droste unsweetened
   cocoa powder.

Pork Tenderloin

Consommé with Poached Oysters and Nori

Pork Tenderloin with Hoisin and Sesame Seeds

Basmati Rice with Tangerines

Stir-Fried Asparagus, Shanxi Vinegar

Fresh Plums and Plum Wine Aspic

Take your guests on an Asian adventure. This dinner will astound them with its familiar ingredients made exotic — and the exotic made approachable.

Almost everything needed for this culinary trip is locally available, including wafer-thin sheets of nori, or roasted seaweed, now found in Asian markets and many supermarkets. The only unfamiliar product is Shanxi vinegar, a soon-to-be-trendy elixir from China, which has all the sex appeal of balsamic vinegar but is deeper and more complex, "brewed" from sorghum, barley, and peas.

Hoisin sauce, another imported Chinese condiment, with a salty-sweet-bitter flavor, imparts great personality to otherwise mild pork tenderloin. The only enemy of this disarmingly simple dish is overcooking.

Tangerines and roasted peanut oil add perfume to the rice. The last of the season's plums provide acidity and a regal purple backdrop to a sheer, shimmering gel of plum wine aspic.

menu notes

Prepare the plum wine aspic and plum wine reduction early in the day or even the day before. The remainder of the menu can be cooked in half an hour if all your ingredients are prepped and ready to go. The plums can be sliced and the dessert assembled just a few minutes before serving.

suggested hors d'oeuvres

Star Anise Tea Eggs (see page 121), Pickled Pink Shrimp (see page 102), and Shanghai Glazed Walnuts (see page 111).

grapenote

A glass of chilled dry sherry (a nutty one, such as Amontillado) or premium sake would make a special match for the consommé. An off-dry white would work well with the main course, but so too would a Cabernet Franc — a Côtes du Castillon from France or a domestic varietal from California (Ironstone or Alexander Vineyards) or Long Island (Alexander Schneider or Pindar). With dessert, a French eau-de-vie made from plums, such as Quetsch or Mirabelle, would be most elegant.

consommé with poached oysters and nori

4 cups chicken broth, homemade or low-sodium canned
16 large fresh oysters, shucked, with their liquor
4 sheets (8 by 7 inches) nori (roasted seaweed) *

- In large pot, bring chicken broth to a boil. Add a pinch of freshly ground white pepper. Lower heat to medium and cook for 5 minutes. Meanwhile, using scissors, cut nori into julienne strips that are 3½ inches long and ¼ inch wide.
- Slip oysters and oyster liquor into consommé. Cook for 1 minute. Add julienne nori. Immediately remove from heat. Using a slotted spoon, divide poached oysters and nori among 4 flat soup plates. Quickly strain hot broth through fine-mesh sieve into bowls. Serve immediately.

serves 4

*
Available in Asian markets and many supermarkets.

pork tenderloin with hoisin and sesame seeds

2-pound pork tenderloin
⅓ cup hoisin sauce
⅓ cup or more sesame seeds, toasted

- Preheat oven to 400°.
- Brush tenderloin with 3 tablespoons hoisin sauce, using a pastry brush or your hands.
- Roll pork in sesame seeds to coat evenly. Increase quantity if pork is not completely coated. Place on baking sheet that has been sprayed with nonstick vegetable spray. Roast for 20 to 25 minutes. Do not overcook.
- Meanwhile, in small pot, combine remaining hoisin sauce and 3 tablespoons cold water. Heat gently until sauce is smooth.
- Remove pork from oven. Let sit for 5 minutes before slicing. Add any pan juices to hoisin sauce. Serve meat with warm sauce.

serves 4

209

basmati rice
with tangerines

3 tangerines
1 tablespoon plus 1 teaspoon roasted peanut
  oil *
1 cup basmati rice

- Cut 1 tangerine through its equator and squeeze to get ¼ cup juice. Set aside.
- Remove rind from remaining 2 tangerines. Using a small sharp knife, remove as much of the white pith from the rind as possible. Finely mince enough of the resulting zest so that you have ½ teaspoon. Julienne the rest into very thin strips until you have ⅛ cup. Using a small sharp knife, cut tangerines into ½-inch pieces, removing any seeds. Set aside.
- In medium pot with cover, heat 1 tablespoon roasted peanut oil. Add rice and cook over medium heat for a few minutes, stirring frequently, until rice begins to take on a little color and smells nutty. Add minced tangerine zest, tangerine juice, 1¾ cups water, and 1 teaspoon salt.
- Cover pot and cook for 20 to 25 minutes until liquid is absorbed. Add tangerines and cook for 30 seconds, just to warm gently. Add freshly grated white pepper and salt to taste, if needed. Fluff with a large fork and transfer to platter. Drizzle with remaining 1 teaspoon oil and scatter julienne zest on top. Serve immediately.

serves 4

* I use Loriva, available in many supermarkets and specialty-food stores.

stir-fried asparagus, shanxi vinegar

1½ pounds thin to medium-thick fresh asparagus
2 tablespoons roasted sesame oil, plus more for serving
3 tablespoons Shanxi vinegar,* plus more for serving

- Cut woody portion from bottom of asparagus. Using a vegetable peeler, peel bottom two-thirds of asparagus. Cut into 2-inch lengths.
- In 12-inch nonstick skillet, heat sesame oil until hot. Add asparagus and stir-fry over high heat for 5 minutes, until asparagus begins to caramelize. Sprinkle with salt and freshly ground black pepper while cooking. After 5 minutes, add vinegar and cook over high heat for 1 minute. Lower heat to medium and cook for 2 minutes, until syrupy.

- Remove from heat. Transfer asparagus to serving platter. Adjust seasonings by adding a pinch of salt and a few drops of sesame oil or Shanxi vinegar. Serve immediately.

serves 4

*A remarkable product unlike anything else. You may substitute a combination of balsamic vinegar and dark soy sauce, but I suggest buying this vinegar. It lasts forever and has many culinary uses. The Chinese take a sip before meals and use it in everything from soups to vegetables. Available from L.T. Longevity Foods, (800) 98-VINEGAR.

211

fresh plums
and plum wine aspic

2 envelopes unflavored gelatin
3 cups Japanese plum wine
1½ pounds (5 or 6 large) ripe purple plums

- In small bowl, put 1 cup cold water and sprinkle on gelatin. Let sit for 1 minute, until dissolved.
- Place 1¾ cups plum wine in small saucepan. Bring to a boil.
- Add dissolved gelatin to boiling wine. Immediately remove from heat, whisking until gelatin is thoroughly dissolved.
- Spray 4 custard cups lightly with nonstick vegetable spray. Fill with plum wine–gelatin mixture. Let cool to room temperature. Place in refrigerator and chill for several hours, until jelled.
- Place remaining plum wine in small saucepan and cook over high heat for several minutes, until reduced to ¾ cup. Transfer to small bowl and chill.
- To serve, wash plums and cut into ⅛-inch-thick slices. Set aside 4 slices. In center of 4 large plates, arrange plums in an overlapping circular pattern. Spoon 2 tablespoons reduced wine over plums. Unmold aspics by quickly dipping in hot water and place in center of sliced plums. Cut reserved plum slices in half and place 2 half slices on top of each aspic. Drizzle with remaining reduced wine. Serve immediately.

serves 4

Deviled Beef Fillet

Carrot, Leek, and Chestnut Soup

Deviled Beef Fillet in Black Olive Crust

Spaghetti Squash with Black Sesame Seeds

Roasted Sweet Potatoes and Shiitakes

Whole Spiced Pears, Mulled Syrup

If this menu were a song, its title would be "Autumn in New York."

Its colors are shades of orange and brownish black: from a bright carrot soup to beef fillet enrobed in black olive puree. Ocher spaghetti squash is speckled with black sesame seeds. Orange sweet potatoes tossed with burnt sienna shiitakes are striking to look at and strike a delicious flavor chord on the palate.

Spiced pears, smelling like autumn, are poached whole in a sweet syrup gently mulled with aromatic spices.

Urbanely stylish, this impressive dinner has only fifteen ingredients and is a minor work of art.

menu notes

The soup and dessert can be made a day ahead or the morning of your party. If you have two ovens, you can prepare the main course and the accompaniments at the same time (at two different temperatures). If you have only one oven, prepare the squash and sweet potato dish one hour before you put the meat in the oven and reheat five to ten minutes (covered) with the fillet. An optional platter of Cocoa Clouds (see page 225), warm from the oven, makes a color-coordinated treat to be served with coffee.

suggested hors d'oeuvres

Brie Croustades with Black Caviar (black; see page 222); The World's Best Pimiento Spread (orange; see page 116), served on Garlic Croûtes (see page 109).

grapenote

To complement the inherent sweetness in this soup, you'll want a white wine with good fruit and a whisper of sweetness. Possibilities include Vouvray; a Riesling (Willie Loos from Germany or Allan Scott from Australia); or a fresh, fruity California blend such as Ironstone Symphonie (a combo of Muscat and white Grenache). The main course deserves a serious Rhône red, such as Cros de la Mure Gigondas, or a Chateauneuf from a good producer such as Guigal, Domaine du Pegau, or Vieux Télègraphe. Serve an ice-cold glass of Poire Williams with dessert.

carrot, leek, and chestnut soup

1½ pounds fresh baby carrots, preferably organic
1 large bunch leeks (about 1½ pounds)
1 10-ounce can whole chestnuts in water

- Peel carrots. Trim leeks so that only very pale green part remains. Save darker green tops for later. Cut leeks in half lengthwise and wash thoroughly.
- Chop carrots and leeks into ½-inch pieces. Drain chestnuts and rinse under cold water.
- Place all ingredients in large pot. Add 6 cups water and 1 teaspoon salt. Bring to a boil. Lower heat to medium, cover, and cook for 1 hour.
- Using a slotted spoon, transfer solid pieces to food processor and process until very, very smooth. Reserve 4 cups cooking liquid.
- Return pureed mixture to pot. Slowly whisk in reserved cooking liquid. Add salt and freshly ground pepper to taste. Set aside.
- Cut dark green tops of leeks into very fine julienne. Cook in small saucepan of boiling salted water until soft, about 5 minutes. Drain.
- Reheat soup. Ladle into flat soup plates. Garnish with cooked julienne leeks.

serves 6 or more (makes about 7½ cups)

deviled beef fillet in black olive crust

2½-pound beef tenderloin (10 by 4 inches)
1¼ cups prepared black olive tapenade or olivada *
1½ cups seasoned dried bread crumbs

- Preheat oven to 475°.
- Tie fillet with kitchen string at ½-inch intervals. Season liberally with salt and freshly ground black pepper. Place in heavy, shallow metal roasting pan. Roast for 10 minutes, turning once.
- Coat roast thickly with 1 cup black olive puree, then with bread crumbs, being sure to cover completely. Return to roasting pan. Continue to cook until desired doneness: 25 minutes for rare, 30 to 35 minutes for medium.
- Meanwhile, put remaining ¼ cup black olive puree in small saucepan. Add 1 cup water. Bring to a boil. Cook until slightly thickened. Season with salt (if needed) and pepper.
- Remove meat from oven and let rest for 5 minutes. Add any pan juices to saucepan. Cut fillet into ¾-inch-thick slices. Pour sauce around meat. Serve immediately.

serves 6

* Available in many supermarkets and specialty-food stores.

spaghetti squash
with black sesame seeds

2 spaghetti squash (2 pounds each)
3 tablespoons unsalted butter, at room temper-
ature
2 tablespoons black sesame seeds

- Preheat oven to 400°.
- Place squash on baking sheet with a little water. Roast for 1 hour.
- Cut squash in half lengthwise and remove seeds. Place cut side down on baking sheet. Cook for 20 to 30 minutes, or until soft.
- Using a large fork, scrape flesh of squash to obtain spaghetti-like strands, being sure to dig deep so that you get all the flesh. You will have about 6 cups. Place squash in bowl. Add butter and salt and finely ground black pepper to taste. Toss well. Serve immediately or reheat gently. Sprinkle with black sesame seeds before serving.

serves 6

roasted sweet potatoes
and shiitakes

2½ pounds (3 or 4 large) sweet potatoes
8 ounces medium shiitake mushrooms
3 tablespoons lemon oil *

- Preheat oven to 400°.
- Peel potatoes using a vegetable peeler. Cut into ¾-inch cubes.
- Trim bottom half of shiitake mushroom stems and discard, leaving caps and upper half of stems attached.
- Place potatoes and shiitakes on baking sheet. Toss with 2 tablespoons lemon oil and 2 table-spoons water. Sprinkle lightly with salt.
- Bake for 1 hour. Potatoes will be tender and lightly browned. (Add a little water or oil during baking if potatoes begin to stick.) Using a spat-ula, turn several times during baking.
- Transfer potatoes and shiitakes to platter. (Or, if serving later, leave on baking sheet and reheat potatoes and shiitakes in a 475° oven for 5 to 6 minutes, or until hot.)
- Drizzle with remaining 1 tablespoon lemon oil. Add salt and freshly ground black pepper to taste.

serves 6

* I use Colavita, available in many supermarkets and specialty-food stores.

215

whole spiced pears,
mulled syrup

2 tablespoons mixed pickling spice
1 cup sugar
**6 large firm Bartlett or Comice pears, with
 stems (½ pound each)**

- Place 8 cups water in large pot with cover. Add
  pickling spice and sugar. Bring to a boil.
- Peel pears with vegetable peeler, leaving stems
  intact. Cut a small slice from bottom of each
  pear so that it can stand upright.
- Place pears in boiling liquid and lower heat to
  medium. Cover and cook for 50 to 55 minutes,
  until pears are tender. Let cool in liquid.
- Remove 3 cups poaching liquid and place in
  small saucepan. Cover pears and refrigerate
  until ready to use.
- Cook poaching liquid over medium heat until
  reduced to ¾ cup syrup.
- To serve, place chilled pears in flat soup plates.
  Pour some poaching liquid in each. Drizzle
  with syrup.

serves 6

holiday celebrations

While this book is suitable

all year round, you may appreciate it most during the holidays. These celebration menus may be more elaborate than others, but it is precisely on such important days that we choose to focus our hearts and minds on putting a great meal on the table.

I fear we may lose these pleasures as our lives become more hurried and harried, so my gift toward the preservation of these holiday celebrations is menus that are easy to make, delicious to eat, and beautiful to look at — all accomplished while reducing the time spent at the supermarket.

Of course, the calendar includes holidays other than those listed here. For Father's Day, for example, try my menu called Beef Shank (see page 148). For an all-fish dinner on Christmas Eve, try my Shrimp and Monkfish (see page 131). And for Oktoberfest (or a Halloween meal for adults), there's a fall dinner featuring Deviled Beef Fillet (see page 213) with all the colors of the season.

The Newish-Jewish Holiday dinner here is appropriate for Rosh Hashanah, Hanukkah, any Sabbath meal, and even Passover. My New Year's Day menu provides a festive meal for an open house and is special enough for anyone's birthday.

Begin each meal with your favorite hors d'oeuvres, or the ones I suggest with each meal. Serve these while your guests gather, along with appropriate libations (see Chapter 4).

All the menus are easily doubled.

As the late, great chef Fernand Point of the fabled three-star restaurant La Pyramide in France said, "At table people enjoy one another above all when one has managed to enchant them."

Now's your chance.

220

New Year's Day

Brie Croustades with Black Caviar

Oysters, Black Radish, Chipolata Sausages

A Duet of Cured Salmons:
 Brown Sugar–Tarragon Gravlax
 Mild-Brine Lenrimmad Lax

Potato "Tortilla"

Champagne Sorbet, Blood Orange Salad

Cocoa Clouds

New Year's Day for us means an open house, and every year the same toasts are offered: to health in the coming year; to my birthday; and to my father's winning touchdown in the Rose Bowl, New Year's Day 1941.

The versatility of this particular buffet menu makes it possible for guests to come and go as they please, all day long, year after year. However, it also makes a gracious four-course sit-down affair. Both are equally celebratory.

menu notes

Prepare the gravlax and brine-cured salmon two days before your party. Prepare the sorbet the day before. The remainder of the meal should be prepared the same day.

suggested hors d'oeuvres

Two quick and easy ones — Cherry Bombs (see page 99) and Prosciutto and Melon Batons (see page 97).

grapenote

A festive mode of ushering in the New Year is with sparklers all the way. Begin with the affordable Iron Horse, Piper Sonoma, or Domaine Chandon. For dessert, switch to a semidry version, such as Schramsberg Crémant. All are from California.

221

brie croustades
with black caviar

½ pound double-cream Brie cheese
3 extra-large eggs
½ cup best-quality black caviar: sevruga, osetra,
   or beluga

- Cut rind from cheese using a small sharp knife. Discard rind. Let cheese sit at room temperature for 30 minutes.
- Preheat oven to 350°.
- Put eggs in bowl of food processor. Cut cheese into 1-inch pieces and add to eggs. Process until very smooth and thick, about 1 minute.
- Spray 2 12-cup 2-inch diameter nonstick muffin tins with nonstick vegetable spray. Spoon 1 tablespoon cheese mixture into each muffin cup. Bake for 9 to 10 minutes, until croustades are well puffed and golden.
- Let croustades sit for 1 minute, then remove from tins using a small flexible spatula. Top each slightly warm (or room-temperature) croustade with 1 teaspoon caviar. (Before topping with caviar, croustades may be rewarmed. Place in pie tin, cover with foil, and heat for 3 minutes in 325° oven.) Serve within 20 minutes.
- *Optional garnish:* Cook 1 extra-large egg in boiling water for about 8 minutes, until hard-boiled. Let cool. Finely chop egg white and sieve the egg yolk. Sprinkle either or both over caviar-topped croustades.

makes 24

oysters, black radish,
chipolata sausages

1 large black radish or daikon, in one piece
   (12 ounces)
72 fresh oysters on the half shell, well chilled *
36 chipolata, ** **or 24 small breakfast sausages**
   (1 ounce each)

- Peel radish. Cut into ⅛-inch-thick slices and then into very fine julienne. Soak in ice water until ready to use.
- Make 6 small mounds of kosher salt around each of 6 large plates. Place 1 oyster on the half shell on each mound. Drain julienne radish and pat dry. Place some on each oyster.
- In large nonstick skillet, quickly cook sausages until browned and hot. Put 3 sausages on each of 12 short skewers. Serve alongside oysters with small oyster forks. Pass the pepper mill.

serves 12

* Have your fish store open the oysters.

** Tiny fresh pork sausages (½-inch in diameter), a specialty of northern Italy. Available in many Italian butcher shops.

a duet of cured salmons:

brown sugar–tarragon gravlax

2½-pound side of salmon, preferably center cut, skin on
2 large bunches fresh tarragon
⅓ cup light brown sugar

- Remove all small bones from fish with tweezers and pat dry. Coarsely chop leaves and stems of 1 bunch tarragon. In small bowl, combine ¼ cup kosher salt, 1 teaspoon coarsely ground white pepper, brown sugar, and chopped tarragon. Rub mixture into salmon flesh. Cover tightly with plastic wrap. Weight down with cast-iron skillets, large cans, or other heavy objects. Refrigerate for 48 hours. Turn after 24 hours, drain off any liquid, wrap again, and weight down.
- Before serving, scrape off seasonings using the blade of a sharp knife. Slice very thinly on the bias, as if it were smoked salmon. Use a long, sharp, narrow knife to gently lift slices off the skin.
- Place slices in an overlapping pattern on platter or individual plates. Chop leaves only of remaining 1 bunch tarragon and scatter over gravlax. Wrap plates tightly in plastic and let sit for 1 hour until ready to serve.

serves 12

mild-brine lenrimmad lax

2½-pound side of salmon, preferably center cut, skin on

- Remove all small bones from fish with tweezers. Rub ⅔ cup kosher salt into salmon flesh. Cover and refrigerate overnight. The next day, rinse fish under cold water.
- *To make brine:* Boil 4 quarts water and 1½ cups kosher salt. Let cool. Place salmon in large container and cover completely with brine. Weight down and refrigerate for 48 hours.
- When ready to serve, remove from brine and pat dry. Serve sliced very thinly on the bias.

serves 12

potato "tortilla"

3 pounds waxy, thin-skinned potatoes
2 sticks unsalted butter
24 extra-large eggs

- Preheat oven to 350°.
- Peel potatoes and slice paper-thin with a thin-bladed sharp knife.
- Melt 7 tablespoons butter in each of 2 large nonstick skillets. Divide potatoes into 2 equal portions and add to skillets, sprinkling with salt and freshly ground black pepper. Sauté over medium-high heat for 1 to 2 minutes. Cover skillets, lower heat, and cook for 16 to 18 minutes, until potatoes are tender and golden but not too soft.
- Meanwhile, beat eggs well with electric mixer. Add 2 teaspoons salt and some pepper. Using remaining 2 tablespoons butter, grease bottoms and sides of 2 10-inch tight-fitting springform pans.
- When potatoes are done, transfer with slotted spoon to pans. Add any pan juices from potatoes to beaten eggs and mix briefly. Pour over potatoes.
- Place pans on 1 or 2 baking sheets and bake for 20 to 25 minutes, until set and golden.
- Let sit for 5 minutes. Loosen sides of tortillas with a knife or flexible rubber spatula. Remove from springform. Cut each tortilla into 12 wedges. Serve hot or at room temperature.
- *Alternative presentation:* Cut into small squares and serve at room temperature as an hors d'oeuvre for a cocktail party.

serves 12

champagne sorbet, blood orange salad

3 cups sugar
2 bottles brut champagne, well chilled
18 small or medium blood oranges

- Put sugar and 3 cups water in medium sauce-pan. Heat for a few minutes, until liquid becomes crystal clear (it will be cloudy at first) and small bubbles begin to form. Remove from heat. You will have 4½ cups simple syrup. Let cool. This will last indefinitely refrigerated in a covered jar.
- *To make champagne sorbet:* Pour champagne and 3 cups simple syrup into electric ice cream maker. Freeze for 50 minutes or according to manufacturer's instructions. (This mixture will take longer to freeze than other ice cream mix-tures because of its high percentage of alcohol.)
- *To make blood orange salad:* Grate rind of enough oranges to make 3 tablespoons grated zest. Set aside.
- Using a small sharp knife, cut rind and all white pith from oranges. Cut oranges into slices slightly less than ¼ inch thick. Place in large bowl with any juices. Add 1 cup simple syrup. Cover and refrigerate until cold.
- To serve, place 8 orange slices and several table-spoons syrup in each of 12 flat soup plates or wine goblets. Top with a scoop of sorbet and garnish with grated orange zest.

serves 12

cocoa clouds

6 extra-large egg whites
6 tablespoons good-quality unsweetened cocoa powder
6 tablespoons superfine sugar

- Preheat oven to 250°.
- In bowl of electric mixer, beat egg whites with a pinch of salt until they form soft peaks. Mix cocoa and sugar together and slowly add to whites. Beat until stiff peaks form.
- Place a piece of parchment paper on baking sheet. Drop a heaping 1½ tablespoons batter on sheet to make each cookie. Bake for 1 hour. Let cool on sheet.

makes 28 cookies

225

Valentine's Day

Wrinkled Potatoes with Salmon Caviar

"Hearts" of Bibb, White Balsamic Vinaigrette

Red Snapper in Champagne Sauce

Broccoli-Ginger Puree

Jasmine Rice with Edible Flowers

Puits d'Amour

What better way to celebrate this day than with "hearts" and "flowers" and other edible expressions of love.

Tiny potatoes filled with an unexpected cottage cheese cream (more romantic than the usual sour cream) lend a lightened counterpoint to coral-hued caviar. The rice is strewn with edible flowers. Only the hearts of Bibb are used for the salad.

Dessert — puff pastry "wells of love" dusted with confectioners' sugar and filled with thick raspberry jam or red currant jelly — is named after the 1843 comic opera *Le Puits d'Amour*.

menu notes

Prepare the dessert several hours before serving.

Make the Broccoli-Ginger Puree before dinner and reheat. You may boil the potatoes for the appetizer early, then "wrinkle" them ten minutes before service. While the potatoes are boiling, prepare the filling and refrigerate.

Prep the salad a few minutes before serving. Simmer the rice while you and your guests are eating the first course. Sauté the red snapper right before service.

suggested hors d'oeuvre

Smoked Salmon Kisses (see page 100).

grapenote

Make a toast to romance with Mirabelle Brut Rosé from California, or splurge with the French Billecart-Salmon Brut Rosé. With the snapper, open a dry, crisp Chardonnay such as Jacob's Creek from Australia, or splurge again with Pernand-Vergelesses, a French white Burgundy.

Save a glass of bubbly per person to make a special Kir Imperial to accompany dessert. Just add a bit of good framboise (from Mathilde or Lucien Jacob) to each glass.

wrinkled potatoes with salmon caviar

1 cup 2 percent small-curd cottage cheese
18 tiny white potatoes (1 to 1¼ inches in diameter; about 1¼ pounds)
6 tablespoons salmon caviar

- Puree cottage cheese in food processor until very, very smooth. Transfer to small bowl. Cover and refrigerate until ready to use.
- Scrub potatoes very well. Put in medium pot and add water to cover by 1 inch. Add ½ cup kosher salt and bring to a boil. Cover pot partially and cook over high heat for 15 to 20 minutes, or until tender.
- Drain potatoes and return to pot. Cook, uncovered, over low heat, shaking pot back and forth frequently, until potatoes are dry and skins are slightly wrinkled. This will take about 10 minutes.
- Cut a small x in top of each potato and squeeze to push potato up a bit. Place ½ tablespoon pureed cottage cheese on each warm potato and top with 1 teaspoon salmon caviar. Serve immediately, 3 potatoes per person.

serves 6

"hearts" of bibb, white balsamic vinaigrette

6 medium heads Bibb lettuce (6 ounces each)
¾ cup plus 2 tablespoons white balsamic vinegar *
6 tablespoons good-quality olive oil

- Wash lettuce, leaving heads intact. Cut each head lengthwise into quarters.
- Place ¾ cup vinegar in small saucepan. Cook over high heat for several minutes, until reduced by one-half. You will have 6 tablespoons. Let cool and set aside.
- In blender or food processor, put olive oil, remaining 2 tablespoons vinegar, and 1 tablespoon cold water. Blend until incorporated. Dressing will be thick and creamy. Add salt and freshly ground black pepper to taste, and blend again.
- Place 4 wedges of lettuce, overlapping slightly, on each of 6 dinner plates. Pour dressing over greens. Drizzle 1 tablespoon reduced balsamic vinegar around wedges. Using a pepper mill, grind black pepper on lettuce and plate. Serve immediately.

serves 6

* Available in most supermarkets. A good brand is Carrara, imported from Italy and distributed by Goya Foods.

red snapper
in champagne sauce

6 8-ounce red snapper fillets, skin on
8 tablespoons unsalted butter, well chilled
1 cup brut champagne or sparkling wine

- Remove any bones from fish. Season fillets lightly with salt and freshly ground white pepper.
- Melt 2 tablespoons butter in each of 2 large non-stick skillets big enough to accommodate fish in one layer.
- Place fish flesh side down in melted butter. Cook over medium heat until opaque and lightly golden. Turn fish over with spatula and increase heat a bit. Cook skin side down until skin begins to crisp. When fish is cooked, transfer to platter.
- Combine pan juices in 1 pan. Quickly add champagne, turn heat to high, and reduce to 1/3 cup. Reduce heat to very low. Cut remaining 4 tablespoons butter into small bits and add to pan, whisking until sauce is thick and creamy. Add a pinch of salt and freshly ground white pepper. Drizzle over fish. Serve immediately.

serves 6

broccoli-ginger puree

4-inch piece fresh ginger
1½ large heads broccoli (2 pounds)
6 tablespoons heavy cream

- Peel ginger with a small sharp knife, then grate on large holes of box grater. Put grated ginger in paper towel and squeeze juice into small cup. You will have about 1½ tablespoons juice. Set aside.
- Bring large pot of salted water to a boil. Cut stems from broccoli, peel, and cut into small pieces. Cut remaining broccoli into florets.
- Add stems to boiling water and cook over medium heat for 5 minutes. Add florets and cook for 8 minutes more, or until broccoli is tender but still bright green.
- Drain broccoli in colander and place in bowl of food processor. Process until broccoli is in small pieces. With the motor running, add ginger juice and cream. Process until very smooth. Add salt and freshly ground black pepper to taste.
- When ready to serve, heat puree in saucepan, adding more cream or water if too thick. Serve immediately.

serves 6

jasmine rice
with edible flowers

12 ounces (about 1¾ cups) jasmine rice
2 cups chicken broth, homemade or low-sodium
canned
12 small edible mixed flowers *

- Rinse rice. In medium saucepan with cover, bring chicken stock and 1½ cups water to a boil. Add rice and bring to a boil again. Cover saucepan and simmer for 20 minutes, or until all the water has been absorbed. Remove from heat and let sit for 3 to 4 minutes.
- Meanwhile, tear petals from flowers so that you have small colorful pieces that look like confetti. You will have about ⅓ to ½ cup petals. Set aside.
- Remove cover from rice and fluff with a large fork. Add salt to taste. Do not add pepper, as the flowers have a peppery taste.
- Transfer rice to large platter. Scatter flowers over rice. Serve immediately.

serves 6

> * Available in many farmer's markets and in the produce section of some supermarkets. You can use a mixture of snapdragons, marigolds, baby carnations, and nasturtiums, for example.

puits d'amour

2 sheets frozen puff pastry (17¼ ounces),
thawed
⅓ cup confectioners' sugar
6 tablespoons best-quality seedless raspberry
jam or red currant jelly

- Preheat oven to 425°.
- While puff pastry dough is cold, roll out each sheet with rolling pin until it is ½ inch larger in width and length. With a 2½-inch round cookie cutter, cut 12 circles from each sheet, for a total of 24. Prick in several places with a fork.
- Cut out centers of 12 circles with 1¼-inch cookie cutter and discard. Brush resulting rings with a little water. Using a spatula, place inverted rings on top of uncut circles. Be careful not to handle sides of cut dough, as pastry will puff unevenly or be lopsided if it is handled too much.
- Place circles on large baking sheet. Bake for 15 minutes, until pastry is well puffed (about 2 inches high) and golden brown. Let cool completely.
- Dust with confectioners' sugar put through a sieve, so that the tops of the pastry rings are thoroughly covered. Very carefully spoon ½ tablespoon jam or jelly into center of each. These are best eaten the same day they are made.

makes 12 pastries

Easter

Crème Fraîche Garlic Dip, Teardrop Tomatoes

Asparagus Mimosa

Lamb Spiced with Ginger and Mint

Glazed Radishes, Braised Leaves

Baked Shallot Custard

Red Papaya Tart, Papaya Sorbet with Papaya "Pepper"

This menu is stylish in a smart, pleasing way.

Stylish: It incorporates some terrific ingredients now readily found in supermarkets, such as crème fraîche and white asparagus, and trendy elements of ginger, mint, and inexpensive cuts of meat.

Smart: Dessert is a twofer, both a tart and a sorbet. Smarter still is what you can do with papaya seeds. Dry them overnight in a 250° oven, then grind in a spice grinder to sprinkle on the sorbet as an enigmatic flavor enhancer.

Pleasing: The food is delicious as all get-out and makes a beautiful presentation — colorful as an Easter parade.

menu notes

Marinate the lamb at least eight hours before cooking. The asparagus and shallot custards can be made several hours before dinner and warmed in the oven. The sorbet and papaya "pepper" can be made the day before. The papaya tart can be assembled right before dinner and baked while you are eating the main course.

suggested hors d'oeuvres

In addition to the teardrop tomatoes, you may also begin with Open-Faced Cucumber-Feta Cocktail Sandwiches (see page 98).

grapenote

With the first course, you need a refreshing Sauvignon Blanc, such as Casa Julia from Chile or Selwyn River from New Zealand. A bit more expensive is a classic Sancerre or Pouilly-Fumé. Merlot is a natural with lamb. There are wonderful inexpensive pickings from the south of France. Or experience the Philippe Lorraine offering from Napa or, if you can find it, a fabulous Italian Merlot made in a Bordeaux style, called Bonzara di Bonacciara. A small glass of Muscat de Beaumes de Venise, slightly chilled, would be delicious with dessert.

crème fraîche garlic dip, teardrop tomatoes

8 ounces crème fraîche
1 medium clove garlic
4 cups tiny red and yellow cherry tomatoes

- Place crème fraîche in small bowl. Push garlic through press and add to crème fraîche with ½ teaspoon kosher salt and a grinding of white pepper. Stir to blend. Makes about 1 cup. Cover and refrigerate for at least 1 hour.
- When ready to serve, wash tomatoes, leaving stems intact. Dry well. Place tomatoes on large decorative platter. Place bowl of crème fraîche on platter. Have your guests dip tomatoes into crème fraîche and then into a small ramekin of kosher salt, if desired.

serves 6 to 8

asparagus mimosa

4 extra-large eggs
10 tablespoons unsalted butter
42 thick green and/or white asparagus

- Boil eggs for 10 minutes. Rinse under cold water and peel. Reserve.
- *To clarify butter:* Melt butter in small heavy saucepan over very low heat. Remove pan from heat and let stand for 5 minutes. Skim foam. Let stand for 5 minutes more and slowly pour clear butter into small bowl, leaving behind milky solids in bottom of pan. You will have about 6 tablespoons clarified butter.
- Trim off tough ends of asparagus. Cook in large pot of boiling salted water until tender, about 5 to 6 minutes.
- Meanwhile, separate egg yolks from whites. Mash yolks with fork and chop whites finely. In small saucepan over low heat, warm clarified butter. Add egg yolks and whites and salt and freshly ground black papper to taste. Keep warm.
- When asparagus are done, drain immediately and arrange on platter. Pour clarified butter mixture over them. The entire dish can be assembled, refrigerated for a few hours, and then reheated, covered, in 375° oven for 15 minutes.

serves 6

lamb spiced with ginger and mint

6-inch piece fresh ginger (about 5 ounces)
1 large bunch fresh mint
4½-pound leg of lamb, butt half, bone in

- Peel ginger using a small sharp knife. Cut into large chunks and place in bowl of food processor. Divide mint into 2 bunches. Wrap one in plastic and refrigerate for later use. Remove leaves from remaining mint and add to ginger. Add 1 teaspoon salt and ½ teaspoon cracked black pepper. Process until a coarse paste forms. Do not overprocess, as you don't want the result to be watery.
- Rub ginger-mint mixture over lamb. Pack some tightly on top of lamb to form a crust. Place in large plastic bag and secure tightly. Marinate in refrigerator for 8 hours.
- When ready to cook, let lamb sit at room temperature for 30 minutes.
- Preheat oven to 375°.
- Using a sharp knife, score top of lamb lightly with lines 1 inch apart. Place in heavy shallow roasting pan and roast for about 18 minutes per pound, or until internal temperature is 145° for medium-rare. You may need to drain fat from pan halfway through cooking.
- Transfer lamb to cutting board. Let rest for 5 minutes, then carve as desired. Serve immediately, garnished with reserved mint.

serves 6 (about 2½ pounds meat)

glazed radishes, braised leaves

4 bunches red radishes with leaves (about ½ pound each)
4 tablespoons unsalted butter
1 tablespoon sugar

- Wash radishes. Using a small sharp knife, remove stems with leaves. Wash leaves well in colander under cold water.
- Cut large radishes in half lengthwise through stem end. Leave smaller radishes whole.
- Place radishes in medium pot. Add just enough cold water to cover and a large pinch of salt. Bring to a boil and cook over high heat for 5 minutes. Radishes will lose some of their color. Remove with slotted spoon. Reserve cooking water.
- In 12-inch nonstick skillet, melt butter. Add radishes and cook over medium heat for 2 minutes. Add sugar and continue to cook for about 5 minutes, until radishes are tender and lightly glazed.
- Meanwhile, bring cooking water to a boil. Add radish greens and cook for 1 minute. Using slotted spoon, put cooked greens in pan with radishes for the last minute of cooking. Add salt to taste, stir well, and serve immediately. This can be made ahead of time and reheated.

serves 6

baked shallot custard

4 ounces medium shallots
1½ cups heavy cream
3 extra-large eggs

- Preheat oven to 350°.
- Peel shallots and trim ends. Place cream and shallots in small saucepan with cover. Bring just to a boil. Reduce heat to very low and cover saucepan. Simmer for 45 minutes, until shallots are very soft. Uncover and remove from heat. Let cool for 15 minutes.
- Place cream and shallots in bowl of food processor with 1 teaspoon salt and a pinch of freshly ground white pepper. Process until very smooth. Add eggs and process until just incorporated. Do not overprocess, or cream will thicken.
- Ladle mixture into 6 5-ounce custard cups, ramekins, or timbales that have been sprayed with nonstick vegetable spray. Place cups in deep baking dish. Pour boiling water in baking dish to come almost all the way up sides of cups.
- Bake for 35 minutes, or until custard is set. Do not overcook. Remove from oven. Let cool for 5 minutes and remove from water bath. Carefully run a small knife around edges of custards to help separate them from cups. Turn out onto platter or individual plates. These can be made ahead of time and refrigerated in their cups, then warmed in a hot-water bath, covered, in 375° oven for 15 minutes.

makes 6 custards

red papaya tart, papaya sorbet with papaya "pepper"

3 pounds tropical red papayas *
¾ cup sugar
1 sheet frozen puff pastry (about 8½ ounces)

- *To make sorbet:* Peel 1½ pounds papayas. Remove seeds and set aside. Cut papaya into chunks and puree in food processor. You should have 1½ cups puree.
- In small saucepan, heat 1 cup water and ½ cup sugar. Cook over medium heat for 5 minutes, then remove from heat. Add puree, mix, and chill well. Freeze in ice cream maker according to manufacturer's directions.
- *To make papaya "pepper":* Preheat oven to 250°. Wash papaya seeds and dry, being sure to remove any fibers. Place on baking sheet. Bake for at least 6 hours to dry completely. Let cool, then grind in spice grinder.
- *To make tart:* Allow pastry to defrost at room temperature. Preheat oven to 400°.
- Roll out pastry with rolling pin and fit into 9½-inch removable-bottom fluted pie tin, pressing pastry up the sides. Remove any excess pastry.

- Peel remaining 1½ pounds papayas and cut lengthwise into ¼-inch-thick slices. Prick bottom of pastry with fork. Sprinkle with 1 tablespoon sugar. Place papaya slices in overlapping pattern to cover bottom completely. Sprinkle with 2 tablespoons sugar. Bake for 30 minutes, then remove from oven.
- Preheat broiler.
- Cover edges of tart with aluminum foil. Sprinkle papaya with remaining 1 tablespoon sugar and put under broiler for 1 minute. Remove immediately. Let cool before serving.
- Cut tart into wedges and serve with sorbet alongside. Sprinkle sorbet with papaya "pepper."

serves 6

* Tropical red papayas are sometimes known as strawberry papayas. Some fruit stores sell them in wedges, like watermelon.

Note: This recipe was inspired by friend and food writer Barbara Kafka.

Mother's Day

Eleven-Inch Parmesan Straws

Chilled Asparagus Bisque with Crabmeat

Pistachio-Crusted Salmon

Spring Vegetables à la Vapeur

Very Lemony Mashed Potatoes

Honeydew and Blueberries: Mixed Fruit Sorbet, Blueberry Drizzle

One of my favorites, this is a foolproof meal that pleases almost everyone — which is getting more difficult these days, as so many people have such personal eating regimes.

The menu is spring incarnate, from bright greens and pinks to pale jade and sky blue. It's full of flavor and surprises: fat-free vegetables taste rich and buttery; creamy mashed potatoes taste light and lemony. And the dessert is a triple-header — fruit, sorbet, and syrup all in one.

To spend as much time with your mother as you can, and as little time in the kitchen as possible, prepare the menu in stages.

menu notes

Parmesan straws can be made way in advance and frozen. Or make them a day ahead and store them in an airtight container. Serve them as an hors d'oeuvre or with the soup course. Both the soup and the sorbet can be made a day ahead.

One hour prior to the meal, make the potatoes, then reheat them before serving. The fish can bake and the vegetables steam while you enjoy your soup.

suggested hors d'oeuvres

If you are serving the Parmesan straws with the soup, choose one simple hors d'oeuvre, such as Zucchini Thimbles with Goat Cheese and Chili Oil (see page 235).

grapenote

Even though it's a bit steep, Mölderbosch Sauvignon Blanc from South Africa makes an extraordinary match for the soup. With the salmon, try an unexpected Pinot Noir: Fleur de Carneros or Talus for the budget; Torii Mor or Panther Creek (both from Oregon's Willamette Valley) otherwise. With dessert, your mother might like a cup of tea.

eleven-inch
parmesan straws

6 sheets phyllo dough
4 tablespoons unsalted butter, melted
**1 cup freshly grated good-quality Parmesan
   cheese**

- Preheat oven to 350°.
- Cut phyllo dough in half widthwise. Brush each half lightly with melted butter, using a pastry brush. Sprinkle each with 2 teaspoons cheese. Roll up tightly like a cigar, so that it is 11 inches long and ½ inch wide. Brush the tops with more melted butter and sprinkle evenly with 1½ to 2 teaspoons cheese.
- Place on ungreased baking sheet. Bake for 10 to 15 minutes, until golden brown and crisp. Serve at room temperature.

makes 12

chilled asparagus bisque
with crabmeat

2 pounds fresh asparagus
2 cups clam juice
½ pound fresh jumbo lump crabmeat

- Wash asparagus. Snap off woody bottoms of stems. Cut into 1-inch lengths.
- In medium-large nonreactive pot, put clam juice, 2 cups water, and any juice from crabmeat. Bring to a boil and add asparagus. Lower heat and simmer about 10 minutes, until tender. Do not overcook, or asparagus will turn an unpleasant gray-green color.
- Transfer contents in several batches to blender. Puree until very smooth. This will take several minutes. Add salt and freshly ground white pepper to taste. Chill for 2 hours, or until very cold.
- To serve, pour into chilled soup cups or flat soup plates and top with crabmeat.

serves 6 (makes about 6 cups)

pistachio-crusted salmon

3-pound side of salmon, skin removed
1 heaping cup (5 ounces) shelled unsalted
  pistachios
½ cup or more prepared pesto *

- Preheat oven to 375°.
- Using tweezers or your fingers, remove any bones running down fish. Place fish on baking sheet.
- Put pistachios in bowl of food processor and process until coarsely ground. Do not over-process, as you want small, discernible pieces, not powder.
- Spread ½ cup pesto thickly on top of salmon, draining off most of the oil from the pesto as you go. You may need more pesto if salmon is not thickly and completely covered.
- Pack ground pistachios on pesto to cover fish evenly. You should have a thick nut crust. Remove any loose nuts that have fallen on the baking sheet to prevent burning.
- Bake for 22 to 24 minutes, or until desired done-ness. Do not overcook. It is important that the fish be juicy and moist.
- Let cool for 2 to 3 minutes. Using a very sharp knife, cut into 6 to 8 portions. Serve immediately, pouring any pan juices over fish.

serves 6 to 8

* Contadina works beautifully in this recipe. Available in the refrigerated section of most supermarkets.

spring vegetables à la vapeur

¾ pound fresh snow peas
¾ pound fresh green beans
3 medium zucchini (about 1 pound)

- Remove little "tails" from snow peas. Trim ends of green beans. Using a small sharp knife, cut beans in half lengthwise. Wash snow peas and beans in colander and drain thoroughly.
- Wash zucchini and dry. Cut 2 zucchini into ⅓-inch cubes. (The best way to do this is to cut the zucchini lengthwise into 3 slices, cut each slice lengthwise into 3 pieces, and then cut crosswise into small cubes.)
- Cut remaining 1 zucchini into 1-inch pieces and place in small saucepan. Cover with water and add ¼ teaspoon salt. Bring to a boil. Lower heat and cook for 15 minutes, until zucchini is very soft.
- Using a slotted spoon, transfer cooked zucchini to bowl of food processor, reserving cooking water. Process until very smooth and creamy, adding almost all the cooking water. The sauce will be thick. You will have about ⅔ cup.
- Bring large pot of water fitted with steamer basket to a boil. Place snow peas and green beans in basket. Place zucchini cubes on top. Cover and steam for 7 minutes.
- Lightly salt vegetables and transfer to platter. Cover with zucchini sauce. Add freshly ground black pepper to taste. Serve immediately. (This is also delicious cold.)

serves 6

237

very lemony
mashed potatoes

**3 pounds large baking and boiling potatoes,
    combined**
3 large lemons
**6 tablespoons unsalted butter, cut into small
    pieces**

- Peel potatoes using a vegetable peeler. Remove any dark spots. Cut potatoes into eighths and place in large pot with cover. Add enough cold water just to cover potatoes. Add 2 teaspoons salt. Bring to a rapid boil. Lower heat to medium, cover, and cook for 20 to 25 minutes, until potatoes are soft but not falling apart.
- Meanwhile, grate rind of lemons on medium holes of box grater so that you have 2 teaspoons grated zest. Cut lemons in half and squeeze ⅔ cup juice. Place juice in small nonstick skillet and cook over medium-high heat until reduced to ½ cup. Set aside.

- When potatoes are done, drain in colander, saving 1 cup cooking water. Put potatoes in large bowl and, using a potato masher, mash until smooth, slowly adding hot cooking water. Add grated lemon zest and reduced lemon juice. Add butter. Continue to mash until creamy. Add salt and freshly ground white pepper to taste. Return potatoes to pot and heat gently before serving.

serves 6 or more (makes about 6 cups)

honeydew and blueberries: mixed fruit sorbet, blueberry drizzle

2½ cups fresh blueberries
1 cup plus 2 tablespoons sugar
1 large ripe honeydew melon (3½ pounds)

- *To make syrup:* Place 1 cup blueberries in small saucepan with ½ cup water and ¼ cup sugar. Bring to a boil. Lower heat and cook for 20 minutes, until syrup is thickened. Place blueberries and syrup in fine-mesh sieve, pushing down hard on berries to extract all the juices. You will have ½ cup blueberry syrup and about 2 tablespoons mashed blueberries. Reserve syrup and blueberries in separate bowls.
- *To make sorbet:* Cut melon in half. Scoop seeds from one half and refrigerate second half for later use. Remove rind and cut melon into 1-inch pieces. You will have approximately 3 cups. Puree melon chunks in food processor with reserved mashed blueberries and 1 tablespoon reserved blueberry syrup. You will have 2½ cups melon-blueberry puree.

- In small saucepan, boil remaining ¾ cup plus 2 tablespoons sugar and 1 cup water for 5 minutes. Add to melon puree and refrigerate until very cold. Place mixture in ice cream maker and process according to manufacturer's directions.
- To serve, remove seeds from remaining melon half. Cut into 6 wedges or make balls using a melon baller, or dice into small cubes. Place a wedge of melon or a mound of melon balls or diced melon on each of 6 large plates. Top each with a scoop of sorbet. Garnish each with ¼ cup of the remaining fresh blueberries and about a tablespoon of the remaining blueberry syrup.

serves 6

239

Fourth of July

Edam-Up Quesadillas

Tri-Tip Fillets in American Red Wine

Smashed Potato Salad

Stoplight Tomatoes: Red, Yellow, and Green

Firecracker Corn

Watermelon Soup, White Chocolate Ice Cream

This is 1-2-3 cooking at its best — an effortless menu that revitalizes a clichéd meat-and-potatoes kind of meal. Proud to be American, it captures the essence of simple ingredients in their prime, configured into democratic new tastes.

menu notes
Marinate the meat for six hours before roasting or grilling. This is also a good time to prepare the potato salad and chipotle butter. The ice cream and soup can be made the day before. An hour before service, prepare the salad fixings and assemble the quesadillas. Serve this meal with a large basket of sourdough rolls.

suggested hors d'oeuvres
How about a bowl of Deviled Pecans (see page 112) to go with some margaritas? Or try a platter of sassy "Smoked" Carnitas (see page 125) or finger-licking Rib Bits (see page 126).

grapenote
How about a pitcher of margaritas to start? (For the kids, a pitcher of Pineapple Lemonade; see page 87.) Patriotic reds to follow: Zinfandel from Alderbrook, Ravenswood, or Pedroncelli Mother Clone Vineyards; at the higher end, a "Zin" from Ferrari Carano or Story Book Mountain.

edam-up quesadillas

12 ounces Edam cheese, in one piece
1 16-ounce jar thick and chunky salsa *
12 8-inch flour tortillas

- Remove rind from cheese. Grate cheese on large holes of box grater. Set aside.
- Put salsa in strainer over bowl to catch liquid. Let sit for 5 minutes. You will have about 1¼ cups drained salsa and ⅓ cup liquid. Reserve.
- *To assemble quesadillas:* Place 1 flour tortilla on flat surface. Distribute about ½ cup grated cheese on top. Dab with 2 to 3 tablespoons drained salsa. Cover with another tortilla. Add ½ cup cheese and 2 tablespoons salsa, then top with a third tortilla. Repeat this process to make 4 triple-decker quesadillas.
- Preheat oven to 300°.
- Heat 10-inch nonstick skillet over medium heat. Place quesadillas in skillet one at a time and cook for 3 minutes, pressing down lightly with spatula. Turn over and cook for 2 to 3 minutes more. Tortillas should be crisp and golden brown. Keep warm on baking sheet in oven. Repeat process until all 4 quesadillas are cooked.
- Cut each quesadilla into 6 pieces. Serve immediately with drained salsa liquid for dunking.

serves 6

 * I use Pace.

tri-tip fillets
in american red wine

2 2-pound tri-tip beef fillets (beef triangles)
2 cups dry red wine (Cabernet Sauvignon,
    Merlot, or Zinfandel)
6 tablespoons soy sauce

- Season beef with freshly ground black pepper. Combine red wine and soy sauce in small bowl. Place beef in plastic bag and pour in wine mixture. Seal tightly. Place in refrigerator on dish (in case it leaks) and marinate for 6 hours, turning bag several times to distribute marinade.
- Preheat oven to 450°.
- Remove beef from marinade. Let sit at room temperature for 30 minutes. Place marinade in small saucepan and cook over medium heat until reduced by one-half, about 1¼ cups.
- Place beef in heavy, shallow metal roasting pan. Roast for 10 to 11 minutes on each side, for a total cooking time of about 22 minutes for rare. Use a meat thermometer and remove meat from oven when it reaches 125°. (Or you may cook on your outdoor grill to desired doneness.)
- Let rest for 5 minutes. Sprinkle with salt and pepper.
- Bring marinade to a boil, lower heat, and cook for 1 to 2 minutes. Using a very sharp knife, cut meat on the bias into ¼-inch-thick slices. Serve with reduced marinade and any collected juices poured over sliced beef.

serves 6

241

smashed potato salad

3 pounds small to medium red new potatoes
2 bunches scallions
2 cups light sour cream

- Scrub potatoes well, but do not peel. Place potatoes in large pot with water just to cover. Add ½ tablespoon salt and bring to a boil. Lower heat, cover pot, and cook for 35 to 40 minutes, until potatoes are soft but not falling apart.
- Meanwhile, trim scallions. Cut off and coarsely chop white parts only, not light or dark green parts, or sauce will be bitter. Reserve green parts. Place white parts in bowl of food processor with sour cream. Process until smooth.
- Cut green parts of scallions into ⅛-inch pieces. Set aside.
- When potatoes are cooked, drain in colander, saving ⅓ cup cooking water. Place potatoes in large bowl, and using a potato masher, mash until some are creamy but some are still in large pieces. While still hot, pour in sour cream mixture and cooking water, and stir well. Add salt and freshly ground white pepper to taste. Add some of the chopped scallion greens, saving some to garnish the salad before serving. Chill well.
- When ready to serve, adjust seasonings. Let come to room temperature, then scatter reserved chopped green scallions on top.

serves 6 or more

stoplight tomatoes: red, yellow, and green

5 large red, 6 large green, and 7 large yellow tomatoes
28 leaves fresh basil
⅔ cup plus 2 tablespoons olive oil

- Trim ends from 5 of each color of tomatoes and cut horizontally into ¼-inch-thick slices. Arrange on large platter, with each color of tomato overlapping in its own long row. Serve with dressings.

- *To make* **Fresh Basil–Green Tomato Oil:** Place ⅔ cup olive oil in blender.
- Trim ends from 1 green tomato. Cut into pieces and puree in blender.
- Bring small pot of salted water to a boil. Add basil leaves and cook for 1 minute. Scoop out leaves and immediately plunge into small bowl of ice water.
- Remove basil from bowl and squeeze out water. Add to green tomato puree and blend well. If there is not quite enough puree, add some cold water to make 1 cup puree. Continue to process until basil is finely minced. Season with salt and freshly ground black pepper to taste.

makes 1 cup

- *To make **Yellow Tomato Coulis:*** Trim ends from 2 yellow tomatoes, then plunge into pot of boiling water. Boil for 1 minute. Remove tomatoes and peel. Cut in half horizontally and squeeze out seeds. Cut into large pieces and place in blender. Add 2 tablespoons olive oil and process until smooth. Add several tablespoons water if too thick. Season with salt and freshly ground black pepper to taste.

makes ¾ cup

firecracker corn

1 stick unsalted butter, at room temperature
1½ canned chipotle peppers in adobo sauce *
12 or more large ears yellow and/or white sweet corn

- Cut butter into 1-inch pieces and place in bowl of electric mixer. Finely chop peppers. You will have about 1½ tablespoons chopped chipotles. Add to butter along with 1 teaspoon adobo sauce and a large pinch of salt. Process until chipotles are incorporated; do not overprocess.
- Pack into 5-ounce ramekin, smoothing top with knife. Drizzle a little adobo sauce on top to "glaze." Refrigerate until ready to use.
- Remove husks and silk from corn. Bring large pot of salted water to a boil. Add corn and cook for 5 minutes. (You may also leave corn in husks, wet them, and cook on an outdoor grill.)
- Serve hot corn with cold chipotle butter and small bowls of salt.

serves 6

* A product of Mexico available in small cans in many supermarkets and specialty-food stores.

watermelon soup,
white chocolate ice cream

10-pound piece ripe watermelon
1 cup plus 5 tablespoons sugar
6 ounces white chocolate

- Divide watermelon into 2 5-pound pieces. Remove seeds from 1 piece. Save ¼ cup seeds as garnish. Discard remaining seeds. Using a melon baller, cut flesh into 1-inch balls. Place in bowl, adding all the accumulated juices, and sprinkle with 1 tablespoon sugar. Cover and refrigerate until ready to serve.

- Remove seeds from second piece of watermelon. Cut flesh into large chunks and place in bowl of food processor. Process until very smooth. You may need to do this in 2 batches. You will have about 6 cups watermelon puree.

- Place puree in medium saucepan. Add ¼ cup sugar and stir. Bring to a boil, then reduce heat to medium-high. Whisking frequently with a small wire whisk, cook until puree is reduced by one-half, about 3 cups. Let cool. Cover and refrigerate until very cold.

- *To make ice cream:* In medium pot, bring 3 cups water, 1 cup sugar, and a pinch of salt to a boil. Chop white chocolate into small pieces (or use white chocolate chips). Reduce heat to medium and add chocolate. Whisk for 2 minutes, until chocolate is melted and mixture is smooth. Remove from heat. Let cool, then refrigerate until cold. Place in ice cream maker (an electric one is preferable) and freeze according to manufacturer's directions.

- To serve, place ½ cup watermelon soup in each of 6 flat soup plates. Top with watermelon balls and a scoop of ice cream. Garnish with a few seeds.

serves 6

Newish-Jewish Holiday

Chicken Confit with Garlic and Thyme

Fourteen-Carrot Chicken Bouillon

Pot Roast Gibson with Dry Vermouth and Onions

Wild Mushroom—Potato Torte

Carrot Puree with Chicken Fat

Fruit Compote in Honey-Lemon Syrup

Little Nut Cakes

Do you have to be Jewish to enjoy this meal? The obvious answer is that this festive menu meets the needs of everyone who doesn't mix dairy products with meat. It easily adapts to kosher constraints — and is even appropriate for Passover, since my Little Nut Cakes are flourless.

Traditional chicken bouillon actually yields three dishes: a soup, carrots pureed with chicken fat into a delicious vegetable, and a confit made from the chicken that flavored the soup and some of its rendered fat.

Pot Roast Gibson (like its namesake cocktail) comprises dry vermouth and onions and is a meltingly tender dish.

This four-course menu speaks to the true spirit of a Jewish household, where enough is never enough.

menu notes
You need to make the chicken bouillon first to prepare the chicken confit and carrot puree. Chill the soup so you can use the congealed fat in both these dishes. Best of all, the entire menu (except the torte) should be made the day before; it is more delicious the next day.

suggested hors d'oeuvres
Serve the Chicken Confit with Garlic and Thyme with Garlic Croûtes (page 109).

grapenote
The first two dishes call for a full, rich Chardonnay, such as Baron Herzog (California) or Yarden (Israel). With the pot roast, a big 1994 St. Estephe from Château Tours des Termes. With dessert? Gan Eden Late Harvest Gewürztraminer. Yes, these are all kosher.

chicken confit
with garlic and thyme

1½ pounds cooked chicken and ¾ cup chicken fat (from Fourteen-Carrot Chicken Bouillon; see the following recipe)
4 large cloves garlic
1 large bunch fresh thyme

- Remove bones and skin from cooked chicken. Discard. Using your fingers, shred 4 cups cooled chicken meat.
- Slice garlic clove very thin. Mix with chicken in large bowl. Pick ¼ cup thyme leaves and add to chicken along with salt and lots of freshly ground black pepper.
- Pack chicken mixture into shallow casserole or nonstick skillet. Melt chicken fat. Reserve 2 tablespoons and pour remaining fat over chicken. Add ¼ cup water. Scatter sprigs of thyme over chicken.
- Cut a piece of waxed paper to fit into the casserole or skillet and cover chicken with it. Simmer for 30 minutes, then let cool. Remove waxed paper and pack chicken into soufflé dish or mold. Pour remaining 2 tablespoons fat on top.
- Refrigerate until cold. Serve on small plates or with Garlic Croûtes (see page 109).

serves 6 to 8

fourteen-carrot
chicken bouillon

14 long, slender carrots, preferably organic (2½ pounds)
4½-pound boiling chicken or fowl
½ teaspoon saffron threads

- Peel carrots and cut into 1-inch pieces.
- Remove giblets from chicken. Wash chicken well. Cut off wing tips and reserve. Put chicken in large heavy pot with cover. Add carrots, 2 teaspoons kosher salt, and ¼ teaspoon whole black peppercorns. Add 12 cups cold water (or more to cover). Bring to a boil.
- Meanwhile, place giblets and wing tips in small nonstick skillet. Discard liver. Cook over medium-high heat for 5 minutes, or until giblets are browned. Add to pot with chicken. Deglaze pan with a little water and also add to chicken.
- When water in pot comes to a boil, lower heat and skim any foam. Cover pot, leaving top askew. Simmer, skimming often, for 2½ hours, adding ¼ teaspoon saffron during last 30 minutes. Turn chicken several times during cooking.
- Remove from heat. With slotted spoon, remove carrots and put in bowl. Remove chicken and put in another bowl.

- Strain remaining broth through fine-mesh sieve into clean pot. Discard residue and cool broth. Place pot in refrigerator until fat congeals. Skim off fat and reserve for Carrot Puree with Chicken Fat (see below) and Chicken Confit with Garlic and Thyme (see the preceding recipe).
- Bring broth to a boil. You will have about 8 to 9 cups. Add remaining ¼ teaspoon saffron. Lower heat and simmer for 30 minutes, or until reduced to 7 cups. Add salt and freshly ground black pepper to taste.
- Remove some carrots from bowl and slice enough to make 1 cup. (Reserve remaining carrots for Carrot Puree with Chicken Fat.) Serve broth hot with sliced carrots and 1 cup thinly sliced or finely diced cooked chicken. (Save remaining chicken for Chicken Confit with Garlic and Thyme.)

serves 6 to 8

carrot puree with chicken fat

- Put reserved carrots from Fourteen-Carrot Chicken Bouillon in bowl of food processor with 2 tablespoons reserved cold chicken fat. Puree until smooth but still retaining some texture; you don't want baby food.
- Add salt and freshly ground black pepper to taste.
- Heat gently in small saucepan with cover.

serves 6 to 8 (makes about 3¼ cups)

pot roast gibson
with dry vermouth
and onions

4½-pound chuck roast
3 pounds onions
1 cup dry vermouth

- Rub chuck roast with salt and freshly ground black pepper. Place on heavy broiler pan and broil on both sides until browned. This will take 1 to 2 minutes per side.
- Peel onions, cut in half through root end, and slice. Place in very large, heavy casserole with cover. Cook over medium heat until onions soften and blacken. Stir constantly with wooden spoon to prevent sticking.
- Add ½ cup dry vermouth and ½ teaspoon whole black peppercorns. Increase heat and cook until vermouth has almost evaporated.
- Add 1 cup water. Place chuck on onions and cover pot. Bring to a boil. Lower heat and simmer for 3 hours, turning meat every 30 minutes.
- After 3 hours, meat will be soft. Transfer to large cutting board. Bring onions and liquid to a boil and cook over high heat for 5 minutes to reduce liquid in pan. Add ¼ cup vermouth and salt to taste. Cook for 5 minutes more, until cooking liquid is rather thick.

- *To make onion sauce:* Transfer ⅓ cup onion mixture to food processor. Puree until smooth. Put in small saucepan. Add remaining ¼ cup vermouth and water to thin, if necessary. Cook until hot. Keep warm.
- Cut meat against the grain into thin slices. Place overlapping slices on warm large platter. Pour onions and liquid from cooking pot over meat. Serve with onion sauce on the side.

serves 6 to 8

wild mushroom–potato torte

½ ounce dried wild mushrooms
1½ pounds large red or Yukon Gold potatoes
4 extra-large eggs, separated

- Place wild mushrooms in small bowl. Add 2 cups boiling water and let sit for 30 minutes. Drain in fine-mesh sieve, reserving liquid. Coarsely chop mushrooms.
- Scrub potatoes, but do not peel. Place in pot, cover with salted water, and bring to a boil. Lower heat to medium, cover, and cook for 30 minutes, or until tender when tested with a sharp knife. Drain in colander. Peel potatoes and place in large bowl.
- Preheat oven to 350°.
- Mash potatoes well with potato masher, adding egg yolks one at a time. Mix in chopped mushrooms, ½ cup mushroom liquid, 1 teaspoon salt, and freshly ground black pepper.
- In bowl of electric mixer, beat egg whites with a pinch of salt until stiff. Fold into potato mixture.
- Spoon mixture into 9-inch springform pan lined with parchment paper or sprayed with nonstick vegetable spray. Bake for 40 minutes, or until set.
- Run a thin sharp knife around the edges of the torte before releasing the spring. Cut into wedges. This can be reheated but is best served immediately from oven.

serves 6 to 8

fruit compote in honey-lemon syrup

2 pounds dried mixed fruit
5 lemons
⅔ cup honey

- In medium heavy pot with cover, put dried fruit. Grate zest of 1 lemon and add to fruit. Cut 1 ungrated lemon into thin slices and reserve. Squeeze remaining lemons to get ½ cup juice. Pour lemon juice and honey over fruit and add 3½ cups water. Bring to a boil.
- Lower heat and cover. Simmer for 15 to 20 minutes, or until fruit is soft. Let cool in liquid, then place reserved lemon slices on top.
- Refrigerate until very cold and serve. It's even better the next day.

serves 8

little nut cakes

2 cups plus 12 whole shelled almonds, with skins (about 9 ounces)
1 cup superfine sugar
2 extra-large eggs plus 2 extra-large egg yolks

- Preheat oven to 325°.
- Place 2 cups almonds in large nonstick skillet. Cook over medium heat for 2 to 3 minutes, until skins darken and you detect a faint nutty aroma. Shake pan to rotate nuts. Let cool for 10 minutes.
- Transfer nuts to food processor. Process until coarsely ground. Add sugar, eggs, and egg yolks, and process briefly. Batter will be thick.
- Line 12-cup muffin tin with paper liners or coat with nonstick vegetable spray. Evenly distribute batter among cups. Center 1 whole almond on each cake. Bake for 25 to 30 minutes, or until slightly browned around edges. Remove cakes from tin and cool.

makes 12 cakes

Thanksgiving

Oyster Bisque

Turkey Ballottine with Fresh Sage and Garlic Jus

Wild Rice with Five-Hour Onions

Roasted Acorn Squash and Carrot Puree

Cranberry Conserve

Slow-Baked Pears, Sauternes Aspic

Sumptuous and sophisticated, this holiday menu boasts familiar components handled with care and leaves you greatly satisfied and full of good cheer.

Classic oyster bisque is nothing more than the bivalves themselves, quickly simmered in their briny liquor with cream and brightened with scallions.

Ballottines, however labor-intensive, are an ideal way to serve lots of guests, as there are no bones or tricky carving angles to deal with. They are also very showy in their classic cylindrical shape. In the French lexicon, ballottines are hot or cold dishes of meat, poultry, game birds, or even fish, where the flesh is boned, stuffed, rolled, and tied with string, then usually wrapped in muslin or in skin, as this one is. Although ballottines are generally braised or poached, my version is slowly roasted.

The five-hour onions and the pears in Sauternes aspic both need slow baking to complete their stunningly intense transformation.

menu notes

Cook onions and pears in the same oven early in the day, leaving the oven free for the remaining dishes. The cranberry conserve and roasted vegetable puree can be made the day before.

suggested hors d'oeuvre

A simple basket of crudités — a fresh vegetable trio (baby carrots, fennel, and blanched green beans) with a 1-2-3 Dip (see page 103).

grapenote

This is a wonderful time to try my Autumn Leaf cocktail (see page 82), made with apple cider, arrack, and freshly squeezed lemon juice. Follow with a menu of American wines: with the bisque, a full-bodied Chardonnay (Belvedere, Geyser Peak, Acacia, or Mueller); with the turkey, a California Rhône-style blend such as Joseph Phelps Vin du Mistral Pastiche, Terre Rouge, or Zaca Mesa Cuvée Z.

251

oyster bisque

4 dozen large fresh oysters, shucked, with their liquor (about 1½ cups liquor)
3 cups heavy cream
1 bunch scallions

- Line fine-mesh sieve with cheesecloth. Pour oyster liquor through cheesecloth to remove sand or grit.
- Place cream in medium heavy saucepan. Cook over medium-high heat for 10 minutes, or until cream thickens a bit. Add strained oyster liquor. Cook over medium heat for 5 minutes.
- Finely chop white part of 1 scallion and add to cream. Reduce heat to medium, add oysters, and cook for 2 to 3 minutes, until oysters are just cooked through and bisque is hot. Add a pinch of salt, if needed.
- Finely chop scallion greens. Ladle bisque into warm flat soup plates, with 4 oysters in each. Garnish with scallion greens and coarsely ground black pepper. Serve immediately.

serves 12

turkey ballottine with fresh sage and garlic jus

16-pound turkey *
1 large head plus 5 cloves garlic
2 large bunches fresh sage

- Early in the day, prepare turkey broth. Place turkey carcass in large heavy pot. Add giblets (except liver), and wing tips. Add cold water to cover; ½ teaspoon whole black peppercorns; 1 head unpeeled garlic, cut in half horizontally; and 6 sage sprigs. Bring to a boil, skimming any foam. Lower heat to medium and cook for 2 hours, skimming periodically.
- Discard carcass and giblets. Strain broth through large fine-mesh sieve, pressing softened garlic through sieve. Place strained broth in large clean pot. Add 1 teaspoon salt and bring to a boil. Lower heat and simmer until broth is reduced to 6 cups. Set aside.
- *To prepare ballottine:* Remove skin from turkey thighs and reserve. Cut meat into ¼- to ½-inch cubes. You will have about 4 cups weighing about 1½ pounds. Place diced turkey in bowl. Finely chop enough sage to make ½ packed cup. Add to diced turkey. Push 4 cloves garlic through garlic press and add to diced turkey with 1 teaspoon salt and freshly ground black pepper. Mix well and let sit while you preheat oven.

- Preheat oven to 325°.
- Lay boned breast flat, flesh side up, on large cutting board or clean flat surface. Position it so there is clearly a lobe to your left and a lobe to your right. Butterfly breast meat so that breast lobes lie flat. Sprinkle lightly with salt and pepper. Place diced turkey mixture across lobes, parallel to your waist, in a long sausage shape in center of turkey breast. You want the mixture to go from end to end. Roll up tightly like a jelly roll. Use reserved thigh skin, if necessary, to cover any exposed meat.
- Tie string tightly around rolled breast at 1-inch intervals. You will have a ballottine that is about 16 inches long. Also tie string around length of breast. Sprinkle lightly with salt.
- Place ballottine in large shallow roasting pan. Add ½ cup broth to pan. Bake for 50 minutes. Baste with pan juices and place turkey wings and turkey legs in pan. Add ½ cup broth. Bake for 50 to 55 minutes, or until meat thermometer reads 140° to 145°. Remove pan from oven. Transfer ballottine, wings, and legs to large platter. Ballottine will continue to cook.

- Add 5½ cups broth to roasting pan, scraping up all the brown pieces. Skim fat and strain through sieve into clean pot. Add 1 small clove garlic pushed through garlic press. Add salt and pepper to taste. Cook over medium heat until reduced to 3 cups.
- Remove all strings from turkey. Cut ballottine into thin slices and serve with wings, legs, and hot garlic jus. Garnish with sage sprigs.

serves 12

* Have butcher prepare turkey as follows: Remove wings and separate tips from wings. Remove legs and thighs. Separate legs from thighs. Bone breast but keep breast and back skin intact. Breast will weigh about 7½ pounds. Keep turkey carcass.

wild rice with five-hour onions

12 medium onions (about 3 pounds), plus ¾ cup finely diced onion
1 stick plus 2 tablespoons unsalted butter
1 pound wild rice

- Preheat oven to 275°.
- Peel whole onions and place in medium heavy pot or casserole with cover. Thinly slice 1 stick butter and scatter over onions. Cover pot and bake for 5 hours. Onions will be golden and give off lots of juices. Set aside.
- One hour before serving, wash rice and drain in colander. Melt remaining 2 tablespoons butter in large heavy pot. Add rice and ¾ cup finely diced onion. Stir with wooden spoon for 5 minutes, or until rice is a bit crisp. Slowly add 2 quarts cold water. Bring to a boil. Add 2 teaspoons salt and freshly ground black pepper.
- Lower heat to medium, cover, and cook for 55 minutes. Uncover pot, increase heat to high, and cook for about 10 minutes, or until rice is tender. Add salt and pepper to taste. Drain in colander, if necessary, to remove excess liquid. Transfer to warm large platter.
- Heat onions gently on top of stove. With slotted spoon, place on rice. Pour onion juices over rice and serve. (This can be easily reheated in oven.)

serves 12

roasted acorn squash and carrot puree

3 large acorn squash (1½ pounds each)
2½ pounds carrots
½ cup apple butter

- Preheat oven to 325°.
- Cut each squash in half and remove seeds. Cut off rind with a small sharp knife. Cut squash into 1-inch cubes.
- Peel carrots and cut into 1-inch pieces. Mix squash and carrots with 5 tablespoons apple butter, ½ teaspoon salt, and freshly ground black pepper. Place mixture on baking sheet big enough to accommodate vegetables in one layer. Add 3 tablespoons water and cover with foil.
- Bake for 1 hour. Remove foil. Add ½ cup water and bake for 20 minutes more.
- Transfer vegetables to food processor and process until very smooth. This must be done in several batches.
- Transfer to medium pot. Add remaining 3 tablespoons apple butter and salt and pepper to taste. Reheat gently before serving. (This dish can also be made early in the day and reheated.)

serves 12 (makes about 6 cups)

cranberry conserve

**1 cup unsulfured molasses, plus more for
serving (optional)**
24 ounces fresh cranberries (about 6 cups)
1 whole nutmeg, for grating

- Put 3 cups water and molasses in medium pot.
Bring to a boil. Add cranberries and return to a
boil.
- Lower heat to a simmer. Add a pinch of salt and
a grinding of black pepper. Cook for 15 minutes,
until all the cranberries have popped and sauce
has thickened. Do not overcook, as sauce will
thicken more when cold.
- Using a small nutmeg grater, grate nutmeg so
that you have almost ¼ teaspoon. Stir into cranberries. Cover and chill. (It will improve with age.)
- Before serving, add a little molasses to sweeten,
if desired. Spoon into serving dish or bowl. Grate
more nutmeg on top.

serves 12 (makes about 4½ cups)

slow-baked pears, sauternes aspic

**12 large firm Comice pears, with stems (about
5½ pounds)**
**2 bottles Sauternes, Moscato, or other white
dessert wine**
2 envelopes unflavored gelatin

- Preheat oven to 275°.
- Wash pears and dry. Place unpeeled pears in very
large casserole (big enough to hold them in one
layer) with cover. Pour wine over pears, adding
water if necessary to cover. Cover casserole
tightly. Bake for 5 hours.
- Remove pears with slotted spoon, reserving liquid. Place pears in shallow casserole. Cool, cover
with plastic wrap, and refrigerate until cold and
ready to serve.
- Reduce reserved liquid so that you have 4 cups.
Sprinkle gelatin over ¼ cup cold water. Let sit for
1 minute, then whisk into hot reduced liquid.
Cook for 1 minute, or until gelatin is dissolved.
Pour liquid through fine-mesh sieve into pan
large enough so that liquid is ½ inch deep. Chill
for 3 to 4 hours, or until mixture is completely
jelled.
- Cut aspic into ½-inch squares. Place in bottom
of 12 flat soup plates and top each with a cold
pear. Pour any accumulated juices over pears.

serves 12

Christmas Eve

Herring Salad with Dill Havarti

Home-Cured Salmon, Sweet Lemon-Mustard Sauce

Caraway Pork Loin in a Salt Crust with Roasted Garlic

Cauliflower-Appenzeller Casserole

Split Pea Puree

Mont Blanc Chantilly

Our pre-Christmas meal (lovely anytime during the winter season) is geographically influenced by Sweden, Norway, Switzerland, and the French Alps — snowy places where a certain Mr. Claus is known to tarry.

Herring and cheese is a classic combination in Sweden, always found together on the smorgasbord. As a salad, they make a delightful starter.

Pork loin, in its Norwegian-inspired caraway coating, is cooked in an igloo of coarse salt.

The special, rounded flavor of Swiss Appenzeller cheese comes from an initial curing in a vat of cider and spices. Its appealing tang turns ordinary cauliflower into an extraordinary vegetable. Keep in mind that while Appenzeller is not a smelly cheese, its distinctive flavor meets the cauliflower head-on.

The dessert derives its name from the highest peak in the Alps — called Mont Blanc in French, Monte Bianco in Italian. If you don't own a ricer,

this is ample justification for buying one. Very recherché, the *mont* (mountain) refers to the chestnut puree topped with a dome of *blanc* (white) chantilly cream. Confectioners' sugar around the edge of the plate looks like freshly fallen snow.

menu notes

If you want an all-fish dinner for your Christmas Eve party, try my winter menu Shrimp and Monkfish (see page 131).

Serve herring and salmon with a variety of store-bought flat breads. Except for the pork loin, which needs to be cooked right before service, the menu can be prepared well in advance.

suggested hors d'oeuvres

Truffled Whitefish Puffs (page 105) and Silver-Dollar Corn Cakes with Bacon and Crème Fraîche (page 125).

grapenote

Do as they do in Sweden: Begin this meal with a shot of aquavit and a beer chaser. Next, sip Hugel Gentil, a rich Alsatian blend of Riesling, Sylvaner, and Gewürztraminer. Give the kids sparkling apple cider. After they're asleep, savor my Brandy Elixir (see page 89) in a large snifter. Warmed by your hands, this will also warm your heart.

herring salad
with dill havarti

16 ounces jarred herring in wine sauce
1 large cucumber
6 ounces dill Havarti cheese

- Place herring in wine sauce in large bowl. You should have about 1²/₃ cups.
- Peel cucumber. Slice lengthwise and remove seeds. Cut into ⅓-inch cubes. You should have about 1½ cups. Add to herring.
- Cut cheese into ⅓-inch cubes. Add to herring and cucumbers. Add freshly ground black pepper and mix. Cover and refrigerate for 30 minutes before serving.

serves 6

home-cured salmon

Prepare either Brown Sugar–Tarragon Gravlax (see page 223) or Mild-Brine Lenrimmad Lax (see page 223), or you may purchase good-quality smoked salmon. Serve with the following 1-2-3 sauce.

sweet lemon-mustard sauce

6 tablespoons sugar
¼ cup distilled white vinegar
½ cup Dijon mustard with lemon *

- Put sugar and vinegar in small bowl and whisk until sugar is dissolved. Whisk in mustard until smooth. Refrigerate for several hours or up to several months. The sauce will thicken when cold.

makes 1 cup

> * Use a French import such as Delouis Fils Moutarde Forte or Citron Frais. You may substitute regular Dijon mustard if necessary.

257

caraway pork loin
in a salt crust
with roasted garlic

2½-pound boned center-cut pork loin
3 cloves plus 6 large heads garlic
¼ cup caraway seeds

- You will need a 3-pound box of kosher salt.
- Season pork with freshly ground white pepper. Push 3 garlic cloves through garlic press and rub all over pork. Let rest for 30 minutes.
- Preheat oven to 450°.
- Pat caraway seeds onto surface of pork.
- In bottom of 6 quart ovenproof casserole, put 1½ pounds kosher salt. Place pork on salt. Cut ¼ inch from tops of garlic heads and place around pork. Cover pork and garlic with remaining 1½ pounds salt, packed tightly. Pour ¼ cup cold water on top.
- Cover casserole and bake for 40 minutes. Remove cover and bake for 25 minutes more. Do not overcook.
- Remove from oven. Let rest 5 minutes. Break open salt crust using a mallet or cleaver. Remove pork and garlic. Let rest for 5 minutes, brushing off any excess salt. Carve pork into ½-inch-thick slices, or thinner, if desired. Pork will be slightly pink. Serve immediately with roasted garlic.

serves 6

cauliflower-appenzeller
casserole

1 very large head cauliflower (about 2½ pounds)
1¼ cups good-quality crushed tomatoes in puree
6 ounces Appenzeller cheese

- Preheat oven to 375°.
- Bring pot of salted water to a boil. Cut cauliflower into large pieces and cook over medium heat for 15 to 20 minutes, or until tender but not too soft.
- Drain cauliflower well in colander. Pat dry. Put in food processor in 2 batches, processing until fairly smooth but with some small pieces. You do not want to liquefy the cauliflower. Transfer to bowl. Stir in 1 cup tomatoes and season with salt and freshly ground black pepper.
- Cut rind off cheese. Cut off a 2-ounce chunk and reserve. Cut remaining cheese into ¼-inch cubes. Add to cauliflower and mix.
- Put cauliflower mixture in shallow oval or square baking dish. Spread evenly with remaining ¼ cup tomatoes. Grate reserved cheese on large holes of box grater and scatter on top. Bake for 15 minutes and serve.

serves 6

split pea puree

1 pound dried green split peas
1 large red onion
3 tablespoons unsalted butter

- Rinse split peas well and remove any stones. Dry well.
- Peel onion and cut into ¼-inch pieces. You will have 1 packed cup diced onion. Reserve extra for garnish, if desired. In medium-large pot, melt 2 tablespoons butter. Add onion and sauté for 5 to 6 minutes, until soft but not browned.
- Add split peas and stir well to incorporate. Add 2½ cups water. Bring to a boil. Lower heat to medium and cook for 20 minutes. Add ½ cup water. Cook for 10 minutes more.
- Add salt and freshly ground black pepper to taste. Cover pot and cook for 30 to 40 minutes, until peas are tender but still retain some texture. If puree is too dry, add a little water and continue to cook for several minutes more.
- Add remaining 1 tablespoon butter and salt and pepper to taste. Serve hot.
- *Optional garnish:* Sprinkle with very finely minced red onion.

serves 6

mont blanc chantilly

1 16-ounce can unsweetened chestnut puree
1½ cups plus 2 tablespoons confectioners' sugar
¾ cup heavy cream

- Reserve 3 tablespoons chestnut puree. Put remaining puree in bowl of electric mixer and blend well with 1¼ cups confectioners' sugar. Mixture will be stiff. In batches, put mixture in potato ricer. Squeeze onto an oval serving platter. Chill until cold.
- Whip heavy cream with reserved chestnut puree, ¼ cup confectioners' sugar, and a pinch of salt until thick and creamy. Do not overwhip. With a flexible rubber spatula, mound whipped cream onto riced puree, leaving a border free of cream. Refrigerate until ready to serve.
- Just before serving, put remaining 2 tablespoons confectioners' sugar in fine-mesh sieve and dust border of chestnut puree and edges of platter.

serves 6

Christmas Day

Smoked Trout and Watercress Salad, Walnut Oil–Green Sauce

Holiday Goose with Prunes and Roasted Chestnuts, Prune Gravy

Red Cabbage with Vinegar and Wildflower Honey

Sweet Potato, Ginger, and Orange Puree

Chunky Celery Root with Caramelized Red Onions

Warm Marzipan-Baked Apples, Apple Cider Granita

This menu brings good tidings.

The holiday season, a time of joy and celebration, should never be thwarted by unrealistic culinary feasts. After all, you don't want to spend the twelve days of Christmas in your kitchen. Rather, here is a way to enjoy them. Except for the main course, which is a golden goose, all the dishes can be made ahead.

This rich and varied repast is a gift to the senses. Its colors are vivid, its flavors are distinct, and it is perfumed with the scents of the season.

I created this menu at the home of my dear friends, Susy Davidson (former food editor of *Food & Wine* magazine), and her husband, Bill Etringer. It is to them (along with their dog, Maggie, who also ate well that day) that I dedicate it. Here's to cherished memories and season's greetings.

menu notes

Early in the day or the day before, you can prepare the granita, red cabbage, sweet potato puree, celery root, and roasted chestnuts. On the day of the party, while the goose is roasting, make the walnut oil–green sauce and fill the apples with marzipan. Pop the apples in the oven immediately after removing the goose, or make them ahead of time and leave them in a warm place in the kitchen. If you want to serve twelve instead of six, cook two geese and simply double the remaining recipes.

suggested hors d'oeuvres

Celery Bites (see page 99) and a "wreath" of Little Radishes with Whipped Goat Cheese and Toasted Cumin (see page 96).

For terrific Christmas cookies, use the dough for Chickpea Flour Cookies (see page 202). Cut out with festive holiday cookie cutters and decorate as desired.

chickpea flour cookies (page 202), mint tea (page 26)

fresh plums and plum wine aspic (page 212)

figs and halvah, honey syrup (page 181)

puits d'amour (page 229), viennese coffee (page 27)

gianduia torta (page 151), cocoa clouds (page 225)

lemon *sorbetto* with rosemary, sweet gremolata (page 185)

honeydew and blueberries:
mixed fruit sorbet, blueberry drizzle (page 239)

watermelon soup, white chocolate ice cream (page 244)

smoked trout and watercress salad, walnut oil–green sauce

6 large smoked trout fillets
3 large bunches fresh watercress
6 tablespoons walnut oil

- Carefully remove skin, if any, from trout fillets. Cut each fillet in half lengthwise. You will have 12 pieces. Set aside.
- Wash watercress and dry well. Trim off all but 1 inch of the stems.
- Bring 3 cups water to a boil. Add ¼ teaspoon salt and half the watercress. Cook for 1 minute, then drain immediately in colander under cold running water. Save ⅔ cup cooking water.
- Place cooked watercress in bowl of food processor and process slowly, adding warm cooking water only until you have a thick paste. With motor running, slowly add 4 tablespoons walnut oil. The dressing should be smooth and fairly thick. Add salt to taste. You will have about ¾ cup dressing.
- *To assemble the salads:* Portion remaining watercress in the center of 6 large plates. Drizzle a little dressing over watercress. Place 2 smoked trout pieces, crisscrossed, on watercress. Drizzle remaining dressing around salad and across the center of trout. Drizzle each plate with 1 teaspoon walnut oil.

serves 6

grapenote

An oak-kissed Chardonnay is the right white for the first course: Deakin Estate from Australia, Lambert Bridge or Bernardus from California. The goose calls for a voluptuous Rhône wine: Serve a solid classic such as Domaine du Trapadis or splurge on a good Châteauneuf du Pape (Beaucastel or La Gardine). A snifter of Calvados is a treat with dessert.

261

holiday goose with prunes and roasted chestnuts, prune gravy

1½ pounds (about 45) fresh chestnuts, in their shells
24 ounces large pitted prunes
10- to 12-pound fresh or thawed frozen goose, with giblets

- Preheat oven to 400°.
- Using a small sharp knife, make an x on the pointed end of each chestnut. Place chestnuts in one layer on baking sheet. Roast for 30 minutes. Let cool for 10 minutes, then peel off shells.
- In large bowl, mix chestnuts with half the pitted prunes. Season with freshly ground black pepper and a pinch of salt. Toss and set aside.
- Reduce oven temperature to 375°.
- *To prepare goose:* Remove giblets. Wrap livers and refrigerate for later use (see page 263). Set remaining giblets aside. Wash goose well, rinsing cavity. Pat dry.
- Cut off tips and first joints of goose wings with a sharp knife. Set aside. Remove any large pockets of fat from goose. Cut off most of large flap of skin near neck, leaving only 2 inches.

- Stuff cavity with chestnut-prune mixture. Using trussing needles and string, tie opening tightly closed so that filling is secure. Wrap strings around legs to secure. Tuck neck flap under bird and place bird on rack in roasting pan. Prick skin all over with the tip of a small sharp knife, being careful not to puncture the flesh. Season lightly with salt and pepper, rubbing them into the skin with your fingers. Roast for 2 hours.
- Meanwhile, make goose stock and prune gravy. In medium saucepan with cover, place giblets (except liver), wing tips and first joints, and 1 teaspoon whole black peppercorns. Add cold water just to cover. Bring to a boil, lower heat to medium, and cook with cover askew for 1 hour, skimming often. Add remaining pitted prunes. Cook for 1½ hours more, continuing to skim and adding water as necesary.
- Using tongs, remove bones and giblets from pot. Strain stock through fine-mesh sieve into clean pot. Reserve prunes. Reduce over medium heat to 3 cups.

- Transfer prunes to food mill and puree to a thick paste. Add 3 to 4 tablespoons prune paste to thickened stock so that you have a dark, thickened, but pourable gravy. Add salt and pepper to taste.
- After 2 hours, check goose with meat thermometer. Breast meat should be 170°. Remove from oven if done, or continue to cook until desired temperature is reached.
- Let goose rest for 15 minutes. Untruss, then remove legs and thighs. Remove chestnuts and prunes and carve breast. Place legs, thighs, sliced breast, chestnuts, and prunes on platter. Pour prune gravy over goose or serve on the side.
- *Optional:* While goose is resting, season goose liver with salt and pepper. Put 2 tablespoons of fat from roasting pan in nonstick skillet. Add liver and cook for several minutes on each side, until firm but still pink in the center. Slice on the bias and add to platter with goose.

serves 6

red cabbage with vinegar and wildflower honey

1 medium red cabbage (2½ pounds)
½ cup apple cider vinegar
5 tablespoons wildflower honey

- Remove any dark outer leaves from cabbage and discard. Remove core and discard.
- Using a sharp knife, shred cabbage into ⅛-inch slices. Do not use food processor, because you don't want cabbage to be too thin.
- Place cabbage in large nonreactive pot with cover. Add cider vinegar, 2 tablespoons honey, 3 cups water, 1 teaspoon whole black peppercorns, and 2 teaspoons kosher salt. Bring to a boil. Lower heat to medium and cover pot. Cook for 2 hours, stirring occasionally. Remove cover and cook for 30 minutes more.
- Drain cabbage in colander, saving all the cooking liquid. Return liquid to pot and add remaining 3 tablespoons honey. Cook over high heat until thick and syrupy, about ¾ cup.
- Return cabbage to pot and mix well with syrup. Add salt to taste, if desired. Cook for 5 minutes more. Reheat before serving.

serves 6

sweet potato, ginger, and orange puree

4 large sweet potatoes (about 3 pounds)
2 juice oranges
2-inch piece fresh ginger

- Scrub potatoes, but do not peel. Place in pot with cold water to cover. Bring to a full boil, then lower heat to medium. Cook for 50 minutes, or until potatoes are very soft.
- Meanwhile, grate rind of 1 orange on fine holes of box grater so that you have 1 teaspoon grated zest. Cut oranges in half and squeeze ⅔ cup juice. Set aside.
- Drain potatoes in colander and peel under cool running water. Cut into large chunks and place in bowl of food processor.
- Using a small sharp knife, peel ginger and mince. You should have almost ¼ cup.
- Add grated orange zest, orange juice, and minced ginger to food processor with potatoes. Process until very smooth. Transfer mixture to saucepan and add salt to taste. Do not add pepper, as the ginger provides enough heat. Reheat gently before serving.

serves 6 (makes 5½ cups)

chunky celery root with caramelized red onions

2 medium celery roots (about 1 pound each)
3 large red onions (about 1½ pounds)
3 tablespoons unsalted butter

- Carefully peel celery root using a small sharp knife. Make sure that all the skin and any dark spots are removed. Wash well. Cut into large chunks and place in saucepan with cold water to cover. Add ½ teaspoon kosher salt and bring to a boil. Lower heat to medium and cook for 30 minutes.
- Meanwhile, peel onions and cut into ⅛-inch-thick slices. Melt 2 tablespoons butter in large nonstick skillet and add sliced onions. Cook over medium-high heat, stirring occasionally, for 30 minutes, or until onions are very soft and dark brown. After first 20 minutes, add a little water and scrape up any browned bits.
- When celery root is soft, drain in colander, saving ¼ cup cooking liquid. Put celery root in bowl. Add remaining 1 tablespoon butter and cooking liquid. Mash well, using a potato masher, making sure to leave small lumps.
- Add mashed celery root to caramelized onions. Stir gently to incorporate. Reheat before serving, adding salt and freshly ground black pepper to taste.

serves 6 (makes about 4 cups)

warm marzipan-baked apples, apple cider granita

1 quart fresh (unpasteurized) apple cider *
6 large Rome apples (½ pound each)
6 ounces marzipan **

- Put 2 cups apple cider in pie tin and place in freezer. Break up ice crystals with a fork every 30 minutes until cider freezes. This should take about 2 hours.
- Preheat oven to 350°.
- Wash apples, but do not peel. Remove cores from apples, leaving 1 inch at the bottom. Fill each apple with approximately 2 tablespoons marzipan, packing it in well and forming a ¼-inch-high mound on top. Flatten slightly to form a ¾-inch-diameter "button."
- Place filled apples in pan large enough to hold them with some space in between. Pour remaining 2 cups cider over apples. Bake for 40 minutes, basting often with cider.

- Transfer apples with slotted spoon to 6 flat soup plates. Put cider from baked apples in small non-stick skillet. Cook until syrupy, then strain through fine-mesh sieve. Pour a little syrup over each apple and let cool.
- Right before you're ready to serve, place granita in bowl of food processor. Process until smooth. Immediately scoop into balls. Serve a scoop of granita on or alongside each apple. Serve immediately.

serves 6

* Available in the produce section of many supermarkets.

** Available canned in most supermarkets and specialty-food stores.

265

New Year's Eve

Hot and Crispy Swiss Truffles

Pumpkin Soup with Cider Syrup

Chateaubriand with Porcini Crust, Wild Mushroom Sauce

Golden Chive Potatoes

Brussels Sprouts with Pancetta and Beef Essence

Eggnog Crème Caramel

It's New Year's Eve: the culmination of a year's worth of entertaining. If you have made your way through this book, you have had a party once a week, cooked more than three hundred new dishes, and had a lot to drink.

So on this big night, the last dinner party of the year, why sweat the small stuff?

Impressive and indulgent, this menu requires almost no last-minute gymnastics, except for frying the lacy cheese truffles, just meant for champagne. Invite your guests to join you in the kitchen.

To prolong the evening, serve a beautiful trio of winter fruits (see page 32) and some home-made candies (see pages 61 and 193) in the living room. This is the time for noisemakers and "Auld Lang Syne." Tomorrow is the time for resolutions.

menu notes

If you are going to serve twelve guests, double all the recipes, but prepare two chateaubriands, not just one longer piece. The soup and dessert can be made a day ahead. The brussels sprouts can be cooked and the meat prepped several hours before serving. The meat and potatoes can be cooked together. This meal deserves the best-quality rolls you can find; warm them for a minute in the oven before serving.

suggested hors d'oeuvres

Pass silver trays of Smoked Salmon Roulades (see page 122) and Endive with Sun-Dried Tomato and Orange Pâté (see page 96).

grapenote

Begin with something sparkling and festive: A fine French champagne such as Heidsieck Monopole or Perrier-Jouet will go beautifully with the crisp cheese truffles and the soup. Next, a great Bordeaux from the 1990 vintage will fit this menu like a velvet slipper. A glass of Moscatel from the sherry producer Barbadillo will complement dessert. At midnight, sip some more champagne, this time a demi-sec, under the mistletoe.

hot and crispy
swiss truffles

1 pound Swiss Emmenthaler cheese
3 cups white cornmeal
vegetable oil or peanut oil, for frying

- Grate cheese on large holes of box grater. Set aside.
- Combine 2½ cups water and 1¼ teaspoons salt in large saucepan. Bring to a boil and gradually stir in 2 cups cornmeal. Cook for 4 to 5 minutes, stirring constantly. When ready, mixture should separate from sides of pan. Remove from heat and stir in cheese. Add freshly ground black pepper and stir until cheese and pepper are thoroughly incorporated.
- When cool, roll mixture into ½-inch balls, then roll balls in remaining cornmeal to coat.
- Pour 2 inches of oil in large pot. Heat oil to 375°. Drop in balls in batches and cook for 2 to 3 minutes, or until golden brown. Drain on paper towels. Sprinkle with salt and serve immediately.

makes about 72 truffles

pumpkin soup
with cider syrup

2 15-ounce cans solid-pack pumpkin (about 3½ cups)
1 quart fresh (unpasteurized) apple cider
1½ cups finely diced onion, packed

- In large saucepan, combine pumpkin, 2 cups apple cider, 2 cups water, onion, ½ teaspoon salt, and freshly ground black pepper. Bring to a boil, lower heat to medium, and cover. Cook for 45 minutes, stirring frequently.
- Meanwhile, put remaining 2 cups cider in small nonstick saucepan and reduce over medium-high heat to 6 tablespoons. Set aside.
- When pumpkin mixture is cooked, transfer to bowl of food processor. Process until very smooth. You may need to do this in 2 batches. Return to saucepan and add salt and pepper to taste.
- Heat soup just before serving. Ladle into flat soup plates and drizzle each with 1 tablespoon cider syrup. Add coarsely ground black pepper. Serve immediately.
- *Optional garnish:* Top with very finely chopped onion.

serves 6 (makes about 7½ cups)

267

chateaubriand
with porcini crust,
wild mushroom sauce

1½ ounces dried porcini mushrooms
3½-pound trimmed chateaubriand or center-
cut beef tenderloin, fat reserved *
4 tablespoons unsalted butter, well chilled and
cut into small pieces

- Preheat oven to 400°.
- Place ½ ounce porcini mushrooms in spice grinder or blender. Process until you have a fine powder. Dredge chateaubriand in mushroom "dust" to cover completely, leaving flat ends exposed. Sprinkle lightly with freshly ground white pepper.
- In large nonstick skillet, melt 2 ounces reserved fat over low heat to make 2 tablespoons melted fat. Remove any large unmelted pieces or any debris.
- Increase heat to high, and when fat is hot, add beef and sear quickly on all sides. You want to create a crust. This should take a few minutes. Transfer beef to heavy shallow roasting pan or baking sheet.
- You may prepare meat up to this point and let sit at room temperature for an hour or two, until you are ready to put it in oven.
- Roast beef for 40 to 50 minutes, checking after 30 minutes with a quick-read meat thermometer. This is essential to ensure a perfectly cooked roast. Roast for about 12 to 15 minutes per pound, or until thermometer reads 125° to 130° for rare.

- While beef is roasting, prepare wild mushroom sauce. In small bowl, place remaining 1 ounce mushrooms and 2 cups boiling water. Let sit for 30 minutes. Remove mushrooms with slotted spoon, then pour liquid through fine-mesh sieve or cheesecloth to remove any grit.
- Place strained mushroom liquid in medium saucepan and bring to a boil. Cut soaked mushrooms into ¼-inch pieces and add to boiling liquid. Lower heat to medium and reduce to 1 cup. Whisk in butter. Add salt and white pepper to taste. Set aside.
- Remove roast from oven when it has reached the desired temperature. Let sit for 5 minutes before carving. Add accumulated juices to mushroom gravy. Cut meat into thick slices. Heat mushroom gravy over high heat for 1 minute, then pour over beef. Serve immediately.

serves 6

* Have your butcher prepare the meat for you: Trim the fat and reserve. Tie the chateaubriand at 1-inch intervals with string. The resulting piece should be 7½ to 8 inches long, with a diameter of 3 inches on the narrow ends and 4½ inches in the center. The net weight should be about 3¼ pounds.

golden chive potatoes

2¼ pounds Yukon Gold potatoes
1 stick unsalted butter
1 bunch fresh chives

- Preheat oven to 400°.
- Peel potatoes and cut into ¾- to 1-inch chunks. Place potatoes in single layer in large cast-iron skillet or shallow casserole.
- Cut butter into small pieces and scatter over potatoes. Pour 1 cup or more cold water to reach one-quarter of the way up the potatoes. Sprinkle with 1 teaspoon salt and mix with large spoon.
- Bake for 1 hour 10 minutes, shaking pan several times during baking. Water will evaporate, and potatoes will become golden brown.
- Transfer potatoes to platter and sprinkle with salt and freshly ground black pepper. Mince chives with a sharp knife so that you have 3 to 4 tablespoons. Add to potatoes and toss. Serve immediately.

serves 6

brussels sprouts with pancetta and beef essence

2 10-ounce packages small fresh brussels
sprouts (1¼ to 1½ pounds) *
4 ounces pancetta, cut into ⅛-inch-thick slices
2 cups beef broth, homemade or low-sodium
canned

- Using a small sharp knife, cut ends from bottoms of brussels sprouts. Place in colander and wash. Drain and dry thoroughly.
- Cut pancetta into ⅛-inch cubes. Divide between 2 10-inch nonstick skillets. Cook over medium heat for 2 to 3 minutes, until some of the fat is rendered. Evenly divide brussels sprouts between skillets. Cook for 1 minute, stirring.
- Add 1 cup broth to each skillet. Continue to cook over medium heat for 15 minutes. Brussels sprouts will be tender, and all the liquid will have evaporated. Season with freshly ground black pepper. Serve immediately or reheat gently with a few tablespoons water.

serves 6

* If brussels sprouts are large, cut them in half lengthwise.

269

eggnog crème caramel

¾ cup sugar
3 cups eggnog *
3 extra-large eggs plus 2 extra-large egg yolks

- Preheat oven to 350°.
- Put sugar in large nonstick skillet. Cook over medium-high heat until sugar melts. Stir with wooden spoon until sugar turns into dark brown caramel with no lumps.
- Immediately pour 2 tablespoons caramel into 6 5-ounce custard cups to cover bottoms. Let harden.
- Put eggnog in medium saucepan and heat almost to a boil. Lower heat and simmer for 1 minute. Remove from heat.
- Place eggs and egg yolks in bowl of electric mixer. Mix well. Slowly add scalded eggnog until just blended. You do not want to incorporate too much air. With a ladle, fill prepared custard cups.
- Place cups in deep pan and carefully pour boiling water into pan almost to tops of cups. Bake for 40 minutes. Remove from oven. Carefully remove custards from water bath. Let cool. Cover with plastic wrap and chill for several hours, until very cold.
- Using a butter knife, carefully cut around edge of each custard to loosen. Turn over in center of 6 flat plates. Caramel will flow onto plate.

serves 6

* Use a commercial brand from the dairy case.

great buffets

Having grown up with parents who were devout restaurant-goers, I learned to love food and buffets. Frequent trips to the great smorgasbords of New York (Scandia and Stockholm), as well as Sunday brunch buffets at the Plaza Hotel, had me hooked on this particularly opulent style of dining.

Being able to eat small portions of lots of things, again and again, pleased me no end, and years later the buffet became my favorite form of entertaining.

The social dynamics differ at a buffet, for there is less pressure on the host and guest to fit into the structure of a seated affair. For the host/cook, critical concerns about the timing of food and service disappear. For the guest, great buffets provide a sense of liberation and a change of pace.

But "liberation" doesn't always mean informality, for many buffets are worthy of guests in black tie, providing the perfect opportunity to use your finest napery, silver, and china. Conversely, a rustic tablescape — a printed cloth and ceramic platters — can take the same food in a different direction, creating an air of informality.

The following buffet menus are constructed from recipes in the book, organized around particular themes and including appropriate grapenotes. Each has a balance of hot and cold items, with no menu having more than one or two that require last-minute preparation. All are designed to be served in pots or pans, or on platters, depending on the dish and the style of your party.

Most of the recipes can be prepared in advance over two or three days. I like to cook early in the morning as I sip strong coffee and listen to the radio. Slowly working my way through the menu is a ritual I love: It's the prelude to the party.

There are several options for these serve-yourself affairs. You can assign seats around a large table or provide adequate seating at small tables around a large room, letting people sit where they wish and encouraging the exchange of partners during the meal.

Depending on the menu, all the dishes, excluding the dessert, can be put out at the same time or split into courses. If you choose courses, you must clear the buffet after each course. In either case, the buffet is cleared and reset for dessert.

Wine can also be self-serve from a lovely wine bar set up on a smaller table or sideboard. I usually offer two whites and two reds. Some wines have an affinity for certain foods, and this kind of entertaining gives people a chance to test wine-food pairings on their own.

274

Wedding Breakfast

Brie Croustades with Black Caviar (page 222)

Smoked Salmon Kisses (page 100)

Crème Fraîche Garlic Dip, Teardrop Tomatoes
(page 231)

Truffled Whitefish Puffs (page 105)

Plugged Honeydew with Prosciutto
(page 137)

Sturgeon with Chive Flowers and Lemon Oil
(page 15)

Scrambled Eggs, Hollandaise-Style (page 17)

Orange-*Orzata* Italian Ices, Angel Food Toast
(page 177)

Pignoli Crunch (page 193)

grapenote
Champagne all the way. Veuve Clicquot Gold Label Brut would
be a celebratory choice. Less expensive but equally memo-
rable would be Iron Horse Wedding Cuvée from California.

A Sumptuous Tea

Smoked Salmon–Horseradish Tea Sandwiches
(page 98)
Open-Faced Cucumber-Feta Tea Sandwiches
(page 98)

Crispy Oatcakes with Cheese and Fruit (page 119)

Champagne Sorbet, Blood Orange Salad
(to be passed in small glasses on a silver tray)
(page 225)

Pithiviers of Apricots and Almond Paste
(page 143)

Marmalade Tart (cut into slivers) (page 21)

Coconut Kisses (page 53)

Cocoa Clouds (page 225)

Pecan Pralines (page 61)

grapenote
Begin with a full-bodied dry sherry such as Oloroso to accompany the savory sandwiches and oatcakes. With the sweeter
offerings, select a demi-sec champagne or soon-to-be trendy
white port, served slightly chilled. And of course, brew a large
pot of black tea served with milk, English-style.

Cocktail Reception

Wrinkled Potatoes with Salmon Caviar (page 227)

Little Radishes with Whipped Goat Cheese and Toasted Cumin (page 96)

Eleven-Inch Parmesan Straws (page 236)

Salmon-in-Blankets (page 105)

Fresh Cod Brandade #1 or #2 (page 114), Garlic Croûtes (page 109)

Blue-Cheese-and-Broccoli-Stuffed Mushrooms (page 124)

Endive with Sun-Dried Tomato and Orange Pâté (page 96)

Sausage and Bay Leaf Brochettes (page 106)

Thai Chicken Skewers (page 124)

Great Fruit and Cheese Combinations (choose one) (page 120)

grapenote
These are largely white-wine dishes, so the two suggested reds are on the lighter side. The whites are both dry and crisp but offer quite different varietal character: Jepson Sauvignon Blanc, Jacob's Creek Chardonnay. Possible reds are Rosemount Grenache/Shiraz, and Italian Dolcetto from a good producer such as De Forville or Vigna del Mandorlo.

Italian Picnic

Prosciutto and Melon Batons (page 97)

Asparagus Tonnato (page 40)

Roasted Tomato and Onion Soup (page 191)

Fennel Salad with Warm *Ricotta Salata,* Lemon Oil (page 170)

Tiny Seashells with Arugula, Garlicky Pepper Oil (page 175)

Swordfish *Peperonata* (page 48)

Cornish Hens Stuffed with Pancetta and Sage (page 205)

Crispy Potatoes with Italian Parsley (page 206)

Fresh Cherries on Ice, Sweet Lemon Mascarpone (page 193)

Gianduia Torta (page 151)

grapenote
Keep the wines Italian. The first white is dry and crisp; the second is richer and fuller: Bertani Due Uve (a blend of Pinot Grigio and Sauvignon Blanc) and a good Soave Classico (from Anselmi or Gini), respectively. These reds are wonderfully interesting: Cantina Sant Agata 'Na Vota Ruchè (made from an ancient Italian grape, a close relative of Grenache) and Foradori Teroldego (the grape used to make Novello). If unobtainable, choose the best Chianti you can afford.

A No-Cook Buffet

Celery Bites (page 99)

A Rainbow of Cheese Truffles (page 120)

Singing Clams (page 101)

Herring Salad with Dill Havarti (page 257)

Apple Cider Cucumber Salad (page 60)

Pear, Endive, and Boursin Salad (page 141)

Sable with Dill Cream (page 28)

Stoplight Tomatoes: Red, Yellow, and Green
   (page 242)

Cantaloupe in Sweet Vermouth, Crushed
   Amaretti (page 168)

grapenote
A pitcher of Martinis (see page 79) or Mimosas (see page 79).
Move on to a white — something minerally, such as a
Sardinian Vermentino or a crisp and steely Chablis. With
dessert, a small snifter of Amaretto.

Le Buffet Français

Eggplant "Caviar" (page 116)

Truffled White Bean Spread (page 112)

Garlic Croûtes (page 109)

Smoked Trout and Watercress Salad, Walnut
   Oil–Green Sauce (page 261)

Bistro Chicken with Goat Cheese and Basil
   (page 56)

Potatoes Boulangère (page 158)

Roasted Pearl Onions, Sherry Vinegar Glaze
   (page 146)

Spring Vegetables à la Vapeur (page 237)

Mesclun Salad, Raspberry Vinaigrette (page 55)

Tartines (page 119)

Puits d'Amour (page 229)

grapenote
Take a 1-2-3 approach with this very French menu. One big
white: Château Le Sartre from Bordeaux. One full-bodied Rosé:
Domaine Bruno Clair 1996 Marsannay Rosé. One lighter-style
red: a good Beaujolais such as Fessy Brouilly. With dessert: Kir
Imperials, made with a moderately priced sparkling wine and
a good dose of framboise.

Pan-Asian Buffet

Sake Olives with Grapefruit (page 111)

Shanghai Glazed Walnuts (page 111)

Pickled Pink Shrimp (page 102)

Shiitake-Scallion Satés (page 44)

Drunken Chicken (page 105) on Stir-Fried
   Asparagus, Shanxi Vinegar (page 211)

Seared Tuna with Coconut Milk and Wasabi
   (page 44)

Basmati Rice with Tangerines (page 210),
   Star Anise Tea Eggs (page 121)

Snow Peas and Baby Corn (page 154)

Ginger-Poached Pineapple (page 155)

Fresh Plums and Plum Wine Aspic (page 212)

grapenote
Offer chilled sake or a pitcher of Sake-tinis (see page 81),
Sapporo beer, and one white and one pink wine: a New
Zealand Sauvignon Blanc (such as Villa Maria or Selwyn River)
and a flavorful Rosé (such as Château d'Aqueria 1996 Tavel
from the Rhône Valley, possessing "green tea on the finish").

Mediterranean Buffet

An Unusual Hummus (page 101)

Pita Chips (page 109)

Roasted Eggplant Wedges, Cilantro Dressing
   (page 172)

Orange and Black Olive Salad (page 48)

Cucumbers in Yogurt Dressing (page 180)

Swordfish Swords with Pomegranate Molasses
   (page 179)

Lemon-Za'atar Chicken (page 200)

Carrots Moroccaine (page 201)

Couscous el Souk (page 172)

Strawberry-Arrack *Sharbat,* Strawberry Salad
   (page 173)

Chickpea Flour Cookies (page 202)

grapenote
These dishes will support heavier wines (both white and red),
but the interesting compare-and-contrast opportunities
come from offering different varietals from different parts
of the world. Try a Chardonnay from Israel (Yarden), a white
Côtes du Rhône, a Syrah from California or Argentina, and a
South African Pinotage.

Le Grand Dessert

Create your own lavish dessert buffet, or "Viennese table," using the following sweet ideas found in this book, listed by category for easy menu planning. Consider the season: Offer a variety of fruits, patisseries, cheeses, sorbets, and the like. Also refer to "Ten-Minute Desserts" on page 304. Choose from a selection of sweet wines (see page 91) or see the grapenote on page 281.

fruit

- Fruit Compote in Honey-Lemon Syrup (page 250)

- Half-Pound Baked Apples, Ginger Cream (page 20)

- Strawberries Catalan (page 147)

- Oranges and Grapefruit in Black Currant Syrup (page 159)

- Whole Spiced Pears, Mulled Syrup (page 216)

- Fresh Plums and Plum Wine Aspic (page 212)

- Real Peach Melba (page 189)

- Ginger-Poached Pineapple (page 155)

- Cantaloupe in Sweet Vermouth, Crushed Amaretti (page 168)

- Fresh Cherries on Ice, Sweet Lemon Mascarpone (page 193)

- Figs and Halvah, Honey Syrup (page 181)

- Spiced Oranges in Cardamom Syrup (page 202)

- Honeydew and Blueberries, Blueberry Drizzle (page 239)

- Watermelon Soup (page 244)

- Slow-Baked Pears, Sauternes Aspic (page 255)

- Warm Marzipan-Baked Apples (page 265)

- Mangoes in Lime Syrup (page 53)

- Star Fruit, Star Anise Syrup (page 46)

- Rhubarb Compote with Toasted Almond Streusel, Brown Sugar Syrup (page 164)

- Strawberry Salad (page 173)

- Blood Orange Salad (page 225)

pastries and cakes

cookies and candies

custards, mousses, and creams

wine jellies

ice creams, sorbets, and granitas

- Black Currant Granita (page 159)

- Orange-*Orzata* Italian Ices (page 177)

- Strawberry-Arrack *Sharbat* (page 173)

- Honey Ice Cream Quenelles (page 163)

- Lemon *Sorbetto* with Rosemary (page 185)

- Champagne Sorbet (page 225)

- Papaya Sorbet with Papaya "Pepper" (page 234)

- Honeydew and Blueberries: Mixed Fruit Sorbet, Blueberry Drizzle (page 239)

- White Chocolate Ice Cream (page 244)

- Apple Cider Granita (page 265)

- Peaches and Bourbon Sorbet, Bourbon Syrup (page 61)

- Granita di Caffé (page 35)

- 'Sgroppino: Venetian Lemon Slush (page 49)

- Granita di Limetta (page 42)

grapenote

The most important caveat is never to serve a dry wine with sweet food — and only with rare exceptions does Cabernet go with chocolate cake (for the same reason). Instead, serve something comparatively sweet: an Asti Spumante, a Moscatel from the Spanish sherry house Barbadillo, Muscat de Beaumes de Venise, or an affordable Sauternes. This might be an interesting time to experiment with a malmsey Madeira, Banyuls, Malvasia, Pedro Ximénez, vintage Port, or Trockenbeerenauslese.

cheese and fruit

- Tartines (page 119)

- Great Fruit and Cheese Combinations (page 120)

healthy
entertaining

An enduring benefit of

cooking with three ingredients is that "fat" often is the fourth ingredient in a recipe and is, therefore, eliminated. Endless experimentation and discovery has led to a slew of voluptuous party dishes that are lower in calories and fat than one might expect. This kind of culinary dress-down results in food that is, ironically, packed with unadulterated, purer tastes.

Imagine a Thanksgiving feast, fat-free and vegetarian. Begin with Pumpkin Soup with Cider Syrup (page 267). Then move to a main-course fall vegetable fantasy featuring Red Cabbage with Vinegar and Wildflower Honey (page 263); Sweet Potato, Ginger, and Orange Puree (page 264); Lentils in Red Wine with Roasted Garlic (page 138); and a crystal bowl of nutmeg-spiced Cranberry Conserve (page 255). For dessert, a refreshing Blood Orange Salad with Champagne Sorbet (page 225), followed by a platter of Cocoa Clouds (page 225), still warm from the oven.

And, yes, only three ingredients per recipe!

Something low cal *and* sensuous? Crudités with Dilled Champagne Cream (page 103),

283

followed by jade green Chilled Asparagus Bisque with Crabmeat (page 236). Next, Lamb Spiced with Ginger and Mint (page 232), sliced rare and served with Baked Shallot Custard (page 233) and Spring Vegetables à la Vapeur (page 237). Slow-Baked Pears with Sauternes Aspic (page 255) make a stunning finale.

Nutritionist par excellence Helen Kimmel, M.S., R.D., and I have defined low-fat recipes as those having 5 grams of fat or less per serving for appetizers, side dishes, and desserts, and less than 10 grams of fat for main courses. Low-calorie recipes contain less than 165 calories for appetizers, side dishes, and desserts, and less than 350 calories for main courses. Fat-free recipes have less than 1 gram of fat per serving.

Combining superlative ingredients simply is the goal in creating exceptional, healthy food. Included in this chapter are 107 low-cal recipes, 59 low-fat recipes, and 44 fat-free recipes. More than half the book can be considered "healthful." Even I was surprised!

Most appealing is the astonishing depth of flavors and the variety of dishes in each category.

Instead of half an ounce of peanuts or cashews (which have about 80 calories and a hefty 7 grams of fat), peruse the spectacular array of low-fat and low-calorie hors d'oeuvres on pages 287 and 290, then decide which you'd rather have!

To prove empirically that health and entertaining are not mutually exclusive, try one of my healthy party menus or create your own. Or wow your guests with one of the seventeen fabulous fat-free desserts.

These delicious dishes will no doubt add an extra dimension of pleasure to your entertaining prowess.

Fat-Free Recipes

(Less than 1 gram of fat per serving)

first courses

- Fourteen-Carrot Chicken Bouillon (without shredded chicken) (page 246)
- Pumpkin Soup with Cider Syrup (page 267)
- Shiitake-Scallion Satés (page 44)
- Lentil Soup with Sherry Vinegar (page 63)
- Dilled Champagne Cream (page 103)
- Apple Cider Cucumber Salad (page 60)
- Roasted Yellow Peppers, Caper–Golden Raisin Emulsion (page 183)

side dishes

- Jasmine Rice with Edible Flowers (page 229)
- Spring Vegetables à la Vapeur (page 237)
- Roasted Acorn Squash and Carrot Puree (page 254)
- Cranberry Conserve (page 255)
- Red Cabbage with Vinegar and Wildflower Honey (page 263)
- Sweet Potato, Ginger, and Orange Puree (page 264)
- Orange-Cucumber Salsa (page 45)
- Lentils in Red Wine with Roasted Garlic (page 138)
- Roasted Pearl Onions, Sherry Vinegar Glaze (page 146)
- Rice Pilaf with Lima Beans and Dill (page 134)
- Couscous el Souk (page 172)

desserts and beverages

Low-Fat Recipes

hors d'oeuvres

(All are calculated per piece. All dips and pâtés are based on 1 tablespoon.)

- Little Radishes with Whipped Goat Cheese and Toasted Cumin (2 gm) (page 96)
- Endive with Sun-Dried Tomato and Orange Pâté (1.5 gm) (page 96)
- Prosciutto and Melon Batons (3 gm) (page 97)
- Smoked Salmon–Horseradish Cocktail Sandwiches (2 gm) (page 98)
- Open-Faced Cucumber-Feta Cocktail Sandwiches (2 gm) (page 98)
- Cherry Bombs (1.5 gm) (page 99)
- Smoked Salmon Kisses (1.5 gm) (page 100)
- Celery Bites (3 gm) (page 99)
- Zucchini Thimbles with Goat Cheese and Chili Oil (3 gm) (page 100)
- Singing Clams (1.5 gm) (page 101)
- Wasabi-Stuffed Shrimp (4 gm) (page 102)
- Pickled Pink Shrimp (1.5 gm) (page 102)
- Green Peppercorn Dip (2 gm) (page 103)
- Truffled Whitefish Puffs (5 gm) (page 105)
- Salmon-in-Blankets (5 gm) (page 105)
- Plum-Glazed Stuffed Mushrooms (5 gm) (page 106)
- Shrimp Tapas (2 gm) (page 107)
- Garlic Croûtes (1.5 gm each) (page 109)
- Pita Chips (2 gm) (page 109)
- Curry Crisps (2 gm) (page 110)
- Chicken Liver and Sun-Dried Tomato Pâté (2 gm) (page 113)
- An Unusual Pâté (2 gm) (page 113)
- Fresh Cod Brandade #1 (1.5 gm) (page 114)
- Eggplant Pâté with Tahina and Pomegranate Molasses (1.5 gm) (page 115)
- Roasted Eggplant and Pesto Spread (1.5 gm) (page 115)
- The World's Best Pimiento Spread (3 gm) (page 116)
- Roasted Garlic–Sapsago Spread (4 gm) (page 117)
- Two-Tone Mussels (1.5 gm) (page 121)
- Star Anise Tea Eggs (3 gm) (page 121)
- Smoked Salmon Roulades (4 gm) (page 122)
- Asparagettes (1.5 gm) (page 123)
- Blue-Cheese-and-Broccoli-Stuffed Mushrooms (3 gm) (page 124)
- Silver-Dollar Corn Cakes with Bacon (4 gm) (page 125)

first courses

- Wrinkled Potatoes with Salmon Caviar (5 gm) (page 227)
- Chilled Asparagus Bisque with Crabmeat (2 gm) (page 236)
- Fourteen-Carrot Chicken Bouillon (with shredded chicken) (2 gm) (page 246)
- Carrot, Leek, and Chestnut Soup (2 gm) (page 214)
- Consommé with Poached Oysters and Nori (2 gm) (page 209)
- Med-Rim Eggplant with Sun-Dried Tomatoes (3 gm) (page 199)
- Asparagus and Shrimp Potage (2 gm) (page 161)
- Truffled Consommé with Vermicelli (2 gm) (page 149)

main courses

- Bluefish on a Bed of Red Onions and Purple Sage (9 gm) (page 183)
- Teriyaki Salmon with Scallions (10 gm) (page 153)

side dishes

- Julienne Carrots with Madeira (4 gm) (page 134)
- Basmati Rice with Tangerines (4 gm) (page 210)
- Corn off the Cob (3 gm) (page 196)
- Cucumbers in Yogurt Dressing (using low-fat yogurt) (2 gm) (page 180)
- Potatoes Boulangère (4 gm) (page 158)
- Carrots Moroccaine (5 gm) (page 201)
- Broccoli-Ginger Puree (5 gm) (page 228)
- Smashed Potato Salad (5 gm) (page 242)
- Wild Mushroom–Potato Torte (4 gm) (page 250)
- Brussels Sprouts with Pancetta and Beef Essence (5 gm) (page 269)
- Borlotti Beans with Tomato and Roasted Garlic (2 gm) (page 41)

desserts
and beverages

- Chickpea Flour Cookies (5 gm) (page 202)

- Coconut Kisses (2 gm) (page 53)

- Amrus (2 gm) (page 85)

- Ginger-Pineapple Frappe (1.5 gm) (page 87)

- Café au Lait (without chocolate) (2 gm)
  (page 27)

Low-Calorie Recipes

hors d'oeuvres

(All are calculated per piece. All dips and pâtés are based on 1 tablespoon.)

- Smoked Salmon Kisses (38 cal) (page 100)
- Celery Bites (27 cal) (page 99)
- Zucchini Thimbles with Goat Cheese and Chili Oil (33 cal) (page 100)
- Singing Clams (23 cal) (page 101)
- Wasabi-Stuffed Shrimp (55 cal) (page 102)
- Pickled Pink Shrimp (35 cal) (page 102)
- Green Peppercorn Dip (20 cal) (page 103)
- Za'atar Pesto (92 cal) (page 103)
- Dilled Champagne Cream (23 cal) (page 103)
- Phyllo and Feta Wraps (85 cal) (page 104)
- Cherry Tomato *Bruschetta* (125 cal) (page 104)
- Truffled Whitefish Puffs (83 cal) (page 105)
- Salmon-in-Blankets (57 cal) (page 105)
- Plum-Glazed Stuffed Mushrooms (69 cal) (page 106)
- Shrimp Tapas (42 cal) (page 107)
- Garlic Croûtes (28 cal) (page 109)
- Pita Chips (33 cal) (page 109)

- Curry Crisps (51 cal) (page 110)
- Chicken Liver and Sun-Dried Tomato Pâté (41 cal) (page 113)
- An Unusual Pâté (38 cal) (page 113)
- Fresh Cod Brandade #1 (20 cal) (page 114)
- Eggplant Pâté with Tahina and Pomegranate Molasses (27 cal) (page 115)
- Roasted Eggplant and Pesto Spread (18 cal) (page 115)
- The World's Best Pimiento Spread (38 cal) (page 116)
- Roasted Garlic–Sapsago Spread (51 cal) (page 117)
- Pesto-Vermouth Spread (65 cal) (page 117)
- Two-Tone Mussels (30 cal) (page 121)
- Star Anise Tea Eggs (40 cal) (page 121)
- Smoked Salmon Roulades (43 cal) (page 122)
- Little Roquefort Biscuits (100 cal) (page 122)
- Asparagettes (25 cal) (page 123)
- Little Radishes with Whipped Goat Cheese and Toasted Cumin (18 cal) (page 96)
- Endive with Sun-Dried Tomato and Orange Pâté (36 cal) (page 96)

first courses

main courses

- Sorrel Frittata (350 cal) (page 17)

- Eggs Fontina Ranchero (250 cal) (page 18)

- Sautéed Shrimp on Red and Green Pepper Confit (350 cal) (page 132)

- Bluefish on a Bed of Red Onions and Purple Sage (270 cal) (page 183)

- Teriyaki Salmon with Scallions (315 cal) (page 153)

- Sage Shrimp and Crispy Pancetta (340 cal) (page 40)

- Swordfish *Peperonata* (330 cal) (page 48)

- A Duet of Cured Salmons: Brown Sugar–Tarragon Gravlax, Mild-Brine Lenrimmad Lax (305 cal, 6-ounce serving) (page 223)

- Lamb Spiced with Ginger and Mint (350 cal, 5-ounce serving) (page 232)

side dishes

- "Hearts" of Bibb, White Balsamic Vinaigrette (125 cal) (page 227)

- Broccoli-Ginger Puree (90 cal) (page 228)

- Spring Vegetables à la Vapeur (36 cal) (page 237)

- Glazed Radishes, Braised Leaves (115 cal) (page 232)

- Baked Shallot Custard (130 cal) (page 233)

- Roasted Acorn Squash and Carrot Puree (140 cal) (page 254)

- Cranberry Conserve (90 cal) (page 255)

- Wild Mushroom–Potato Torte (130 cal) (page 250)

- Red Cabbage with Vinegar and Wildflower Honey (105 cal) (page 263)

- Chunky Celery Root with Caramelized Red Onions (155 cal) (page 264)

- Brussels Sprouts with Pancetta and Beef Essence (106 cal) (page 269)

- Roasted Pearl Onions, Sherry Vinegar Glaze (104 cal) (page 146)

- Olive Oil Biscuits, Hot from the Oven (99 cal) (page 133)

- Julienne Carrots with Madeira (103 cal) (page 134)

- Spaghetti Squash with Black Sesame Seeds (105 cal) (page 215)

desserts and beverages

- Chickpea Flour Cookies (100 cal) (page 202)
- Coconut Kisses (50 cal) (page 53)
- Pecan Pralines (156 cal) (page 61)
- Slow-Baked Pears, Sauternes Aspic (165 cal) (page 255)
- Cocoa Clouds (13 cal) (page 225)
- Carrot-Apple Smoothie (121 cal) (page 85)
- Ginger-Pineapple Frappe (120 cal) (page 87)
- Moroccan Grape Drink (165 cal) (page 86)
- Rosemary Lemonade (130 cal) (page 86)
- Mint Tea (1 tablespoon sugar) (45 cal) (page 26)
- Lemon "Tea" (30 cal) (page 26)
- Café au Lait (without chocolate; 1 tablespoon sugar) (83 cal) (page 27)

- Stir-Fried Asparagus, Shanxi Vinegar (100 cal) (page 211)
- Crispy Potatoes with Italian Parsley (155 cal) (page 206)
- Sautéed Cherry Tomatoes (125 cal) (page 188)
- Cucumbers in Yogurt Dressing (using low-fat yogurt) (75 cal) (page 180)
- Almond-Crusted Baked Tomatoes (160 cal) (page 176)
- Slow-Cooked Baby Carrots (138 cal) (page 167)
- Potatoes Boulangère (165 cal) (page 158)
- Chopped Broccoli Rabe and Roasted Red Onions (126 cal) (page 206)
- Roasted Beet Puree with Allspice (without fried beets) (126 cal) (page 158)
- Baked Fennel with Garlic Bread Crumbs (145 cal) (page 150)
- Carrots Moroccaine (92 cal) (page 201)
- Orange-Cucumber Salsa (80 cal) (page 45)
- Apple Cider Cucumber Salad (75 cal) (page 60)

Healthy Party Menus

(Under 675 calories)

Consommé with Poached Oysters and Nori
  (page 209)

Teriyaki Salmon with Scallions (page 153)

Broccoli-Ginger Puree (page 228)

Stir-Fried Asparagus, Shanxi Vinegar (page 221)

Tangerines

  ℛ

"Hearts" of Bibb, White Balsamic Vinaigrette
  (page 227)

Bluefish on a Bed of Red Onions and Purple Sage
  (page 183)

Roasted Yellow Peppers, Caper–Golden Raisin
  Emulsion (page 183)

Julienne Carrots with Madeira (page 134)

Cocoa Clouds (4) (page 225)

  ℛ

Chilled Asparagus Bisque with Crabmeat
  (page 236)

A Duet of Cured Salmons (6 ounces) (page 223)

Cucumbers in Yogurt Dressing (page 180)

Wrinkled Potatoes with Salmon Caviar (page 227)

Melon

  ℛ

Lentil Soup with Sherry Vinegar (page 63)

Swordfish *Peperonata* (page 48)

Crispy Potatoes with Italian Parsley (page 206)

Spring Vegetables à la Vapeur (page 237)

Globe Grapes

  ℛ

Fourteen-Carrot Chicken Bouillon (page 246)

Lamb Spiced with Ginger and Mint (page 232)

Baked Shallot Custard (page 233)

Salad of Arugula and Currants (page 52)

Coconut Kisses and Cocoa Clouds (1 each)
  (pages 53, 225)

  ℛ

Truffled Consommé with Vermicelli (page 149)

Sage Shrimp and Crispy Pancetta (page 40)

Potatoes Boulangère (page 158)

Italian Plums

Low-Fat Supper

Med-Rim Eggplant with Sun-Dried Tomatoes
(page 199)

Bluefish on a Bed of Red Onions and Purple Sage
(page 183)

Corn off the Cob (page 196)

Smashed Potato Salad (page 242)

Orange-*Orzata* Italian Ices, Angel Food Toast
(page 177)

Fat-Free Dessert Party

Ginger-Poached Pineapple (page 155)

Spiced Oranges in Cardamom Syrup (page 202)

Fresh Plums and Plum Wine Aspic (page 212)

Whole Spiced Pears, Mulled Syrup (page 216)

Lemon *Sorbetto* with Rosemary, Sweet Gremolata
(page 185)

Cocoa Clouds (page 225)

spontaneous entertaining

Great taste is timeless.

Some dishes reach perfection in a matter of minutes; some require hours in a slow oven or over a low flame to release, transform, or transfix a recipe's inherent flavors.

All the recipes in this chapter, however, can be ready for company in thirty minutes or less, including ten-minute desserts to impress your guests. Using these lists, you can create your own smart menus for spur-of-the-moment entertaining.

For example, the fastest four-course party menu I can think of, using the recipes in this book, is Penne Pasta à la Vodka (page 34) to begin, a main course of Salmon Roasted in Butter (page 137) with Sautéed Cherry Tomatoes (page 188) and Sautéed Spinach with "Burnt" Almonds (page 146), a salad of "Hearts" of Bibb with White Balsamic Vinaigrette (page 227), and any Ten-Minute Dessert (pages 304–305).

All you need is a beautiful tablecloth, your best china, and a bottle or two of Pinot Noir!

Some of these recipes rely on new specialty foods available today in most supermarkets.

My list of store-bought "conveniences" seems to get shorter, and more interesting, the more I delve into this style of cooking. It includes pesto sauce; *salsa verde* (with tomatillos); sun-dried tomatoes in oil; rolled anchovies; chipotle peppers in adobo; coconut milk; hoisin sauce; flavor-packed oils such as lemon, rosemary, roasted peanut, and truffle; and appetite-tingling vinegars such as sherry, balsamic, raspberry, apple cider, and the deliciously complex Shanxi from China. Most are available in good supermarkets.

Also indispensable are basic homemade recipes, always available in my pantry or fridge, for last-minute entertaining. These include my omnipresent jars of Garlic Oil, Rosemary Mayonnaise, Simple Syrup, Vanilla Sugar, and Ginger Sugar (recipes follow).

With these few staples, you can rustle up a 1-2-3 party in great style. For example, use the Simple Syrup for fixing a "retro" cocktail; serve a first course of stir-fried asparagus and shiitakes in Garlic Oil; grill swordfish "chops" with halved red and yellow tomatoes, then add a dollop of Rosemary Mayonnaise; finish with a coupe of thinly sliced peaches sprinkled with Ginger Sugar and topped with crème fraîche.

For similar unstructured recipes for daytime entertaining, refer to "1-2-3 Breakfast Ideas" (pages 13–14) and "1-2-3 Lunch Ideas" (pages 65–67).

Being prepared is a prerequisite for being a great host. At our house, we welcome the unexpected and have found that spontaneity is the mother of culinary adventure.

Also included in this chapter is "It's a Nice Touch," ideas related to food, drink, and style. These are the little things that make the big impressions. They don't cost much money, but they provide a wealth of pleasure.

A Few Basic Recipes

garlic oil

1 cup olive oil
8 large cloves garlic
1 good-quality dried bay leaf

- Put oil in small saucepan. Add garlic and heat gently for 5 minutes, or until small bubbles form on top. Turn off heat. Add bay leaf and ¼ teaspoon whole black peppercorns. Let cool. Remove bay leaf and transfer oil to jar. Cover and refrigerate. Use within 2 weeks.
- The store-bought garlic oils I like are all-natural Boyajian, Consorzio, and Zeta/Land of Canaan Natural Oils from Israel.

makes 1 cup

rosemary mayonnaise

2 teaspoons distilled white vinegar
2 teaspoons minced fresh rosemary
1 cup mayonnaise

- Place vinegar and rosemary in small bowl. Let sit for 5 minutes. Add mayonnaise. Stir well. Add a pinch of freshly ground white pepper and stir to combine. Transfer to jar. Cover and refrigerate. Will keep for several months.

makes 1 cup

simple syrup

2 cups sugar

- In small saucepan, combine sugar and 2 cups water. Cook over high heat, stirring often, bringing just to a boil, about 2 minutes. Lower heat to medium and cook for about 3 minutes, until sugar is dissolved and syrup is clear. Remove from heat and let cool. Transfer syrup to jar. Cover and refrigerate. Will keep indefinitely.

makes 3 cups

vanilla sugar

2 cups sugar
1 long, pliable vanilla bean

- Put sugar in medium bowl. Split vanilla bean in half lengthwise. With the tip of a knife, scrape out vanilla seeds, reserving split bean, and add seeds to sugar. Mix well with your fingertips, making sure seeds are well distributed (they are moist and tend to stick together). Stick split bean into sugar. Cover tightly and store in dry place. Will keep indefinitely.

makes 2 cups

ginger sugar

1 cup sugar
2 teaspoons ground ginger

- Mix sugar and ginger together in small bowl until thoroughly blended. Cover tightly and store in dry place. Will keep indefinitely.

makes 1 cup

Under Thirty-Minute Recipes

hors d'oeuvres

- Sips and Bits (page 77)
- 1-2-3 Snacks (page 78)
- Quick and Easy (page 95)
- Pita Chips (page 109)
- Curry Crisps (page 110)
- Brie Croustades with Black Caviar (page 222)
- Hot and Crispy Swiss Truffles (page 267)
- Olive Oil Biscuits, Hot from the Oven (page 133)
- Tartines (page 119)
- Silver-Dollar Corn Cakes with Bacon and Crème Fraîche (page 125)

first courses

- Oysters, Black Radish, Chipolata Sausages (page 222)
- "Hearts" of Bibb, White Balsamic Vinaigrette (page 227)
- Oyster Bisque (page 252)
- Smoked Trout and Watercress Salad, Walnut Oil–Green Sauce (page 261)
- Stoplight Tomatoes: Red, Yellow, and Green (page 242)
- Edam-Up Quesadillas (page 241)
- Consommé with Poached Oysters and Nori (page 209)
- Asparagus Tonnato (page 40)
- Sturgeon with Chive Flowers and Lemon Oil (pages 15)
- Sable with Dill Cream (page 16)
- Penne Pasta à la Vodka (page 34)
- Salad of Arugula and Currants (page 52)
- Mesclun Salad, Raspberry Vinaigrette (page 55)

main courses

side dishes

- Breakfast Sausages on Rosemary Branches (page 19)
- Macadamia Rice with Basil (page 45)
- Smoky Grits and Sweet Pea Casserole (page 60)
- Saffron Rice and Brie (page 188)
- Sautéed Cherry Tomatoes (page 188)
- Corn off the Cob (page 196)
- Whole Wheat Couscous with Grilled Scallions (page 201)
- Carrots Moroccaine (page 201)
- Stir-Fried Asparagus, Shanxi Vinegar (page 211)
- Broccoli-Ginger Puree (page 228)
- Jasmine Rice with Edible Flowers (page 229)
- Glazed Radishes, Braised Leaves (page 232)
- Spring Vegetables à la Vapeur (page 237)

- Firecracker Corn (page 243)
- Brussels Sprouts with Pancetta and Beef Essence (page 269)
- Julienne Carrots with Madeira (page 134)
- Rice Pilaf with Lima Beans and Dill (page 134)
- Sautéed Spinach with "Burnt" Almonds (page 146)
- Polenta-Peas-Parmesan (page 150)
- Snow Peas and Baby Corn (page 154)
- *Haricots Verts* à la Crème (page 163)
- Couscous el Souk (page 172)
- Big Portobellos Filled with Creamed Spinach and Pernod (page 175)
- Warm Salad of Wilted Kale and Bacon (page 184)
- Almond-Crusted Baked Tomatoes (page 176)
- Bulgur with Pine Nuts and Cilantro (page 180)

Ten-Minute Desserts

- Fresh Cherries on Ice, Sweet Lemon Mascarpone (see page 193).

- Figs and Halvah, Honey Syrup (see page 181).

- Cut ripe peaches in half. Replace stone with a nugget of marzipan. Sprinkle with orange-flower water and bake at 450° for 5 minutes.

- Cut fresh figs in half lengthwise. Pour clotted or clabbered cream (available in many specialty-food stores) over the figs and drizzle with an exceptional honey (acacia, eucalyptus, tupelo, wildflower, or raspberry blossom).

- Place grapefruit segments in flat soup plates. Pour on green Chartreuse and garnish with candied violets.

- Cut the rind from a variety of oranges. Cut the oranges into thin slices and dust heavily with confectioners' sugar and ground cinnamon.

- Spoon mascarpone into wineglasses. Top with fresh raspberries and a drizzle of crème de cassis.

- Cut batons of ripe fresh pineapple. Serve with a sauce of jarred wet walnuts thinned with spiced rum.

- Gently warm imported marmalade. Spoon over mounds of ricotta cheese and serve with Savoiardi biscuits (available in many super-markets and Italian markets).

- Splash balsamic vinegar onto ripe, halved straw-berries. Top with cracked black pepper and good-quality strawberry sorbet.

- Prepare a salad of ripe mango, cut into small chunks, and fresh raspberries. Put in chilled wineglasses and cover with Sauternes.

- Insert wooden ice cream sticks or coffee stirrers into frozen Yodels. Serve next to a mound of fresh orange segments tossed with Grand Marnier.

- Make tiny ice cream sandwiches from thin chocolate wafer cookies and your favorite ice cream. Roll the edges in chocolate sprinkles.

- Buy a fabulous chocolate cake. Decorate with edible silver shavings and jarred cherries in brandy.

- Fill small store-bought meringue shells with lemon curd. Top with fresh blueberries. Crush one extra meringue shell and scatter the crumbs on the berries.

- Slice ripe nectarines into thin wedges. Place in large martini glasses. Pour equal amounts of Campari and Simple Syrup (see page 299) over the fruit.

- Make a "Paris-Brest": Split a glazed yeast dough-nut (from a doughnut shop) horizontally. Fill with small scoops of cherry vanilla ice cream or whipped cream sweetened with confectioners' sugar, piped through a pastry bag. Replace top and dust heavily with confectioners' sugar.

- Peel ripe pears and cut into thin wedges. Place in flat soup plates. Melt bittersweet chocolate and pour over pears. Top with a quenelle of vanilla ice cream.

- Blanch fresh peaches for 1 minute in boiling water. Peel, then dice into small cubes. Place in wineglasses, splash with chilled peach schnapps, and garnish with a fine julienne of fresh basil.

- "Hostess" cupcake: Scoop out the center of a chocolate cupcake. Fill with pistachio ice cream and cover with melted milk chocolate.

- Cut a thick slice of baked farmer cheese. Serve with fresh berries and a drizzle of aromatic honey.

- Overlap thin slices of guava paste and goat cheese. Serve with nut biscotti, slightly warmed.

- Buy an angel food cake. Make a pink icing of lemon confectioners' sugar and pureed straw-berries. Glaze the entire cake. Serve with fresh halved strawberries.

- Buy napoleons from a wonderful bakery. Place washed and dried raspberries on top. Glaze with melted currant jelly, using a pastry brush.

- Toast thick wedges of panettone. Soak with rum and Simple Syrup (see page 299).

- Make a salad of ripe honeydew melon and fresh pineapple chunks. Scatter with toasted coconut.

- Drinks with Dessert (see page 90).

- Great Fruit and Cheese Combinations (see page 120).

A Month of Sundaes

- Vanilla ice cream, melted Valrhona chocolate, salted peanuts (known as a tin roof sundae)

- Chocolate ice cream, single-malt Scotch, finely ground hazelnut coffee

- Lemon sorbet, crème de menthe, raspberries

- Chocolate chip ice cream, sun-dried cherries soaked for 8 minutes in Oloroso sherry

- Chocolate sorbet, passion fruit sorbet, preserved ginger in syrup

- Coffee ice cream, dried apricots soaked for 5 minutes in Armagnac

- Orange sherbet, vanilla ice cream, orange-flower water

- Mango sorbet, canned lychee nuts, fresh blackberries

- Strawberry ice cream, blueberries, blueberry liqueur

- *Sorbets 1-2-3* served in champagne flutes with a corresponding liqueur and a *gaufrette,** or chocolate cigarette.

- Lemon sorbet with Marc de Gewürztraminer, Marc de Bourgogne, or Grappa

- Apricot sorbet with apricot liqueur

- Pear sorbet with Poire Williams

- Strawberry sorbet with strawberry liqueur

- Chocolate sorbet with Kahlúa or crème de cacao

- Passion fruit sorbet with Alizé

- Orange sorbet with Curaçao

- Margarita sorbet with *anejo* Tequila

* Les Gavottes *gaufrettes* are distributed in this country by A&A Food Products.

It's a Nice Touch

- Provide overnight guests with a decanter of brandy, slippers, and a bowl of lemonlike Japanese *yuzu* (or use regular lemons) to fill the room with color and to squeeze into a hot bath.

- For breakfast, serve three syrups (to drizzle over pancakes, toast, or even hot cereal) in beautiful glass cruets: real maple syrup, blueberry syrup, and vanilla syrup (made by adding an equal amount of water to Vanilla Sugar, see page 300, and boiling until dissolved and slightly thickened).

- In the powder room, put a bowl of fresh bay leaves, a large scented candle, or a pile of small plush towels.

- Give dinner guests a small gift to take home: Pignoli Crunch (see page 193) wrapped in linen and tied with raffia; Brandy Elixir (see page 89) in a stunning small bottle; or little cellophane bags (found in party stores) filled with seasonal candy, gold chocolate coins, or Jordan almonds.

- Things to collect in a bowl: stylish matchbooks from around the world, wrapped sugar cubes, or little jars of jam from room service breakfast trays. (These make great breakfast table centerpieces.)

- To serve with hot tea drinks: rock candy stirrers, long cinnamon sticks, or sour cherry preserves.

- Serve cold drinks with a decorative pitcher of Simple Syrup (see page 299) and a long silver spoon.

- Present fresh berries or sliced fruits with a European-style "sugar shaker" (looks like a very large saltshaker) filled with Vanilla or Ginger Sugar (see page 300).

- Serve a good ham sandwich with three varieties of mustard, each spooned into a small ramekin.

- Fill a pepper mill with Tellicherry peppercorns, white peppercorns, and coriander seeds for a "house blend."

- Offer a triptych of salts: Use Flavored Salts (see page 110) or kosher salt, fine sea salt, and *sel gris* from Brittany (available in specialty-food stores).

- Save wide strips of citrus rind in a small bowl. Let dry, and when brittle, snip bits over soups, pastas, sauces, or salads, in front of your guests.

- Serve morning coffee in French breakfast bowls (also great for ice cream).

- Offer chilled sake in traditional small cedar boxes (available at Asian specialty stores).

- Use fresh rosemary branches as a "utensil" for drizzling honey over fruit or cheese.

- Use sturdy blades of lemongrass, stalks of sugar cane, or slender grapevine branches to "skewer" chunks of fresh fruit or morsels of chicken or beef for grilling.

- Present beautiful lacquered chopsticks with Asian-influenced dishes.

- Mound small chunks of Parmigiano-Reggiano on a plate with a Mouli grater alongside and pass at the table.

- Serve a triad of hot sauces on a small tray, from mild to incendiary.

- To gussy up any plain-Jane chocolate cake, garnish with tissue-paper-thin sheets of edible silver, available in many specialty-food stores.

- Plate painting: Always have raspberry sauce or thick chocolate sauce in squeeze bottles in your refrigerator. Squeeze as you please.

- Cocoa stencil: To decorate a dessert plate, lay a fork on the plate, dust heavily with cocoa powder passed through a sieve, and carefully remove the fork.

- For formal dinners, create a white-on-white tablescape: white plates, candles, flowers, napkins, and strands of fake pearls.

- For more casual dinners, decorate the table in primary colors: red, yellow, and blue.

- Dyed "Easter" eggs are beautiful anytime. Find an old-fashioned egg stand at a flea market, use mix-and-match eggcups, or spray-paint a cardboard egg container a vivid color, or gold or silver, to make a fabulous morning centerpiece.

- Change the pattern or style of plates for each course.

- Present food in unexpected vessels. For example, serve cookies in small boxes lined with tissue paper.

- Serve small hors d'oeuvres in a Japanese bento box.

- Keep several "logs" of compound (flavored) butters in your freezer: lemon-tarragon, chive, and sun-dried tomato. Slice as desired and present on a small plate lined with a few lemon leaves. Serve with warm bread or atop vegetables, fish, or veal.

- Tie long, graceful bread sticks with thin grosgrain ribbon.

- Present scooped-out cherry tomatoes stuffed with a favorite filling in little paper candy cups to look like bonbons.

- Serve hot toast English-style in a classic silver toast caddy, found in antique stores and at flea markets.

- Present oysters or clams on the half shell on a tall, wire Paris bistro shellfish stand, available in many restaurant supply stores. Serve with thinly sliced brown bread and a ramekin of salted butter. Pass the pepper mill.

- Use antique linen kitchen towels as napkins. Tuck into large, interesting napkin rings.

- Find a colorful insulated cozy at a flea market to cover your hot teapot.

- Make your own elegant eaux-de-vie. Begin with a beautiful long-necked bottle and fill with fresh cherries and kirsch, or fresh raspberries and framboise.

- Dip small washed fruits (seedless grapes — green, red, champagne — in fall; cherries, blueberries, or strawberries in summer) in beaten egg whites and roll heavily in sugar. Let dry. Serve after coffee.

- Set the table with unusual or oversize flatware. Serve fish with fish knives; "sauced" dishes with flat "sauce spoons."

- Serve caviar in a chilled martini glass with a twist of lemon and a mother-of-pearl spoon.

- To end a meal on a high, sprinkle cocoa-dusted chocolate truffles with chili powder.

- Collect antique *porte-couteaux* for placing knives on the dinner table. Also good for chopsticks.

- Serve up a tray of steamed white washcloths after a sticky course. Also a nice way to begin a meal for weary travelers.

- For dessert, wrap a perfectly ripe whole fruit — pear, apple, or peach — in ultrathin tissue paper. Present on a small plate with a dessert fork and knife.

321